french

Gaëlle Graham

D0048860

TEACH YOURSELF BOOKS

For UK order queries: please contact Bookpoint Ltd, 39 Milton Park, Abingdon, Oxon OX14 4TD. Telephone: (44) 01235 400414, Fax: (44) 01235 400454. Lines are open from 9.00–6.00, Monday to Saturday, with a 24 hour message answering service. Email address: orders@bookpoint.co.uk

For U.S.A. & Canada order queries: please contact NTC/Contemporary Publishing, 4255 West Touhy Avenue, Lincolnwood, Illinois 60646–1975, U.S.A. Telephone: (847) 679 5500, Fax: (847) 679 2494.

Long renowned as the authoritative source for self-guided learning – with more than 30 million copies sold worldwide – the *Teach Yourself* series includes over 200 titles in the fields of languages, crafts, hobbies, sports, and other leisure activities.

Teach Yourself French is also available in the form of a pack containing this book and a cassette. If you have been unable to obtain the pack, the cassette can be ordered separately through your bookseller.

British Library Cataloguing in Publication Data
A catalogue entry for this title is available from The British Library.

Library of Congress Catalog Card Number: 98-65810

First published in UK 1998 by Hodder Headline Plc, 338 Euston Road, London, NW1 3BH.

First published in US 1998 by NTC/Contemporary Publishing, 4255 West Touhy Avenue, Lincolnwood (Chicago), Illinois 60646–1975 U.S.A.

The 'Teach Yourself' name and logo are registered trade marks of Hodder & Stoughton Ltd.

Copyright © 1998 Gaëlle Graham

Advisory Editor: Paul Coggle, University of Kent at Canterbury

Typeset by Transet Limited, Coventry, England.
Printed in Great Britain for Hodder & Stoughton Educational, a division of Hodder Headline Plc, 338 Euston Road, London NW1 3BH by Cox & Wyman Ltd, Reading, Berkshire.

Impression number   10 9 8 7 6 5 ·
Year   2002 2001 2000 1999

CONTENTS

INTRODUCTION

Welcome to *Teach Yourself French!*

The aim of this book

If you are an adult learner with no previous knowledge of French and studying on your own, then this is the course for you. Perhaps you are taking up French again after a break from it, or you are intending to learn with the support of a class? Again, you will find this course very well suited to your purposes.

The language you will learn is introduced through everyday situations. The emphasis is first and foremost on using French, but we also aim to give you an idea of how the language works, so that you can create sentences of your own.

The course covers all four of the basic skills – listening and speaking, reading and writing. If you are working on your own, the cassette will be all the more important, as it will provide you with the essential opportunity to listen to French and to speak it within a controlled framework. You should therefore try to get a copy of the cassette if you haven't already got one.

The structure of the course

The course book contains 25 course units plus a reference section at the back. There is also a 90-minute audio cassette which you must have if you are going to get maximum benefit from the course.

Each course unit contains most or all of the following:

Statement of aims

At the beginning of each unit there is a list of what you can expect to learn by the end of that unit.

Presentation of new language

This is usually in the form of dialogues 🗣, on the audio 📼 💿 and in the book or in reading passages 📖. Some assistance with vocabulary is also given in the **Mots-clefs**, *keywords boxes* 🔑. The language is presented in manageable chunks, building carefully on what you have learned in earlier units.

Practice of new language ✔

Practice is graded so that activities which require mainly recognition come first. As you grow confident, in manipulating the language forms you will be encouraged to write and speak the language yourself.

Language structures (*Comment ça marche?*) 📷

In these sections you will learn how to construct your own sentences correctly.

Pronunciation and intonation (*Comment ça se prononce?*)

The best way to acquire good pronunciation and intonation is to listen to the native speakers on the cassette and to try to imitate them. However, as certain sounds in French are very unfamiliar we include specific advice on pronunciation within the course units.

Information on French-speaking countries (*Point info*)

Here you will find information on various aspects of everyday life such as the level of formality that is appropriate when you talk to strangers, and how the health service works if you should fall ill.

You will find five **Self-assessment tests (unités de révision)** at different stages in the book. These differ from the practice materials in that the main point is for you to test yourself and judge whether you have successfully mastered the language so far and whether you are ready to move on.

The **reference** section contains: a glossary of grammar terms, a key to the activities, transcripts of the cassettes, a French–English glossary.

Study tips

Language learning is a bit like jogging – you need to do it regularly for it to do any good! Ideally, you should find a 'Study Buddy' to work through the course with you. This way you will have someone to try out your French on. And when the going gets tough, you will have someone to chivvy you until you reach your target.

At the beginning of each course unit make sure that you are clear about what you can expect to learn. Read any background information that is provided, then listen to the first dialogue on the cassette. Try to get the gist of what is being said before you look at the printed text in the book. Refer to the printed text and the **Mots-clefs** in order to study the dialogues in more detail.

Don't fall into the trap of thinking that you have 'done that' when you have listened to the cassette a couple of times and worked through the dialogues in the book. You may recognise what you have heard or read, but you almost certainly still have some way to go before you can produce the language of the dialogues correctly and fluently. This is why we recommend that you keep listening to the cassette at every opportunity – sitting on the tube or bus, waiting at the dentist's or stuck in a traffic jam in the car – using what would otherwise be 'dead' time. Of course, you must also be internalising what you hear and making sense of it – just playing it in the background without really paying attention is not enough!

Some of the recordings are listening-only exercises. The temptation may be to go straight to the transcriptions at the back of the book, but try not to do this. The whole point of listening exercises is to improve your listening skills. You will not do this by reading first. The transcriptions are there to help you if you get stuck.

As you work your way through the exercises, check your answers carefully in the back of the book. It is easy to overlook your own mistakes. If you have a study buddy it's a good idea to check each other's answers. Most of the exercises have fixed answers, but some are a bit more open-ended, especially when we are asking you to talk about yourself. Then, in most cases, we give you model answers which you can adapt for your own purposes.

We have tried to make the grammar explanations as user-friendly as possible, since we recognise that many people find grammar daunting. But in the end, it is up to you just how much time you spend on studying and sorting out the grammar points. Some people find that they can do better by getting an ear for what sounds right, others need to know in detail how the language is put together.

Before you move on to a new unit always check that you know all the new words and phrases in the current unit. Trying to recall the context in which words and phrases were used may help you learn them better.

We hope that you enjoy working your way through **Teach Yourself French**. Don't get discouraged. Mastering a new language does take time and perseverance and sometimes things can seem just too difficult. But then you'll come back another day and things will begin to make more sense again.

Beyond the course book

Where can I find real language?

Don't expect to be able to understand everything you hear or read straight away. If you watch French-speaking programmes on TV or buy a French magazine you should not get discouraged when you realise how quickly native-speakers speak and how much vocabulary there is still to learn. Just concentrate on a small extract – either a video/audio clip or a short article – and work through it till you have mastered it. In this way, you will find that your command of French increases steadily.

Sources of real French

■ Newspapers (*Le Monde, Libération, Le Figaro* – the weekend issue is particularly interesting)
■ Magazines (*Le Nouvel Observateur, Cosmopolitan, Elle, Marie-Claire, Les Cahiers du Cinéma, Première*)
■ Satellite TV channels (For films: Ciné Cinéma, Paris Première. For news: CNN and Euronews)
■ Radio stations on long wave (France Inter 162, RTL, Europe Un)
■ World Wide Web sites (e.g. http://www.yahoo.France)
■ In London you can get information and activities at l'Institut Français, 17 Queensberry Place, London SW7 2DT (telephone 0171 838 2154)

French in the modern world

Outside France, French is the first language for large communities in Belgium, Luxembourg and Switzerland. France also has four overseas **départements** which come under French administration and are part of the French Republic: Guadeloupe, Martinique, Réunion and Guyane. There are two territorial collectivities: Mayotte and St Pierre et Miquelon and other overseas territories which include Polynésie Française, Nouvelle Calédonie, îles Wallis-et-Futuna, terres Australes et Antarctiques (terre Adélie, îles Kerguelen, Crozet, St Paul).

French is also spoken in countries which have been under French rule in the past. In North Africa, French is the second language after Arabic in Tunisia, Algeria and Morocco. The same applies to many central African countries such as Senegal. There is still an ageing population which speaks and understands French in Vietnam. In North America, Louisiana still has some vestiges of the French language. In Canada, in the province of Quebec French is spoken by many people as their first language. French in Quebec has developed differently from the French spoken in France. The accent and the intonations are very different and it has more or less become a language in its own right although its speakers can understand and communicate with French people without difficulty.

1 | SALUTATIONS
Greetings

In this unit you will learn:

- how to say hello
- greetings for different times of the day
- greetings for special occasions
- a few places in the town
- food and drinks
- about gender and number

1 *Simple greetings*

You may be starting to learn French because you would like to be able to communicate with people you meet for business or leisure when you travel to France or other parts of the world where French is spoken. It might be because you have French acquaintances visiting you or because your children are learning French at school. Communicating starts with very few words or, indeed, without words at all, for example shaking hands with someone, which French people do whether they are meeting friends or meeting people for the first time. It is usual to give close acquaintances two, three or even four kisses on the cheeks, depending on the region. If you watch young people at the terrace of a café for example you will see how spontaneous and communicative it all is!

The first few words are very important but also very simple. You will feel a great sense of satisfaction and achievement when you greet someone as if you have been speaking French all your life.

If you have the audio, listen to the following people saying *hello* and *goodbye*. It is day time:

Bonjour!   *Hello!*
Bonjour monsieur!   *Hello! (to a man)*
Bonjour Madame Martin!   *Hello! (to a woman – Mrs Martin)*
Salut Dominique!   *Hi!/Hello! (to a friend or acquaintance – Dominique)*
Au revoir mademoiselle!   *Goodbye (to a young, unmarried woman)*
À bientôt! À tout à l'heure!   *See you soon!*

Note that if you know someone's name, for example a neighbour, you greet them with their full name. Otherwise you greet them as **madame, monsieur** or **mademoiselle**. You usually use first names for family and close friends.

In addition, you need to know the correct greeting for each time of day:

Bonjour!   *Hello (any time in daytime)!*   **Bonsoir!**   *Good evening!*
Bon après-midi!   *Good afternoon!*   **Bonne nuit!**   *Good night!*

À vous maintenant! *Now it's your turn!*

1 Bonjour!

Say the appropriate greeting to the following people:

(a) Hello to Madame Corre
(b) Goodbye to Marie-Claire

(c) Good night to Paul

(d) Good afternoon to a young woman at the cash desk in the supermarket

(e) Hi to Marcel

(f) See you soon to Monsieur Jarre

Raise your voice slightly at the end of each word or expression and make the last syllable linger a little. Now listen to the audio to check whether you have got it right. If you do not have the audio just look up the answer at the back of the book.

2 Comment ça va? *How are you?*

Listen to the conversation between two neighbours and see whether you can tell who is feeling fine and who is feeling 'so so!'.

Madame Lebrun	Bonjour Monsieur Blanchard, comment ça va?
Monsieur Blanchard	Ça va bien merci et vous Madame Lebrun?
Madame Lebrun	Oh, comme ci, comme ça! Allez! Au revoir Monsieur Blanchard.

Point info:

Info is short for *information. Les informations* also means the news on the radio or TV.

■ When asking somebody **Comment ça va?** it is not intended that the other person should give a full health bulletin in reply. Most of the time people reply **Ça va, ça va!** or **Ça va bien merci!** If someone replies **Comme ci, comme ça!** it indicates that all is not well, things could be better, but the person is unlikely to disclose more unless they are asked further questions.

■ When you listen to French people talking you are very likely to hear **Allez!** which comes from **Aller** *to go*.
It is almost impossible to translate **Allez!** but you are likely to hear it said before greetings, especially (but not always) when people want to indicate that they wish to terminate the conversation. It roughly means *Well then* I'll leave you to your food or to your fishing, or to whatever the other person is doing or about to do:

Allez, à bientôt!
Allez, bon appétit! (to someone eating or about to start a meal)
Allez, bonne pêche! (to someone fishing or collecting shellfish on the beach)

À vous maintenant! *Now it's your turn!*

2 Cherchez la bonne phrase *Find the right expression*

Listen to some more greetings on the audio. Try to match them to the correct English expressions.

1) Allez, bon voyage!	(a) Have a good weekend!
2) Bon week-end!	(b) Happy birthday!
3) Allez, bonne route!	(c) Have a good journey!
4) Bonnes vacances!	(d) Happy new year!
5) Bonne Année!	(e) Have a safe car journey!
6) Bon anniversaire!	(f) Have a good holiday!

Check your answers at the back of the book.

3 A votre santé! *To your good health!*

French people always find a good reason to drink a toast. You will hear:

A votre santé!	*To your (good) health!*	These are said to all those assembled, or individually to someone you would address formally.
A la vôtre!	*To yours!*	
A ta santé!	*To your (good) health!*	These are said to one person you know well.
À la tienne!	*To yours!*	
Santé!	*Good health! Cheers!*	

À vous maintenant! *Now it's your turn!*

3 Quelle est la fête? *What's the celebration?*

Listen to the audio. You will hear three very short scenes. You have to decide what is being celebrated in each of of them:

Dialogue 1
- Bonne Année!
- À votre santé!
- Santé!
- À la vôtre!

A la vôtre!

Are they celebrating:

a) a good holiday b) a wedding c) New Year?

Dialogue 2
- Bon Anniversaire Françoise!
- À la santé de Françoise!
- À la tienne Françoise!
- À la vôtre!

Are they celebrating:

a) a good journey b) a birthday c) a good holiday?

Dialogue 3
– À la santé des mariés!
– À la santé d'Estelle et Paul!
– À la vôtre!

Are they celebrating:

a) a wedding   b) an anniversary   c) New Year

Vive les mariés!

| **Vive les mariés!** | *Long live the bride and groom!* |

4 *Buying something in a shop or in a café*

All you need to know is the name of what you would like to buy and how
to ask for the price. Saying *please* and *thank you* will help you feel confident
that you can express yourself, even if you are only using a few words.

S'il vous plaît (S.V.P.) *please*	**C'est combien?** *How much is it?*
Merci *thank you*	**L'addition s'il vous plaît!** *The*
Merci bien *thanks a lot*	*bill please*

Un sandwich et un coca S.V.P!

69 À vous maintenant! *Now it's your turn!*

4 Où sont-ils? *Where are they?*

Look at the illustrations and listen to the three short dialogues.

Dialogue 1
Are the people (a) at home (b) at a grocery shop (c) in a taxi?

Dialogue 2
Are the people (a) in church (b) in a café (c) at a grocery shop?

Dialogue 3
Are the people (a) at the station (b) in the street (c) at a grocery shop?

Now check your answers by reading the dialogues you have just heard.

Dialogue 1
– Taxi! Taxi! La gare du Nord s'il vous plaît!
– Oui madame!

Dialogue 2
– Un café, une bière et un sandwich au fromage s'il vous plaît.
– Oui monsieur.
– L'addition s'il vous plaît.

Dialogue 3
– Une baguette, un camembert et un kilo de pommes s'il vous plaît.
– Oui mademoiselle!
– Merci bien. C'est combien?
– Trente-deux francs mademoiselle.

5 Cherchez les mots *Look for the words*

Look again at the three dialogues above and find the French expressions for the following:

(a) a kilo of apples
(b) thirty-two francs
(c) a cheese sandwich
(d) a beer
(e) the station

Now check your answers at the back of the book.

5 Dans la rue *In the street*

You want to find out where some places are in the village. The important thing is to know what to ask for, then people will point you in the right direction.

Pardon madame, la boulangerie s'il vous plaît?	*Excuse me, where is the baker's please?*

Try to guess which places are mentioned in the following examples.

(a) Pardon monsieur, la poste s'il vous plaît?
(b) Pardon mademoiselle, l'office du tourisme s'il vous plaît?
(c) Pardon madame, le supermarché s'il vous plaît?
(d) Pardon madame, le garage Citroën s'il vous plaît?

Comment ça marche? *How does it work?*

So far you may have noticed three different ways of spelling the word for *good*:

Bon voyage!
Bonne année!
Bonnes vacances!

This is because in French, nouns (words which represent objects, people or ideas) have a gender; they can be either feminine or masculine. **Un voyage** *a journey* is masculine, **une année** *a year* is feminine, **des vacances** *holidays* is feminine but also plural.

The gender of nouns does not follow any logical pattern so you will need to be aware of the gender of every noun you learn.

Bon, bonne and **bons, bonnes** are four forms of the same adjective (a word which describes a noun) and they have the same gender as the nouns they describe, so we have masculine and feminine adjectives which can both be singular or plural.

French adjectives are spelt differently according to their genders. Generally (but not always) an -**e** at the end of an adjective is for feminine, an -**s** is for plural.

More examples:

If we take two other nouns **un raisin** *grape* (masc.) and **une pomme** *apple* (fem.) we have four spellings for **bon**:

un **bon** raisin *a good grape*   une **bonne** pomme *a good apple*
des **bons** raisins *good grapes*   des **bonnes** pommes *good apples*

des = *some/more than one*

Comment ça se prononce? *How does it sound?*

■ **Ça va** – C with a cedilla (ç) sounds like an **s**. It is only used in front of **a, o** and **u**: ça [sa], ço [so] and çu [su].
Note that there is no cedilla in **merci** and that in **comme ci, comme ça** – only **ça** needs a cedilla.

■ **Comment** – the -**t** at the end is silent and -**en**- is pronounced in a nasal fashion.

■ **Année, santé, enchanté, présente, appétit** all have an **e** with an acute accent. It changes the neutral **e** sound into one close to the final sound in *ready*.

■ **Bon** **a**ppétit – the two words are pronounced as if they were one. Because the second word starts with a vowel the -**n** of **bon** is linked to the **a**- of **appétit**, making **bon** sound like **bonne**. The same happens with **bon après-midi**.

◢ À vous maintenant! *Now it's your turn!*

6 La liste de provisions *the shopping list*

Make your own shopping list using all the words for food and drinks in
the unit.

1 kilo de pommes

BONNE CHANCE!
(Good luck!)

2 | **PREMIERS CONTACTS**
Meeting people

In this unit you will learn:

■ how to give and understand information about marital status, family links, age and profession

■ numbers up to sixty-nine

■ four verbs: **être** *to be*, **parler** *to speak*, **s'appeler** *to be called*, **avoir** *to have*

1 Enchanté de faire votre connaissance

 There is a wedding in the family. People have travelled from all over the place. At the dinner table two people who have never met before find out each other's names and where they come from.

 Listen a first time to the audio.

(a) What is the man's first name?
(b) What is the woman's first name?

Listen once more.

(c) Where is Claire from?
(d) Where is Alain from?

Now read the dialogue:

Homme	Bonjour, je m'appelle Alain. Et vous, comment vous appelez-vous?
Femme	Je m'appelle Claire.
Homme	Enchanté de faire votre connaissance, Claire! Vous êtes d'où?
Femme	Je suis de Paris. Et vous?
Homme	Moi, je suis de Marseille.

un **homme** *a man*	**Je m'appelle** *My name is …*
une **femme** *a woman*	**Vous êtes d'où?** *Where are you*
Comment vous **appelez-vous?**	*from?*
What is your name?	**moi** *me*

Find the French for:

(d) I am from Paris.

(e) Pleased to meet you.

To say where you are from you can name a town or a country:

Je suis de Bordeaux

Je suis de Londres

Je suis du Pays de Galles

Je suis des États-Unis

Je suis de New York

Je suis du Canada

I am from Wales

I am from the United States

À vous maintenant!

1 D'où êtes-vous?

You are François or Françoise, a guest at the wedding. You are from Boulogne. Fill in your part of the dialogue.

Lucien Bonjour, je m'appelle Lucien. Et vous, comment vous appelez-vous?

Vous (a) …

Lucien Enchanté de faire votre connaissance. D'où êtes-vous?

Vous (b) …

Lucien Je suis de Bruxelles.

Now do the exercise again, using your own identity.

Comment ça marche?

1 Des nombres et des chiffres *Numbers and figures*

The following table should allow you to work out numbers from 0 to 69

0	**zéro**	10	**dix**	21	**vingt et un**
1	**un**	11	**onze**	22	**vingt-deux**
2	**deux**	12	**douze**	23	**vingt-trois**
3	**trois**	13	**treize**	30	**trente**
4	**quatre**	14	**quatorze**	31	**trente et un**
5	**cinq**	15	**quinze**	32	**trente-deux**
6	**six**	16	**seize**	40	**quarante**
7	**sept**	17	**dix-sept**	50	**cinquante**
8	**huit**	18	**dix-huit**	60	**soixante**
9	**neuf**	19	**dix-neuf**	61	**soixante et un**
		20	**vingt**	69	**soixante-neuf**

À vous maintenant!

2 Le loto

Look at this LOTO grid and answer the questions which follow.

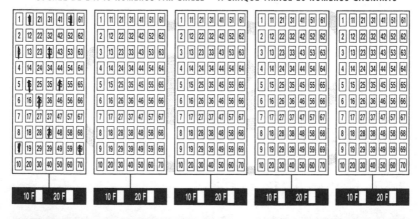

(a) For each grid how many numbers can you tick?

(b) How many winning numbers are drawn? On Wednesdays and Saturdays there are two draws.

(c) How much does it cost if you have two draws? If you have one draw?

Listen to the audio. Write down all the numbers you hear and find out if you have any of the winning numbers.

Point info

Did you know that the French National Lottery started in 1918 to fund the war widows' pensions, soldiers' disability pensions and the upkeep and education of the First World War orphans?

In 1933 it became officially **la Loterie Nationale** and it existed as such until 1990. The lottery is now run by a body called **La Française des Jeux**.

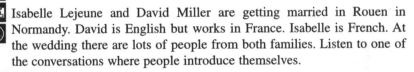

2 Je suis la mère d'Isabelle

Isabelle Lejeune and David Miller are getting married in Rouen in Normandy. David is English but works in France. Isabelle is French. At the wedding there are lots of people from both families. Listen to one of the conversations where people introduce themselves.

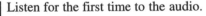

Listen for the first time to the audio.

(a) Who is Hélène Lejeune?

(b) Whose aunt is Anne Thompson?

Listen once more.

(c) Is Anne Thompson English?

(d) What is her husband's name?

Listen a final time.

(e) Where does she live?

Listen to the audio as many times as you need.

Madame Lejeune	Bonjour Madame, je m'appelle Hélène Lejeune. Je suis la mère d'Isabelle. Et vous comment vous appelez-vous?
Anne Thompson	Enchantée de faire votre connaissance. Je m'appelle Anne Thompson, je suis la tante de David.
Madame Lejeune	Ah, vous êtes anglaise?
Anne Thompson	Non, non, je suis française. Je suis mariée à Mark Thompson, l'oncle de David. J'habite en Angleterre.
Madame Lejeune	Ah très bien! Enchantée!
Anne Thompson	Voici mon fils Raphaël et voilà ma fille Sophie. Raphaël, Sophie, je vous présente Madame Lejeune, la maman d'Isabelle.
Sophie et Raphaël	Bonjour Madame.

 Now read the written dialogue and try to find out how to say the following in French:

(f)   I live in England
(g)   David's aunt
(h)   Let me introduce you to Madame ...
(i)   My son
(j)   My daughter

Check your answers at the back of the book.

Comment ça marche?

2 Voici/voilà *This is/that is*

Voici is used when introducing a first person, standing next to you.
Voilà is for introducing a second person, possibly standing further away from you.

More generally:

Voici is for pointing out someone or something close by.
Voilà is for pointing out someone or something slightly further away from you.

3 La famille

1   2   3   4   5

1) Voici Jacques, le frère de Monsieur Norbert.
2) Voici Gaétan, le fils des Norbert.
3) Voici Madame Norbert.
4) Voici Monsieur Norbert.
5) Et voilà Joëlle, la fille des Norbert.

Voici la famille Charcot   **et**   **voilà la famille Bastide**

3 Tu as quel âge?

 The children at the wedding are getting to know one another.

Read what they say.

Camille	Bonjour, je m'appelle Camille ... et toi comment tu t'appelles?
Sophie	Moi, je m'appelle Sophie. Et mon frère s'appelle Raphaël.
Camille	Moi je suis la sœur d'Isabelle. Je n'ai pas de frère.
Sophie	Tu as quel âge?
Camille	J'ai douze ans.
Sophie	Ah moi aussi j'ai douze ans! Mon frère, il a quatorze ans.

la sœur	*the sister*	**ma sœur**	*my sister*
le frère	*the brother*	**mon frère**	*my brother*
moi *me*		**toi** *you*	

Note that to say *my* in French you must use **ma** in front of a feminine word and **mon** in front of a masculine word.

Find the French for the following:

(a) I am twelve years old.
(b) My brother, he is fourteen.
(c) I don't have a brother.
(d) Me too!
(e) How old are you?

Comment ça se prononce?

In French, words tend to be linked together, particularly when the second of two words starts with a vowel. When saying her age Camille says: **J'ai douze ans**. These four short words are heard as two groups of sounds: [*jai douzan*].

Sophie says of her brother **Il a quatorze ans** which, again, is heard as two sets of sounds: [*ila quatorzan*].

It is important to know how the numbers are spelt because the last letter of the number is always linked with **an(s)** *year*. Here are some more examples:

Isabelle? Elle a vingt-cinq ans. [*ella vintcincan*]

Danielle? Elle a trente ans. [*ella trentan*]

Note that the **e** at the end of **trente, quarante**, etc. is not heard.

Arnaud? Il a neuf ans. [*ila neuvan*]

(an **f** sounds like a **v** when linking two words)

À vous maintenant!

3 Quel âge avez-vous?

Try saying the following:

(a) I am twenty-one years old.
(b) He is thirty-eight.
(c) She is sixty-nine.
(d) He is forty.

Now listen to the audio to hear the answers.

4 Vous parlez français?

Still at the wedding, Hélène and Anne discuss which language is spoken in the Thompson household.

Listen to the audio a few times and see whether you can answer the following questions.

(a) Which two languages are mentioned?
(b) Does she speak English or French with Mark, her husband?
(c) What does Mark teach?

Hélène Lejeune	Vous parlez français avec les enfants?
Anne Thompson	Oui, je parle français à la maison. Les enfants parlent couramment les deux langues.
Hélène Lejeune	Et avec Mark?
Anne Thompson	Avec mon mari je parle français ou anglais, cela dépend. Il parle bien le français, il est professeur de français.

avec	*with*	**couramment**	*fluently*
à la maison	*at home*	**mon mari**	*my husband*
les enfants	*the children*	**professeur**	*teacher*

 Find the French for the following in the dialogue.

(d) He is a French teacher.
(e) It depends.
(f) I speak French or English.
(g) I speak French at home.
(h) The children speak both languages fluently.
(i) He speaks French well.

📻 Comment ça marche?

Verbs

In this unit you have already come across four important verbs. (A verb is the part of the language used to indicate an action or state of things.) Here is what you have learnt so far:

Être *to be*

> **Je suis** française.
> **Je suis** mariée.
> **Il est** anglais.
> **Il est** professeur.
> **Vous êtes** anglaise?

> *I am French.*
> *I am married.*
> *He is English.*
> *He is a teacher.*
> *Are you English?*

Être indicates a state of things.

Avoir *to have*

> **J'ai** trente ans.
> **Il a** dix ans.
> **Elle a** vingt-cinq ans.
> **Je n'ai pas** de frère.

> *I am (have) thirty (years).*
> *He is ten.*
> *She is twenty-five.*
> *I don't have a brother.*

S'appeler *to be called*

This a reflexive verb, that is, the subject and the object of the verb are one and the same. Word for word **s'appeler** means *to call oneself*.

Comment **vous appelez-vous**?	*What's your name?* (lit. *How do you call yourself?*)
Je m'appelle Anne.	*I am called Anne.*
Comment **tu t'appelles**?	*What's your name?* (when speaking to a child or someone you know well)

Parler *to speak*

Je parle français.	*I speak French.*
Je parle anglais.	*I speak English.*
Vous parlez français?	*Do you speak French?*
Ils parlent français.	*They speak French.* (the **nt** in **ils parlent** is not pronounced)

À vous maintenant!

4 Cherchez la bonne phrase

Link the English sentences to the equivalent French expressions.

1   I am not married.
2   What's his name?
3   He has a brother and a sister.
4   I don't have a sister.
5   I don't speak English.

(a)   Je n'ai pas de sœur.
(b)   Je ne parle pas anglais.
(c)   Je ne suis pas mariée.
(d)   Il a un frère et une sœur.
(e)   Comment il s'appelle?

5 Qui est-ce?

Who is it? Read the explanations below and say what the family link is likely to be:

Your father? Your cousin? Your aunt? Your brother? Your grand-mother?

(a)   C'est la mère de mon père.
(b)   C'est le mari de ma mère.
(c)   C'est la sœur de mon père.
(d)   C'est la fille du frère de ma mère.
(e)   C'est le fils de mes parents.

3 | ON FAIT CONNAISSANCE
Getting to know someone

In this unit you will learn how to

■ introduce yourself fully
■ understand what other people say about themselves
■ talk and ask about professions, leisure activities, likes and dislikes
■ talk further about marital status and families

1 En stage *On a training course*

A group of people of all ages and backgrounds are on a weekend course (**un stage**) in Paris preparing for an amateur photography expedition to Vietnam. The first thing they do is a self introduction exercise to get to know one another.

The course participants (**les stagiaires**) have been asked to say the following things about themselves:

■ Name
■ Age
■ Town/area where they live
■ Marital status + family details
■ Profession
■ Languages spoken
■ Likes (leisure, hobbies)
■ Dislikes

They all give the information in different ways, so listen for the expressions they use to say their name, their profession and what they like or dislike .

Listen to what the first person says and then stop the audio. You may need to listen more than once to understand what is being said.

Natalie Le Hénaff

J'aime faire de la photographie.

Je n'aime pas faire le ménage.

Without looking at the text below can you answer the following questions about Natalie?

(a) How old is she?
(b) Is she married?
(c) How many children does she have?
(d) Does she speak English?
(e) Can you tell at least one thing she likes doing?

Listen to the audio again but this time you may look at the text.

"Bonjour! Je m'appelle Natalie Le Hénaff. J'ai trente-six ans.
J'habite à Vannes en Bretagne.
Je suis mariée. J'ai deux enfants, un garçon et une fille.
Je suis professeur d'histoire dans un collège.
Je parle français, anglais et espagnol.
J'aime aller au cinéma, voyager, lire et faire de la photographie.
Je n'aime pas faire le ménage."

From the text above can you tell which French expressions Natalie uses to say the following things?

(f) I am a history teacher.
(g) I love travelling.
(h) I live in Vannes in Britanny.
(i) I love going to the cinema.
(j) I don't like doing the housework.

Comment ça marche?

1 Saying your job

In French there is no indefinite article (*a* or *an* in English) in front of the name of a profession.

Natalie says she is a history teacher in a secondary school :

Je suis professeur d'histoire dans un collège.

The next person, Antoine Durand, (see page 30) says he is a sound engineer for a French TV channel, France 3:

Je suis ingénieur du son à France 3.

The omission of the indefinite article also applies when Antoine says he is a bachelor:

Je suis célibataire.

(**Célibataire** is used for both unmarried men and women)

2 How to express likes

- **J'aime** *(I like/love)*
- **J'aime bien** *(I like / I quite like)*
- **J'aime beaucoup...** *(I like... a lot)*
- **J'adore** *(I adore /love)*

Je becomes **j'** in front of **aime** because **aime** starts with a vowel. The same rule applies with **adore** and with all other verbs starting with a vowel. **e** is the only letter which can be replaced by an apostrophe in front of a vowel.

3 ... and dislikes:

■ **Je n'aime pas**

To make a verb negative (the equivalent of adding *not* in English), use **ne ... pas** (**ne** + verb + **pas**). Here **ne** becomes **n'** before a vowel (**aime**):

Je n'aime pas faire le ménage. *I don't like doing the housework.*

You can also use expressions such as:

■ **Je déteste** or **J'ai horreur de**... *I really don't like / I hate...*

Comment ça se prononce?

Look back at what Natalie says and find all the apostrophes. In each case, an apostrophe replaces an -e because the word that follows begins with a vowel or an **h**:

There is also one example of **de** losing its **e** in front of a vowel sound: **professeur d'histoire**. Here and in **j'habite**, the **h** is silent.

All these expressions are pronounced as if they were one word:

je **m**appelle/ **j**ai / **j**abite / **j**aime / je **n**aime pas / professeur **d**istoire.

Antoine Durand

Try to answer the following questions about Antoine after listening to the next part of the audio a few times:

(a) How old is he?
(b) Where does he live?
(c) What foreign language does he speak?
(d) What does he like doing best?

Now look at the text:

"Alors moi, mon nom c'est Antoine Durand. J'ai vingt-neuf ans.
Je demeure à Paris.
Je suis célibataire.
Je suis ingénieur du son à France 3.
Je parle français et allemand.
J'aime bien regarder des films et le sport à la télé. J'adore la photographie et les voyages.
J'ai horreur des voitures, alors je vais au travail à vélo."

Using the text above find out the following expressions:

(e) I live in Paris.
(f) I like watching films on TV.
(g) I hate cars.
(h) I go to work by bike.

Comment ça marche?

4 Alors

As soon as you hear French people talking amongst themselves you will hear **alors** or **bon, alors** or **oui, alors**. It loosely means **then** or **so**, similar to someone saying *well / so then…* in English. It is used to fill a gap in the conversation. It also means *therefore*.

Task: Find two different uses of **alors** in what Antoine Durand says.

Monique Duval

Listen to the next part of the audio and answer the following questions about Monique:

(a) How old is she?
(b) Who is Pierre?
(c) Where does she work?
(d) Does she speak English?
(e) How does she feel about football on TV?

Now read the text below:

"Bonjour, je m'appelle Monique Duval. J'ai quarante-cinq ans.
Je suis de Dijon.
Je suis mariée avec Pierre mais je n'ai pas d'enfants.
Je travaille à la poste.
Je parle un peu l'anglais et j'apprends le vietnamien.
J'aime beaucoup le sport, les voyages et la photographie.
Je déteste le football à la télévision."

Using the text above find out the following expressions:

(f) I work at the post office.
(g) I speak a little bit of English.
(h) I don't have any children.
(i) I am learning Vietnamese.

Pierre Duval

Listen to Pierre speaking on the audio and answer the following questions:

(a) How old is Pierre?
(b) What is his wife's name?
(c) Where does he work?
(d) Where does he live?

Now read the text of what Pierre said:

"Alors je me présente: je m'appelle Duval Pierre.
J'ai cinquante-deux ans. J'habite à Dijon.
Je suis marié avec Monique.
Ma mère est veuve et elle habite chez nous.
Je travaille chez Renault.

Je comprends un peu l'anglais.
J'adore les voyages et la lecture.
Je n'aime pas la télé sauf les documentaires sur les voyages."

The following words help you to understand what Pierre is saying.

avec	with	sauf	except
chez	at	veuve	widow/widowed (woman)

Using the text above find out the following expressions:

(e) My mother is a widow.
(f) I work at Renault.
(g) She lives with us.
(h) I love travel and reading.
(i) I don't like TV except travel documentaries.
(j) I understand English a little.

Comment ça marche?

5 Le nom de famille

When French people are introducing themselves in a formal way they often mention their surname first and then their first name:

Note that Pierre Duval says: **Je m'appelle Duval Pierre.** This is also the way names are written on envelopes for administrative or commercial purposes:

Monsieur Duval Pierre
16 Avenue de la Gare
DIJON

6 Quelles questions?

There is always more than one way to ask a question. Here are standard questions and answers about personal details.

Topics	Questions	Answers
Name	Comment vous appelez-vous? Quel est votre nom?	Je m'appelle Nathalie. Mon nom c'est Josianne.
Age	Quel âge avez-vous? Vous avez quel âge?	J'ai trente-deux ans. J'ai cinquante ans.
Where living	Où habitez-vous? Où est-ce que vous habitez? Où est-ce que vous demeurez?	J'habite à Nantes. Je demeure à Bordeaux.
Marital status	Vous êtes marié(e)?	Oui, je suis marié(e). Non, je suis célibataire.
Profession	Quelle est votre profession? Quel est votre métier? Quel travail faites-vous? Où est-ce que vous travaillez?	Je suis dentiste. Je suis dans le commerce. Je travaille chez Renault.
Languages	Quelles langues parlez-vous? Vous parlez anglais?	Je parle français et anglais. Oui, un petit peu.
Likes	Vous aimez le cinéma? Vous aimez le football?	Oui, j'adore le cinéma. Non, j'ai horreur du football.

 # À vous maintenant!

1 Je m'appelle ...

You are a participant on the Paris photography course. Try to make a statement giving the following information:

- Your name is Anne-Marie Pélerin
- You are 45
- You live in Boulogne
- You are a dentist
- You speak French, English and German
- You love football and photography

2 Questions et réponses

You will need to look back at the statements made by the people on the photography course. In the box overleaf enter the missing questions or the missing answers.

Names	Questions	Answers
Natalie	Comment vous appelez-vous?	
Antoine	Quel âge avez-vous?	
Natalie		Je suis professeur d'histoire
Monique	Où travaillez-vous?	
Pierre		J'habite à Dijon
Antoine		Je parle français et allemand
Monique		Oui, j'aime beaucoup le sport
Pierre	Vous êtes marié?	

3 Vrai ou faux?

The following statements are not all accurate. Looking back at our four course participants say which statements are true (**vrai**) and which ones are false (**faux**):

(a) Monique apprend le chinois.
(b) Pierre et Monique ont deux enfants.
(c) Natalie aime aller au cinéma.
(d) Antoine est célibataire.
(e) Antoine habite à Paris.
(f) Pierre travaille chez Citroën.

4 | UN VOYAGE EN BATEAU
A boat trip

In this unit you will learn how to:

  ask where something is situated
  understand some directions
  ask if something you need is available
  ask most forms of questions
  say what you would like to do
  count to 101

Travelling to France on a cross-Channel Ferry you may find that most of the staff are French. Although they are likely to speak English, use the opportunity to try out your French!

1 Au pont cinq

Sarah Burgess is travelling to France with a French friend, Dominique Périer. They have left their car on the car deck (**le pont**) and now they are looking for their cabin.

Listen to the audio once through, then answer these questions:

(a) On which deck is their car?
(b) On which deck is their cabin?

Listen again.

(c) Where do they go to find out? On which deck is it?
(d) Is it morning or evening?
(e) Did you get the number of the cabin?

Now read the dialogue.

Dominique	Bon, la voiture est au pont cinq. Maintenant allons à la cabine.
Sarah	Où se trouve notre cabine?
Dominique	Je ne sais pas. Allons au bureau d'information au pont sept.
Membre de l'équipage	Bonsoir madame.
Dominique	Bonsoir, j'ai réservé une cabine.
Membre de l'équipage	Oui, c'est à quel nom?
Dominique	Périer, Dominique Périer.
Membre de l'équipage	Oui, alors c'est la cabine 017 au pont huit. Prenez l'escalier à gauche.
Sarah	Allons-y.

la voiture *the car*	**c'est à quel nom?** *which name?*
je ne sais pas *I don't know*	**l'escalier** *the staircase*
membre de l'équipage *a member of the crew*	**à gauche** *on the left*
	allons-y *let's go*

You may be able to work out some words and expressions for yourself. Link the English phrases below to the equivalent French expressions:

1) Where is our cabin?
2) Let's go to the information desk.
3) Take the staircase on the left.
4) I have reserved a cabin.
5) The car is on deck five.

(a) Prenez l'escalier à gauche.
(b) J'ai réservé une cabine.
(c) La voiture est au pont cinq.
(d) Où est notre cabine?
(e) Allons au bureau d'information.

🎲 Comment ça marche?

1 Où se trouve...?/Où est...?

To ask where a place is use either **où se trouve...?** or **où est...?** These two expressions are totally interchangeable:

Où se trouve le bar?	*Where is the bar?* (lit. *where does the bar find itself?*
Où est le bar?	*Where is the bar?*

Remember, if a noun is in the plural form, the verb will also be in the plural form:

Où se **trouvent** les toilettes?/Où **sont** les toilettes s'il vous plaît?

2 à, à la, au, aux

These are prepositions. They are used to indicate a direction (to, at, in...) and are placed immediately before a noun.

Although all four words mean the same, you use the one that matches the gender (feminine or masculine) and number (one: singular, more than one: plural) of the noun it precedes.

■ **à** is generally used before the name of a place:
Allons **à Paris**. *Let's go to Paris.*

■ **à la** is used in front of a feminine noun:
Allons **à la cabine**. *Let's go to the cabin.*

■ **au** is used in front of a masculine noun. **au** is a contraction of **à + le**:
La voiture est **au garage**. *The car is in the garage.*

■ **aux** is used in front of a plural noun, either feminine or masculine. It is a contraction of **à + les**:
Allons **aux cabines téléphoniques**. *Let's go to the telephone kiosks.*

🐦 À vous maintenant!

1 Dans le bateau

Now it is your turn to ask questions about various locations on the boat. Look at the four diagrams of the boat overleaf. The first one shows a plan of the boat; the others show various places on decks 7, 8 and 9.

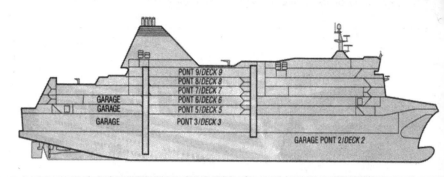

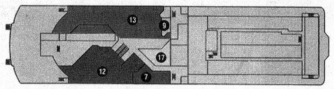

Pont 9

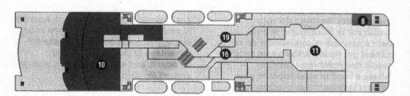

Pont 8

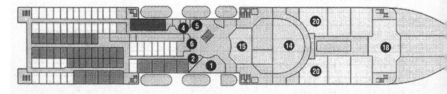

Pont 7

Here are some of the places that you can identify on the three decks.

1)	Bureau d'information	PONT 7	a)	*Self-Service Restaurant*
2)	Bureau de change	PONT 7	b)	*Baggage room*
4)	Cabines téléphoniques	PONT 7	c)	*Children's playroom*
6)	Local à bagages	PONT 7	d)	*Information desk*
7)	Salle de jeux enfants	PONT 9	e)	*The duty free shops*
11)	Restaurant Self-Service	PONT 8	f)	*Bureau de change*
12)	Salon de thé	PONT 9	g)	*Telephone kiosks*
13)	Le Bar "Le Derby"	PONT 9	h)	*Tea Shop*
15)	Les boutiques hors taxes	PONT 7	i)	*Newsagent*
17)	Le kiosque	PONT 9	j)	*"Le Derby" Bar*

Match the French names of places on the boat with their English equivalents. The numbers in the first column correspond to numbers on the diagrams of the decks opposite.

2 Répondez aux passagers

Look at the plan of the boat and imagine that you are a member of the crew answering passengers' questions.

Exemple:
Passager Le restaurant self-service s'il vous plaît?
Membre de l'équipage C'est au pont huit Monsieur.

Madame is used for a woman passenger (**passagère**), **monsieur** for a male passenger (**passager**).

How would you reply to these questions?

(a) **Passager** Pardon, la boutique duty free s'il vous plaît?
    Membre de l'équipage ...
(b) **Passagère** Où est le salon de thé, s'il vous plaît?
    Membre de l'équipage ...
(c) **Petit garçon** S'il vous plaît madame, où sont les jeux pour les enfants?
    Membre de l'équipage ...
(d) **Passager** Le bar c'est à quel pont?
    Membre de l'équipage ...
(e) **Passagère** Il y a un bureau de change s'il vous plaît?
    Membre de l'équipage ...

Comment ça marche?

3 Un passager, une passagère

Nouns finishing with **-er** tend to change to **-ère** in the feminine form.

Other examples are:

masculine	**feminine**	
le boulanger	la boulangère	*the baker*
le fermier	la fermière	*the farmer*
le boucher	la bouchère	*the butcher*

2 Est-ce qu'il y a un cinéma?

Sarah and Dominique are exploring the boat. What do they find?

Listen once to the audio and answer these questions:

(a) Is there a cinema on the boat?
(b) Are they going to see *A Hundred and One Dalmatians*?

Listen again.

(c) What film are they going to see?
(d) Is the film they are going to see at 23.00 or at 23.30?
(e) How much does it cost to get in?

Now look at the script:

Sarah   Est-ce q'il y a un cinéma sur le bateau?
Dominique   Oui il y a deux salons vidéo. On y va?
Sarah   Oui d'accord!
Dominique   Il y a deux films. À quelle heure?
Sarah   Alors, il y a *Star Wars* à vingt-trois heures et à vingt-trois heures trente il y a *Cent Un Dalmatiens*.
Dominique   Moi j'adore *Star Wars*! Et toi? Qu'est-ce que tu voudrais voir?
Sarah   Moi aussi je voudrais voir *Star Wars*. C'est combien?
Dominique   C'est 45 francs.

On y va? *Let's go?* (**On** is frequently used in conversation to express a collective action). **Oui d'accord** *Yes O.K.*	**Je voudrais + verb** *I would like to...* **Je voudrais voir** *I would like to see* **salon** *lounge* **salle** *room*

Link these English phrases to the equivalent French expressions from the script:

1) What about you?
2) At 23.30 there is *101 Dalmatians*.
3) What would you like to see?
4) Me too.

(a) Qu'est-ce que tu voudrais voir?
(b) Moi aussi.
(c) Et toi?
(d) À vingt-trois heures trente il y a *101 Dalmatiens*.

Comment ça se prononce?

In French there is a tendency for groups of words to be pronounced as if all the letters were linked up. This applies to the following:

Il y a [ilia] Y a t-il? [iatil] Est-ce qu'il y a? [eskilia]

However it is not always possible to link up all words. Although **est une** can be linked [etune], **et une** cannot. The **t** of **et** cannot be linked with the following word **une** despite the fact that it starts with a vowel. Doing so would alter the sound of **et** *and* to **est** *is*.

So in **un homme et une femme** (*a man and a woman*) **et** and **une** must be pronounced quite separately to avoid the meaning *a man is a woman*!

Comment ça marche?

4 Des nombres et des chiffres de 70 à 101

70 **soixante-dix** [60 + 10]	90 **quatre-vingt-dix**
71 **soixante et onze** [60 + 11]	91 **quatre-vingt-onze**
72 **soixante-douze**	92 **quatre-vingt-douze**
79 **soixante-dix-neuf**	99 **quatre-vingt-dix-neuf**
80 **quatre-vingts*** [4 × 20]	100 **cent**
81 **quatre-vingt-un**	101 **cent-un**
89 **quatre-vingt-neuf**	

*Only **quatre-vingts** is spelt with -**s** for plural (four twenties)

Point info

In some francophone countries 70, 80 and 90 are said differently:

70 is **septante** in Belgium, Switzerland and in the Democratic Republic of Congo

80 is **octante** in Belgium and Quebec
80 is **huitante** in Switzerland
90 is **nonante** in Belgium and Switzerland

À vous maintenant!

3 C'est combien?

Sarah and Dominique are at the duty free shop. They are checking the price of drinks and cigarettes.

Listen to the audio and answer these questions:

(a) How much is the Cognac?
(b) How much is the whisky?
(c) How much are the cigarettes?
(d) How much is the gin?

5 | ON VISITE LA VIEILLE VILLE
Visiting the old town

In this unit you will learn:

- how to ask for various places in a town
- how to follow and give directions
- how to count from 102 to 10 500
- some adjectives
- the imperative

1 Pour aller à ...?

Some tourists have just arrived in St Malo after their crossing on the ferry. They visit the old town, **la Vieille Ville**, which in St Malo is normally referred to as **L'intra muros** (the Latin phrase for 'inside the walls').

In this dialogue the tourist is asking for the station but the passer-by is not sure whether she means the bus station (**la gare routière**) or the railway station (**la gare SNCF**).

Point info

SNCF stands for **S**ociété **N**ationale des **C**hemins de fer **F**rançais (*National Board of French Railways*).

First read the key directions:

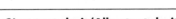

C'est tout droit/Allez tout droit   *It is straight ahead/Go straight on*
C'est à droite/Tournez à droite   *It is on the right/Turn right*
C'est la première rue à gauche/Prenez la première rue à gauche
   It is the first road on the left/Take the first road on the left
C'est la deuxième rue à droite/Prenez la deuxième rue à droite
   It is the second road on the right/Take the second road on the right
C'est la troisième rue sur votre gauche/Prenez la troisième rue sur
   votre gauche   *It is the third road on your left/Take the third road on your left*

Now listen to the audio and choose the correct answer.

(a) Can you tell whether the tourist is looking for:
 1) the bus station
 2) the railway station?

(b) Is it :
 1) the first street on the left and the next one on the right?
 2) the first one on the left and then straight ahead?

(c) How far away is it?
 1) one kilometre?
 2) one hundred metres?
 3) two hundred metres?
 4) more than two hundred metres?

Now listen to the audio again and read the dialogue.

Touriste	Pour aller à la gare s'il vous plaît madame?
Passante	La gare routière ou la gare SNCF?
Touriste	Euh, la gare SNCF...
Passante	Oui alors vous prenez la première rue à gauche et c'est tout droit.
Touriste	C'est loin?
Passante	Non c'est tout près. C'est à deux cents mètres, au maximum.
Touriste	Merci beaucoup madame.

 Link the English phrases to the equivalent French expressions

1) at the most
2) Is it far?
3) It's two hundred metres away.
4) It's straight ahead.
5) Take the first street on the left.
6) It's very near.

(a) C'est à deux cents mètres.
(b) C'est tout près.
(c) C'est loin?
(d) Prenez la première rue à gauche.
(e) au maximum
(f) C'est tout droit.

Comment ça marche?

1 Feminine and masculine adjectives:

You are already aware that there are feminine and masculine nouns in French. Similarly, adjectives describe the nouns they are linked up with and are feminine or masculine according to the gender of the nouns they accompany.

In French adjectives can be placed before or after nouns, although changing the position of an adjective can modify the meaning of the phrase. In many cases -e is added for the feminine form of the adjective and -s is added for the plural:

Masculine

un village	*a village*
un **joli** village	*a pretty village*
des **jolis petits** villages	*pretty little villages*
un **grand** château	*a big castle*
des **grands** châteaux	*big castles*

Feminine

une ville	*a town*
une **jolie** ville	*a pretty town*
des **jolies petites** villes	*pretty little towns*
une **grande** maison	*a big house*
des **grandes** maisons	*big houses*

But many adjectives change more radically from the masculine to the feminine:

le **vieux** port	*the old port*	la **vieille** ville	*the old town*
le **premier** jour du mois	*the first day of the month*	la **première** rue à gauche	*the first street on the left*

Masculine adjectives ending in -e remain the same in the feminine form:

le bonnet **rouge**	*the red hat*	la fleur **rouge**	*the red flower*
le **deuxième** magasin	*the second shop*	la **deuxième** rue	*the second street*

2 Some ordinal numbers

These are adjectives indicating a ranking position:

3rd	**troisième**	20th	**vingtième**
4th	**quatrième**	36th	**trente-sixième**
10th	**dixième**	100th	**centième**
15th	**quinzième**	1000th	**millième**

2 Vous tournez à gauche

As Sarah and Dominique leave the port they decide to visit Saint Malo before continuing with their journey. They ask for directions.

Listen to the audio once through, and answer the questions.

(a) Who would like to visit the old town?
(b) Whom do they ask for directions?

Listen again.

(c) Is the old town far from the port?
(d) Are there problems with parking?

Now read the text.

Dominique	Je ne connais pas St Malo. Je voudrais bien visiter la Vieille Ville. Et toi, tu connais?
Sarah	Non je ne connais pas. On y va! Demande la direction au monsieur, là.
Dominique	Pardon monsieur. Pour aller à la Vieille Ville s'il vous plaît?
Un passant	Oh c'est tout près d'ici! Alors vous allez au rond point et là vous tournez à gauche. La Vieille Ville est à cinq cents mètres à gauche.
Sarah	Merci monsieur. Il y a un parking pas trop loin?
Passant	Pas de problèmes avec le stationnement à St Malo, il y a plusieurs grands parkings.
Dominique	C'est parfait! Merci monsieur!
Passant	De rien mesdemoiselles!

Link the English phrases to the equivalent French expressions.

1) there
2) at the roundabout
3) I don't know St Malo.
4) It's perfect!
5) Ask the way.
6) no problem with parking
7) several large car parks

(a) Je ne connais pas St Malo.
(b) C'est parfait!
(c) Demande la direction.
(d) pas de problème avec le stationnement
(e) plusieurs grands parkings.
(f) là
(g) au rond point

Comment ça marche?

3 Savoir *and* connaître

The verbs **savoir** and **connaître** both mean *to know*: **je sais** (*I know a fact*), **je connais** (*I know a place, something or someone*).

Je ne sais pas où c'est.	*I don't know where it is.*
Je ne connais pas la ville.	*I don't know the town.*

4 Directions: the imperative

Here are some verbs used for directions: **aller** *to go*, **prendre** *to take*, **tourner** *to turn*, **continuer** *to carry on*.

When someone is giving directions or orders they use a verb form called the imperative (*Go...!, Take...!, Turn...!*). If the directions are given to a stranger or someone the speaker is not acquainted with, the form of the verb used is different from the form used for family or friends or children.

To an adult:

Allez jusqu'au château, **tournez** à gauche puis **prenez** la deuxième rue à droite.

To a child or to an adult you know well:

Va jusqu'au château, **tourne** à gauche puis **prends** la deuxième rue à droite.

jusqu'à/jusqu'au	*as far as*	**puis**	*then*

5 Vous *and* tu

There are two ways of addressing people in French:

Vous to individuals who are not friends or relatives, and to more than one person (**vouvoyer** is the verb which describes the action of addressing someone as **vous**).

Tu to a friend, relative or young child (**tutoyer** is the verb which describes the action of addressing someone as **tu**).

6 Directions: the present tense

It is also possible to use the present tense to give directions:

Vous allez jusqu'au château, **vous tournez** à gauche puis **vous prenez** la deuxième rue à droite. *You go as far as the château, you turn left then you take the second road on the right.*

☑ À vous maintenant!

1 Vous tournez à gauche encore

Look back at the dialogue on page 46.

(a) Can you find examples of people saying **tu** to one another?
(b) Can you find examples where someone gives directions using the
    present tense rather than the imperative?

2 La piscine, s'il vous plaît?

Look at the diagram below (this is not an accurate map of St Malo). The
ten places numbered on the diagram are listed in the key words box.

You are standing at the star, answering the questions of passers-by.
Choose the correct reply.

INTRA-MUROS

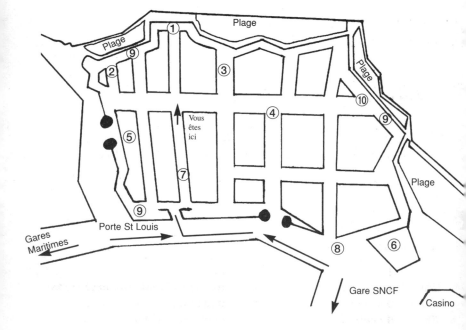

1 la piscine *the swimming pool*	**6 le château** *the castle*
2 le musée *the museum*	**7 la Grand'Rue** *the High Street*
3 la cathédrale *the cathedral*	**8 l'Office de Tourisme** *the Tourist Office*
4 le marché aux poissons *the fish market*	**9 les remparts** *the ramparts*
5 le marché aux légumes *the vegetable market*	**10 le petit aquarium** *the small aquarium*

Question 1   La piscine s'il vous plaît?
Réponse   (a) C'est sur votre gauche. (b) C'est à droite. (c) Continuez tout droit.
Question 2   La Grand' Rue SVP?
Réponse   (a) C'est ici la Grand'Rue. (b) C'est à gauche. (c) Prenez la deuxième rue à droite.
Question 3   Pour aller au marché aux poissons SVP?
Réponse   (a) Vous prenez la deuxième rue à gauche. (b) Allez tout droit. (c) Vous tournez à droite et c'est la deuxième rue sur votre droite.

3 Quelle question?

This time you are still standing at the same spot but you are asking the questions.

Question 1   …
Réponse   Alors vous tournez à droite et vous continuez tout droit. C'est à deux cent cinquante mètres.
Question 2   …
Réponse   Oui, alors tournez à droite et c'est la première rue à gauche.
Question 3   …
Réponse   Tournez à gauche et prenez la deuxième rue à droite.

Comment ça marche?

7 Des nombres et des chiffres de 102 à 10500

102	**cent deux**	1000	**mille**
170	**cent soixante-dix**	1900	**mille neuf cents/dix-neuf cents**
200	**deux cents**	2000	**deux mille**
900	**neuf cents**	2020	**deux mille vingt**
926	**neuf cent vingt-six**	10500	**dix mille cinq cents**

Note that when there is more than one hundred, **cent** is spelt with an **s** but if another number follows, the **s** is dropped:

deux cents *200*   but   **deux cent cinq** *205*

Point info

St Malo cité historique

St Malo was founded in the 6th century by the Welsh monk MacLow. It is the birth place of many sailors and discoverers. One of the most famous is Jacques Cartier who discovered Canada in the 16th century. There are still very strong links between St Malo and Canada, especially with Quebec. It is not unusual to see the Canadian flag flying in St Malo.

 # À vous maintenant!

4 Répondez aux touristes

It is your turn to answer questions asked by tourists.

Listen to the audio and answer the questions you will hear.

You need to know that:
- the castle is on the left
- the tourist office is straight ahead
- the swimming pool is on the right
- the museum is 200 metres away
- the cathedral is very near

R1 | PREMIÈRE UNITÉ DE RÉVISION

Profils

Listen to the audio several times. You will hear information which should allow you to complete these profiles of two friends. Fill them in in French. You may need to revise what you have learnt so far.

A	B
Nom:	Nom:
Prénom:	Prénom:
Âge:	Âge:
Adresse:	Adresse:
Numéro de téléphone:	Numéro de téléphone:
Nationalité:	Nationalité:
Nationalité du père:	Nationalité du père:
Nationalité de la mère:	Nationalité de la mère:
Profession:	Profession:
Lieu de travail:	Lieu de travail:
Aime:	Aime:
N'aime pas:	N'aime pas:

2 Une promenade à Saint Malo

Follow the directions on the map and say what your starting point is and where you are going.

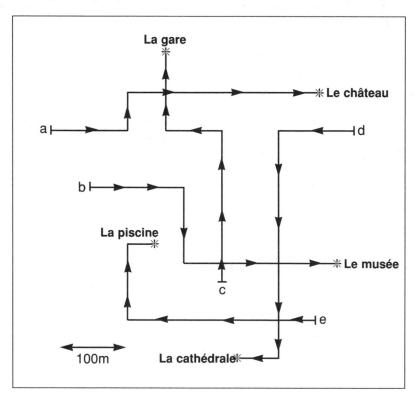

Exemple:

Alors pour aller au musée vous allez vers la droite. Après cent cinquante mètres vous tournez à droite. Continuez sur cent mètres et vous tournez à gauche et le musée est à deux cents mètres.

Réponse: From b) to the museum

1) Pour aller à la gare vous allez tout droit. Après deux cents mètres vous tournez à gauche. Vous continuez encore sur cent mètres, puis vous tournez à droite et la gare est à cent mètres environ.

2) Pour aller à la piscine vous allez vers la gauche, vous allez tout droit sur deux cent cinquante mètres. Vous tournez à droite. Vous continuez sur cent mètres et vous tournez encore à droite. La piscine est à cinquante mètres.

3) Pour aller à la cathédrale? Vous allez vers la gauche. Vous tournez à gauche après cent mètres. Vous continuez sur trois cents mètres et vous tournez à droite. La cathédrale est à cinquante mètres.

4) Alors, pour aller au château vous allez vers la droite. Après cent mètres vous tournez à gauche. Vous tournez à droite après cinquante mètres et vous continuez sur deux cent cinquante mètres pour arriver au château.

3 Orthographe des nombres *Spelling of numbers*

Read the card and say what spelling rule applies for 20 and 100.

6 OÙ STATIONNER?
Where to park?

In this unit you will learn

■ how to understand instructions for car parking
■ a bit about French money
■ the time
■ how to talk about daily routine

1 Où stationner?

Dominique and Sarah are trying to find a car park space. They have a guide to all the parking zones in St Malo which they got from the Tourist Office: **l'Office de Tourisme** or **le Syndicat d'Initiative** (the name varies from town to town but they are interchangeable).

You are likely to hear a lot of French people refer to a car park as **un parking** but in an effort by various governments to remove the English and American influence on the French language you will notice that the official name for a car park is **une zone de stationnement**. On parking notices and tickets you will see:

Stationnement gratuit *free parking*

Stationnement payant *pay-parking*

Stationnement interdit *Parking forbidden / No parking*

Stationnement autorisé *Parking allowed*

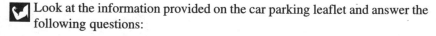 Look at the information provided on the car parking leaflet and answer the following questions:

STATIONNEMENT EN FONCTION DE VOS BESOINS.

compagnie Générale de Stationnement

Stationnement payant de courte durée, <u>2 H 30</u> maximum.
Tarifs: 0h15 = 1 F.
-1h = 4 F. - 2h = 8 F.
-2h30 = 10 F.

Stationnement payant de longue durée, <u>24 H</u> maximum.
Tarifs: 1h = 4 F.
-2h = 8 F. -3h = 10 F.
-4h = 15 F. -8h = 25 F.
-10h = 30 F.

INFORMATIONS ET CONTACTS
• Service du Stationnement. Horaires d'ouverture: du lundi au samedi de 9 H à 19 H.

NOTA:
Stationnement gratuit de 19h. à 9h

■ Stationnement interdit.
■ Stationnement libre et gratuit. Plusieurs centaines de places.

1) What is the maximum amount of time you can stay in the short-stay car park?
2) Match the following:
   (a) short stay
   (b) long stay
   (y) courte durée
   (z) longue durée
3) Say how long cars can be left in:
   (a) short stay car parks
   (b) long stay car parks
4) How much would you have to pay for four hours in the long-stay car park?
5) How many free parking spaces are there around the town?
6) Look at the parking ticket below. How long did the driver stay in the car park?

2 Tu as de la monnaie?

Listen to the audio and then answer these questions.

1) Which type of car park did Sarah and Dominique use?
   (a) long stay   (c) free
   (b) short stay
2) How long did they plan to stay?
3) How much did they pay?
4) How did they pay?

   Tick the coins they used and say how many of each type they used:
   (a) 50 Centimes   b) 1F   c) 2F
   (d) 5F   e) 10F

Now read the text.

Sarah	Tiens! Il y a des places au parking là-bas sur le quai.
Dominique	D'accord. C'est une zone de stationnement payant de longue durée. Tu as de la monnaie?
Sarah	Oui un peu. Il faut combien?
Dominique	Je ne sais pas. On reste combien de temps?
Sarah	Trois ou quatre heures.
Dominique	Alors quatre heures, cela fait quinze francs. J'ai deux pièces de deux francs et deux de cinquante centimes, c'est tout!
Sarah	Pas de problème, moi j'ai deux pièces de cinq francs.
Dominique	Quelle heure est-il?
Sarah	Il est dix heures et quart, donc on a jusqu'à deux heures et quart.
Dominique	Voilà notre ticket. Fin de stationnement autorisé: quatorze heures quinze.

Tiens!	*Look!*	**donc**	*therefore*
là-bas	*over there*	**voilà**	*here is*
C'est tout!	*That's all!*		

Link the following English phrases to the correct French expressions.

1) Are there spaces on the quay?   (a) Quelle heure est-il?
2) How long will we stay?   (b) Fin de stationnement autorisé
3) How much do we need?   (c) On a jusqu'à deux heures et quart.
4) What time is it?   (d) On reste combien de temps?

5) We've got until a quarter   (e) Il y a des places sur le quai?
   past two.

6) End of authorised parking   (f) Il faut combien?

Comment ça marche?

1 More new verbs

■ **Tiens!** is the imperative form for the verb **tenir** *to hold* but it is
frequently used as an expression of surprise *Look!* or **Tiens! Tiens!**
Well! Well!

■ **Cela fait quinze francs.** *That makes it 15 F.* **Fait** is the verb **faire**
to do /to make in the present tense.

■ **Il faut combien?** literally means *How much is necessary/ required?*
but it is best translated as *How much do we need?* The verb **falloir**
means *to need / to have to.* It is only ever used with the pronoun **il**
it in an impersonal form.

could also be translated as *one must*:

Il faut manger pour vivre   *One must eat in order to live*
Il faut souffrir pour être   *One must suffer to be beautiful!*
    beau / belle!

(**beau** is masculine, **belle** is feminine.)

■ **On** is also an impersonal pronoun meaning *one*, but it is frequently
used in conversation instead of **nous** *we.*

2 Formal and informal ways of asking questions

Most everyday conversations between people are informal. This is
reflected in the way people ask questions.

In all cases the questionning is shown in the tone of voice which rises on
the last syllables.

FORMAL	INFORMAL
As-tu de la monnaie?	Tu as de la monnaie?
Est-ce que tu as de la monnaie?	
Quelle heure est-il?	Il est quelle heure?
Combien faut-il?	Il faut combien?
Combien de temps reste-t-on?*	On reste combien de temps?

* see **On** above.

3 Des faux amis *False friends*

There are a few French words which are deceptively similar to English words although their meanings are quite different. There are two examples in the dialogue above:

■ **rester** *to stay*:
On **reste** combien de temps? *How long are we staying?*
(*to rest* is **se reposer** e.g. **je me repose** *I am resting*)

■ **de la monnaie** *change*
Tu as de la **monnaie**? *Have you got any change?*
Une pièce de monnaie is *a coin* (although **pièce** is usually used on its own).
Similarly **un billet** *a note* is short for **un billet de banque** *a bank note*.
(Money is **de l'argent**. Note that **argent** is also the word for silver.)

✍ À vous maintenant!

1 Remplissez les blancs

Choose some of the words from **Des faux amis** to complete the following sentences.

(a) You are in a shop and you would like to get some change.
  J'ai un billet de 500F. Vous pouvez me faire la _____ SVP?
(b) Je suis fatiguée. Je _____ _____ cinq minutes.
(c) On _____ quatre heures ici.
(d) Oh le joli bracelet en _____!
(e) Oh là là! C'est 1000F. Je n'ai pas d'_____.

3 À l'heure française

Two adults and two children have been asked three similar questions about their daily routine – **la routine quotidienne:**

1) *At what time do you get up in the morning?*
2) *At what time do you have lunch?*
3) *At what time do you go to bed?*

Questions aux adultes	Questions aux enfants
1) Vous vous levez à quelle heure le matin?	Tu te lèves à quelle heure?
2) Vous prenez votre déjeuner à quelle heure?	Tu prends ton déjeuner à quelle heure?
3) À quelle heure est-ce que vous vous couchez?	Tu te couches à quelle heure?

Before you listen to the audio, first check the French for the days of the week (page 64). Now look at the verbs in the three questions.

Se lever *to get up* and **se coucher** *to go to bed* are reflexive verbs. The first reflexive verb you came across in this book was **s'appeler** *to be called*, (page 24). **Vous vous levez** literally means *you get yourself up*. The subject and the object of the action is the same person (**vous** *you*, in this case) in reflexive verbs.

Vous prenez / tu prends are the present tense of the verb **prendre** *to take*. To say you have a meal in French, you normally say **je prends...**

Look again at the three questions above.

(a) What are the two expressions used for saying *'your lunch'* (one to an adult and the other to a child)?

(b) Now listen to the audio and fill in this grid:

	Question 1 (a)	Question 2 (b)	Question 3 (c)
Femme	7.30	?	?
Homme	?	1.00-1.30	?
Fille	?	12.00	?
Garçon	6.45	?	?

(c) Who gets up between ten o'clock and half past ten on a Sunday morning?

(d) At what time does the boy claim he sometimes goes to bed at the weekend?

📻 Comment ça marche?

4 L'heure

There is a general tendency to use the twenty-four-hour clock in France. It is used for transport timetables (**les horaires**), TV programmes (**les programmes de télévision**), computers (**les ordinateurs**), the Internet (**l'Internet**), working hours (**les horaires de travail**), school timetables (**les emplois du temps scolaires**), etc...

Most people use a mixture of the more traditional way of telling the time and of the twenty-four-hour clock:

4h00   il est quatre heures / il est seize heures

4h15   il est quatre heures et quart / il est seize heures quinze

4h30   il est quatre heures et demie / il est seize heures trente

4h45   il est cinq heures moins le quart / il est seize heures quarante-cinq

12h00 il est midi (*midday*) / il est minuit (*midnight*)

🐾 À vous maintenant!

2 Quelle heure est-il?

Listen to the audio and write down the correct letter for each time you hear next to each of the following times:

1) 1h20 ( )   2) 23h45 ( )   3) 17h05 ( )   4) 12h30 ( )

5) 8h56 ( )   6) 11h15 ( )   7) 3h00 ( )   8) 6h45 ( )

3 Matin ou après-midi?

Il est quatre heures du matin ou quatre heures de l'après-midi?

The distinction a.m. and p.m. has never been used in French. Listen to the audio to hear what people say when there is a need to make a distinction between morning and afternoon/evening.

(a) What time is it for Jean-Pierre in Paris?
(b) What time is it for Martine in Sydney?

4 À Gagner!

Anyone watching the nature programme on **la Cinquième** can win a prize. Read the competition details and then answer the questions on page 62.

(a) Which TV channel do you have to watch?
(b) Give the two dates and times when the programme is on.
(c) What is the question?

5 Le manoir de Jacques Cartier

Un peu de lecture! Remember Jacques Cartier, the famous sailor from St Malo and discoverer of Canada?

You can visit le Manoir de Limœlou, his manor house, but when exactly? (Check with **Les jours de la semaine et les mois de l'année**, page 64.)

Visite commentée
du Manoir de Jacques Cartier

Musée ouvert toute l'année
Accès aux visites guidées
Tous les jours du 1er juillet au 31 août
sauf week-end du 1er septembre au 30 juin

Horaires des visites
du 1er juin au 30 septembre
de 10 heures à 11 h 30 et de 14 h 30 à 18 heures
du 1er octobre au 31 mai
à 10 heures et à 15 heures.

Prix réduit pour écoles
et groupes de 10 personnes minimum
(uniquement sur réservation)

Gratuit pour :
Enfants au-dessous de 5 ans.

(a) Between which dates is it open every day of the week?
(b) Could you visit le Manoir de Limœlou the first week-end in September?

(c) In July what are the opening times?

(d) In May what time of day is it open?

(e) Who can get a reduction? Under what condition?

(f) How much does it cost for a child under the age of five to visit Jacques Cartier's Manor House?

(g) Find the French expressions for the following:

■ museum open all year round

■ every day from 1st July to 31 August

(h) Can you spot a difference between French and English in the way that days and months are written?

Comment ça marche?

5 Tout le, toute la, tous les, toutes les

In front of nouns these words are adjectives (respectively masculine, feminine, masculine plural and feminine plural according to the noun they are used with). They mean *all* or *every*:

Il faut visiter **toute** la ville et **toutes** les vieilles rues.	*We must visit the whole town and all the old streets.*
J'adore **tout** le village et **tous** les monuments historiques.	*I love the whole village and all the historic monuments.*

Look at your answers to (g) and (h) above: **toute** agrees with **l'année** (fem.) and **tous** agrees with **les jours** (masc. pl.).

Tous les jours ils arrivent en retard (*late*)

6 Les jours de la semaine et les mois de l'année:

Les jours de la semaine			
L: lundi	*Monday*	**V: vendredi**	*Friday*
M: mardi	*Tuesday*	**S: samedi**	*Saturday*
M: mercredi	*Wednesday*	**D: dimanche**	*Sunday*
J: jeudi	*Thursday*		

There is a saint for each day of the year. Until recently French children could only be given a name which appeared on this calendar. Many people celebrate their name day as well as their birthday.

1998

7 L'HÉBERGEMENT
Accommodation

In this unit you will learn how to:

■ find a hotel
■ book a hotel room
■ ask for various facilities

Point info

À l'office de tourisme

Most French towns have **un Office de Tourisme**. The tourist office is an ideal place for you to get information and advice, **renseignements et conseils** whether you are on holiday or on a business trip, **en vacances ou en voyage d'affaires**. It can help you find somewhere to stay, somewhere to eat and also something interesting to do. Some offices will do the booking for you but if not they will give you all the information you need. As a general principle they deal with:

Hébergement
Where to stay

Restauration
Where to eat

Loisirs
What to do – leisure

1 Choisir un hôtel

You need to know which facilities you are looking for in order to choose somewhere to stay.

Match the following French and English expressions.

1) Une chambre simple
2) Une chambre double

  (a) Full board (breakfast + dinner)
  (b) A room for a disabled person

3) Une chambre familiale
(avec un grand lit +
un lit pour enfant)
4) Une chambre pour personne
handicapée
5) Pension (petit déjeuner + dîner)
6) Demi-pension (petit déjeuner)

(c) A single room
(d) Half-board (breakfast)
(e) A double room
(f) A family room (with a double bed + a bed for a child)

Now match the symbols below and the French explanations to their English equivalents.

1 Facilités pour handicapés / pour voyageurs à mobilité réduite	(a) Main credit cards accepted
2 Ouvert toute l'année	(b) Bath & toilets
3 Catégorie (une /deux/ trois/quatre étoiles)	(c) Garage / private car park
4 Douches et wc	(d) Sea view
5 Salle de bains et wc	(e) Swimming pool
6 Garage / parking privé	(f) Children's games
7 Restaurant	(g) Lift
8 Principales cartes de crédit acceptées	(h) Facilities for disabled visitors
9 TV en chambres	(i) TV in rooms
10 Vue sur la mer	(j) Open all year round
11 Piscine	(k) Category (1/2/3/4 stars)
12 Ascenceur	(l) Pets welcomed
13 Jeux pour enfants	(m) Showers & toilets
14 Animaux acceptés	(n) Restaurant

2 Quelques renseignements

At the tourist office four tourists are requesting special facilities.

Listen to the audio, then answer these questions.

1) First tourist requires _____   2) Second tourist requires_____
3) Third tourist requires_____   4) Fourth tourist requires _____

Premier touriste	Je voudrais une chambre pour deux personnes pour une nuit dans un hôtel trois étoiles, avec vue sur la mer.
Deuxième touriste	J'ai un petit chien alors je cherche un hôtel où l'on accepte les animaux.
Troisième touriste	Je voudrais une chambre pour une personne dans un hôtel pas trop cher, avec restaurant et piscine.
Quatrième touriste	Ma fille est handicapée et elle a un fauteuil roulant. Nous voudrions une grande chambre pour trois personnes dans un hôtel avec ascenceur.

Comment ça marche?

1 Des verbes!

There are three groups of verbs

Group 1: verbs ending with **-er**. They very nearly all follow a regular pattern (**aller** is an exception).
Group 2: verbs ending with **-ir**. Some of them follow a regular pattern.
Group 3: mostly verbs ending with **-re/-oir**. They are mostly irregular verbs.

Vouloir *to want*

This is a very useful verb to express a wish / something you would like. As in English, it is more polite to use the conditional tense, rather than the present tense: *I would like* rather than *I want*.

Compare:

Je veux une glace!   *I want an icecream!*

and ....

Je voudrais une chambre   *I would like a room with two beds.*
à deux lits.

Nous voudrions louer des vélos.   *We would like to hire bikes.*

Chercher *to look for*

This is an easy verb to use. It is an **-er** verb because its infinitive (basic form) ends with **-er**. It is also a regular verb which means that it should provide you with a good example of how all regular **-er** verbs function.

Look carefully at the table below. It will provide you with some necessary information about French verbs in the present tense:

je cherche	Lit. *I look for* but best translated as *I am looking for*	**nous cherchons** **vous cherchez**	*we are looking for* *you are looking for* (see **vouvoyer** page 47)
tu cherches	*you are looking for* (see **tutoyer** page 47)	**ils/elles**	*they are looking for*
elle/il cherche **on cherche**	*she/he/it is looking for* Lit. *one is looking for* but best translated as *we are looking for*	**cherchent**	(It is pronounced the same way as **il/elle cherche**)

☑ À vous maintenant!

1 Je voudrais une chambre double

Say what accommodation you require :

(a) I am looking for a single room in a hotel with sea view.
(b) I would like a double room in a hotel.
(c) We are looking for a hotel with a swimming pool. (use **nous**)
(d) We would like a hotel room for the weekend. (use **on**)

3 Quel mode d'hébergement choisir? *Which kind of accommodation should you choose?*

Point info

Tourism and business tourism (**le tourisme d'affaires**) are booming in France and there are now lots of places to stay to choose from. Apart from the traditional range of hotels in towns there are also much cheaper and sometimes more convenient ranges of accommodation in out-of-town hotels, often in commercial estates (**zones commerciales**) or close to motorways (**les autoroutes**). **Hôtels Formule 1, Etap Hôtels, Hôtels**

Première Classe, Hôtels Campanile are mushrooming all over France and Europe.

Camping is still very popular in the summer and for young people there are youth hostels (**auberges de jeunesse** – **centres de rencontres internationales**) but the fastest growing area for accommodation is the equivalent of the English bed and breakfast (**chambres d'hôtes**) with the cost of breakfast included (**nuit + petit déjeuner**). Many of them are located in genuine farmhouses and are registered with **Gîtes de France**.

Chambre d'Hôtes à la ferme

La chambre d'hôtes à la ferme, c'est le "bed and breakfast" à la française chez des agriculteurs. Que ce soit pour une ou plusieurs nuits, vous serez reçus "à la ferme". Le matin, vos hôtes vous serviront un petit déjeuner campagnard. Dans certains cas, il vous sera même possible de prendre vos repas chez l'habitant (table d'hôtes). La chambre labellisée "gîtes de France", c'est l'assurance de bénéficier d'un accueil de qualité dans un cadre chaleureux.

Read the text above and find the French words or phrases for:

(a) at farmers' homes
(b) either for one or several nights
(c) a country breakfast
(d) your hosts will serve you

Services "plus" *Extras*

Now read the leaflet overleaf from Campanile and make your own vocabulary list. Find the French words for the following objects:

(a) toothpaste
(b) baby bottle warmer
(c) hair dryer
(d) toothbrush
(e) shaving cream
(f) a fax*

* This a new expression for fax, again created in an effort to move away from English and American influence on the French language. However **un fax** is still used most of the time.

Services "Plus" • Service "Extras"

• Dans la plupart de nos hôtels, possibilité de prendre une chambre 24h/24 grâce à notre système de paiement par carte bancaire		• In most of our hotels, possibility to take a room 24 hours a day thanks to our automatic payment system operating by credit card.
• Renseignements - réservation de votre prochaine étape chez Campanile		• Information - Booking your next stopover at Campanile
• Envoi d'une télécopie		• Sending a fax
• Vente de boissons (non alcoolisées)		• (Non alcoholic) beverages on sale
• La boutique Campanile : rasoir, crème à raser, dentifrice, nécessaire à couture, brosse à dents...		• The Campanile boutique : razor, shaving cream, toothpaste, sewing kits, toothbrush...
• Prêt d'un fer à repasser, sèche-cheveux, oreillers synthétiques, chauffe-biberon		• At your disposal : an iron, hair dryer, synthetic pillows, baby bottle warmer

4 Un petit hôtel

Having spent half a day in St Malo, Sarah and Dominique have decided that they want to see more of the town and the area around it (**la ville et ses environs/ses alentours**). They decide to stay for a few days (**quelques jours**) but are not sure about what to do and where to stay. At the tourist office they find that there is a lot of choice:

Listen to the audio and answer these questions.

(a) Are the two women likely to find something not too expensive for a few nights?

(b) Would they like a hotel with a restaurant?

Listen again.

(c) Do most hotels offer breakfast?

(d) Can they arrange hotel bookings for customers at the Tourist Office?

Now read the dialogue.

Dominique   Pardon monsieur, pouvez-vous nous renseigner? Nous passons quelques jours dans la région et nous cherchons un petit hôtel pas trop cher.

Employé   Oui, alors cela devrait être possible. Il y a beaucoup de petits hôtels deux étoiles qui sont très bien. Voici notre brochure... Vous voulez un hôtel avec ou sans restaurant?

Sarah   Sans restaurant. Il y a beaucoup de restaurants à St Malo.

Employé   Oh oui et la plupart des hôtels servent le petit déjeuner de toute façon.

Dominique   Vous vous chargez des réservations?

Employé   Non, je suis désolé madame! Nous ne nous chargeons pas des réservations, mais si vous voulez je peux téléphoner à l'hôtel de votre choix pour vérifier qu'il y a des chambres disponibles.

sans *without*	**disponible(s)** *available*	
la plupart *most*	**vérifier** *to check*	
de toute façon *in any case*		

Find the French expressions for the following:

(e) It must be possible.

(f) Could you give us some information?

(g) Do you take care of reservations?

(h) No, I am afraid not (madame)!

(i) We are spending a few days in the area.

Comment ça marche?

2 Encore des verbes

There are several new verbs or new verb forms in the dialogue.

Vouloir *to want/to like to* (see page 67)

■ It is used with **vous** here:

Vous voulez un hôtel?   *Would you like a hotel?*

Voulez-vous une chambre?   *Would you like a room?*

Devoir *ought to/must*

■ In the present tense it mainly means *must*:
    Je dois partir. *I must go.*

■ Just as **je voudrais** is a conditional form of **vouloir**, so **je devrais**
I ought to is a conditional form of **devoir**:
    Je devrais téléphoner à ma mère. *I ought to phone my mother.*

■ In the dialogue **devoir** is used with **cela** *that / it* (often shortened to **ça**
as in **ça va?** see page 14):
    Cela/ça devrait être bon. *It ought to be good.*

Servir *to serve*

There are two examples of **servir** in this unit:

■ The first is in the dialogue:
    Les hôtels servent le petit déjeuner. *Hotels serve breakfast.*
Note that **-ent** at the end is the plural form and you cannot hear it. The
singular form would be:
    L'hôtel sert le petit déjeuner à partir de huit heures. *The hotel*
    serves breakfast from 8.00am.

■ The other is in **Chambre d'hôtes à la ferme** (page 69):

    Vos hôtes vous serviront un petit déjeuner campagnard. *Your hosts*
    will serve you a country breakfast.
    Ils serviront *they will serve* is the future tense of the verb **servir**,

Se charger de *to take responsibility for something*

■ Je me charge de tout! *I'll take care of everything!* This is a reflexive
verb:

L'Office de Tourisme de St Malo ne se charge pas des réservations.
This is best translated as *St Malo's Tourist Office does not deal with
reservations.*

☑ À vous maintenant!

2 Chargez-vous de vos réservations avec l'Internet!

Take care of your own bookings with the Internet. If you have access to
the Internet you can use **Yahoo France** as a server. Go to **Tourisme** and
then **Hébergement**, and choose the region of France you want to visit.

Here is the information provided by the Hôtel du Palais at St Malo:

HÔTEL**
DU
PALAIS

Hôtel situé dans la partie haute de la vieille ville: l'Intra Muros. Proche des remparts et de la plage, ainsi que des rues commerçantes très animées tout en restant dans un environnement dégagé et calme. Accès aisé en voiture en toutes saisons.

CHAMBRES
18 Chambres – Toilettes, WC – Douche ou bain – Ascenseur
Télévision, Chaînes françaises et anglaises – Petit déjeuner

Prix de base: Chambre double (2 personnes) 220 Fr à 330 Fr

(a) Where is l'Hôtel du Palais situated?
(b) How many rooms have they got?
(c) Would you be able to watch EastEnders?
(d) What other facilities do they offer?
(e) What is their basic price for a double room?

8 | À L'HÔTEL
At the hotel

In this unit you will learn:

■ how to express a preference and make some comparisons
■ how to book a hotel, indicate requirements, understand instructions
■ the alphabet, how to use accents and spell names
■ **du, de la, des**
■ the pronouns **le, la, les**
■ **vouloir, pouvoir, prendre**

1 Quel hôtel choisir?

 Monsieur and Madame Olivier have some difficulties choosing a hotel. The choice is between:

L'HÔTEL **DE LA** GARE **   (*Station Hotel*)
L'HÔTEL **DE L'**ÉGLISE *   (*Church Hotel*)
L'HÔTEL **DU** CENTRE ****   (*Centre Hotel*)
L'HÔTEL **DES** VOYAGEURS ***   (*Travellers' Hotel*)

Listen once to the audio, then answer these questions:

(a) Which hotel does Monsieur Olivier suggest in the first place?
(b) He gives three reasons for his choice. Name one of them.

Listen to the audio again.

(c) Where is l'Hôtel des Voyageurs situated?
(d) Who makes the final choice?
(e) What reason is given for the choice?

Now read the dialogue:

Madame Olivier   Alors quel hôtel choisis-tu?
Monsieur Olivier   Pas de problèmes, descendons à l'Hôtel de la Gare.

C'est tout près de la gare. C'est plus pratique, c'est plus facile avec les bagages et c'est l'hôtel le moins cher!

Madame Olivier   Oui d'accord mais il y a aussi l'Hôtel des Voyageurs. C'est aussi tout près de la gare! Alors, quel hôtel choisis-tu?

Monsieur Olivier   Oh je te laisse choisir, c'est plus simple!

Madame Olivier   Dans ce cas je choisis l'Hôtel du Centre. C'est plus loin de la gare mais c'est certainement plus confortable!

Link the following English phrases to the equivalent French expressions:

1) It's further from the station.	(a) Oui, d'accord mais...
2) Yes OK but...	(b) C'est plus pratique.
3) It's the cheapest.	(c) C'est plus loin de la gare.
4) It's certainly more comfortable.	(d) Je te laisse choisir.
5) It's more convenient.	(e) C'est certainement plus confortable.
6) It's easier.	(f) C'est le moins cher.
7) I'll let you choose.	(h) C'est plus facile.

Comment ça marche?

1 Du, de la, de l', des

The names of the four hotels on page 74 have been used to show that there are four different ways to say *of the*.

Notice the word order in French: *Hotel of the station* rather than *Station hotel*.

You use **du, de la, de l'** or **des** according to the gender and number of the noun which follows. This can be illustrated with the following names of streets (**rues**) or town squares (**places**):

De + feminine noun = **de la**	**Rue de la Cité**
De + masculine noun = **du**	**Rue du Port**
De + singular noun beginning with a vowel or mute h = **de l'**	**Rue de l'Europe**
De + plural noun (fem. or masc.) = **des**	**Place des Québécois**

2 **Choisir** *to choose*

In Unit 7 (page 68) you met the verb **chercher**, an -er verb with a regular pattern. Similarly **choisir** which belongs to the second group of verbs (those regular verbs ending in **-ir**) is a useful model for other **-ir** verbs. (Unfortunately quite a few verbs ending in **-ir** are irregular and belong to the third group of verbs.) The letters in bold below show the pattern.

Choisir *in the present tense*

je chois**is**	*I choose/I am choosing*	nous choisis**sons**	*we choose*
tu chois**is**	*you choose*	vous choisi**ssez**	*you choose*
il/elle chois**it**	*he/she/it/I am choosing*	ils/elles choisi**ssent**	*they choose*

3 **Plus** *more* and **moins** *less*

In order to make a comparison you need at least two comparable things: **C'est plus pratique** effectively means that the Station Hotel is more convenient in terms of location than the other three hotels. **C'est plus pratique** is therefore a short cut for: L'Hôtel de la Gare est **plus** pratique **que** l'Hôtel du Centre, etc. (*more convenient than...*).

■ In more formal speech the sentence would start with **Il est ...**
Il est plus pratique de descendre* à l'Hôtel de la Gare que de descendre à l'Hôtel du Centre.

  * **Descendre** usually means *to go down, to alight* but here it means *to put up at a hotel*. In the dialogue **Descendons à l'Hôtel de la Gare** simply means *Let's go to ...*

■ **C'est moins cher** is a short cut for: L'Hôtel de la Gare est **moins** cher **que** l'Hôtel du Centre (*less expensive than.../cheaper than ...*)
■ **C'est le moins cher** (*it's the least expensive/it's the cheapest*)

À vous maintenant!

1 À qui sont les valises?

Three suitcases have been left in the corridor. Whose are they?

Look at the people and at the three suitcases and say whether the following statements are true or false (**vrai ou faux**).

(a) C'est la valise de la mère.
(b) C'est la valise du père.
(c) C'est la valise des enfants.

2 Nommez les cafés!

Choose the correct words to complete the name of each café.

    EUROPE   **VIEILLE VILLE**   **PORT**   **AMIS** (*friends*)

(a) Café des ____   (b) Café du ____
(c) Café de la ____   (d) Café de l'____

3 Jeu du café mystère

The name of a café, the name of a hotel and a name for the part of a town are hidden in the grid. Can you find them?

Mots cachés *hidden words*

```
C Q A D H B G T I C R V
H A P D E O U Y T N H I
S Q F X G L -T W T T Y E
H O T E L D U P O R T I
R E G T D F M E D A W L
T G H W A E F P F M F L
A N G L A I S V I L L E
A M G L B I S Q C R U P
B C V N F T H W A Q S F
```

4 Un peu de publicité

What are the two selling points mentioned in this advert for the SEAT Ibiza?

Seat Ibiza SE. C'est une des moins chères, et c'est une des plus riches.

2 À l'hôtel de la Plage**

 Monsieur and Madame Landré are at the reception desk (**au bureau de réception**) of the Beach Hotel.

 Listen once to the audio and answer these qeustions:

(a) Have Monsieur and Madame Landré reserved a room?
(b) How long do they intend to stay ?

Listen to the audio again.

(c) On which floor is their room?
(d) What is their room number?

Listen one more time.

(e) At what time is breakfast?

(f) At what time does the hotel door close?

Now read the dialogue:

Réceptionniste	Bonsoir monsieur-dame. Vous désirez?
Madame Landré	Nous avons réservé une chambre pour deux personnes, pour deux nuits.
Réceptionniste	Bien, c'est à quel nom?
Madame Landré	Landré, Jacques et Martinc Landré.
Réceptionniste	Cela s'épelle comment?
Monsieur Landré	L-a-n-d-r-e accent aigu.
Réceptionniste	Ah oui, voilà. Une chambre double pour deux nuits. Alors vous avez la chambre vingt-cinq au troisième étage. L'ascenceur est au bout du couloir. Voici votre clef. Vous prendrez le petit déjeuner?
Madame Landré	Euh oui! C'est à quelle heure?
Réceptionniste	Alors le petit déjeuner est servi dans la salle à manger de huit heures à dix heures mais vous pouvez le prendre dans votre chambre si vous voulez.
Monsieur Landré	Nous le prendrons dans la salle à manger, merci.
Réceptionniste	Très bien. Si vous avez besoin de quoi que ce soit, n'hésitez pas à m'appeler. Si vous sortez, gardez votre clef avec vous parce que la porte de l'hôtel ferme à vingt-trois heures. Bon séjour à l'Hôtel de la Plage, Monsieur et Madame Landré!
M. et Mme Landré	Merci bien Mademoiselle.

Vous désirez?   *What can I do for you?* (**désirer** *to wish/desire*)
Cela s'épelle comment?   *How do you spell it/how is it spelt?*
au bout du couloir   *at the end of the corridor*
la salle à manger   *the dining room*
avoir besoin de ...   *to need ...*
quoi que ce soit   *what ever it is*
parce que   *because**
*Another word for *because* is **car** but it is more formal and it is used less frequently in speech and more often in formal written French.

Link the following English phrases to the equivalent French expressions:

1) on the third floor
2) Do not hesitate to call me.
3) if you go out
4) Keep your key.
5) Have a good stay!
6) The hotel door closes at...
7) We have reserved a room.

(a) si vous sortez
(b) Nous avons réservé une chambre.
(c) La porte de l'hôtel ferme à...
(d) N'hésitez pas à m'appeler.
(e) au troisième étage
(f) Gardez votre clef.
(g) Bon séjour!

Comment ça se prononce?

Monsieur Landré was asked how to spell his name (**Cela s'épelle comment?**) If you need to spell your name, you will need to know the French alphabet – listen to it on the audio and repeat it:

A,B,C,D,E,F,G,H,I,J,K,L,M,N,O,P,Q,R,S,T,U,V,W(double V),X,Y (I grec),Z

In addition to spelling the letters you also need to spell accents and other signs. Listen to them and repeat them:

é = e accent aigu
è = e accent grave
ê = e accent circonflexe (also â, î, ô, û - often in place of **s** in earlier language e.g. ho**s**tel has become hô**t**el, pa**s**te – pâte, ba**s**tard – bâtard, ho**s**pital – hôpital)
ë = e tréma (used to keep two vowel sounds separate e.g. **Noël**)
ç = cédille
Examples of double letters: deux c, deux f, deux m, deux s, etc.

À vous maintenant!

5 Écoutez et écrivez

Listen to the way people spell their names and write down what you hear:

1 Sylvie _____
2 _____ Leberre
3 _____ _____
4 Now can you spell your name in French?

Comment ça marche?

4 Pronouns: le, la , les

The receptionist says:

Vous pouvez le prendre dans votre chambre... *You can take it in your room ...*

Le refers to **le petit déjeuner** *breakfast*. **Le** here is a pronoun, a word which stands in for a noun, although not necessarily in the same position. At a later stage you will learn how to use a whole range of pronouns but for the moment it is important to understand the difference between the articles **le**, **la**, and **les** which mean *the* and come in front of nouns, and the pronouns **le**, **la** and **les** which replace nouns altogether:

Vous prendrez le **petit déjeuner**?
Oui nous **le** prendrons.   *Yes we will have it.*
Vous gardez **la clef**?
Oui je **la** garde.   *Yes I am keeping it.*
Tu gardes **les clefs**?
Oui je **les** garde.   *Yes I am keeping them.*

5 Vouloir, pouvoir, prendre

These three verbs belong to the third group of verbs (mostly irregular which means that they do not all have the same spelling pattern). Here they are in the present tense.

Vouloir *to want* in the present tense

je veux	*I want*	nous voul**ons**	*we want*
tu veux	*you want*	vous voul**ez**	*you want*
il/elle/on	*he/she/one*	ils /elles	*they want*
veut	*wants*	veul**ent**	

Pouvoir *to be able to*

je peux	*I can*	nous pouv**ons**	*we can*
tu peux	*you can*	vous pouv**ez**	*you can*
il/elle/on	*he/she/one*	ils/elles	*they can*
peut	*can*	peuv**ent**	

Prendre *to take*

je prends	*I take*	nous pren**ons**	*we take*
tu prends	*you take*	vous pren**ez**	*you take*
il/elle/on	*he/she/one*	ils/elles	*they take*
prend	*takes*	prenn**ent**	

You now know enough about verbs to look them up in the Verb table appendix (see page 307). However you do not have to check endings every time you want to use a verb. For instance you know that when you use **vous** in the present tense the ending of the verb is likely to be **-ez**, and with **nous** the ending is **-ons**.

6 Verb + infinitive

Vous pouvez prendre le petit *You can have breakfast in your*
déjeuner dans votre chambre. *room.*

In this sentence **prendre** is in the infinitive (the basic form of the verb). That is simply because when one verb follows another, the second one remains in the infinitive, except after **avoir** *to have* and **être** *to be*.

☑ À vous maintenant!

6 Pouvoir et prendre

(a) It is your turn to find the correct endings for the verb **pouvoir** *can* and for the verb **prendre** *to take*.

The first column is a list of the pronouns *I, you*, etc. (referred to as subject pronouns). Link each pronoun to the correct part of the verb listed in the second column (each pronoun can be linked to more than one verb form). Try to do this without referring back to **Comment ça marche?**, to see if you have learnt them.

Je	pouvez
Tu	prends
Il	prennent
Elle	prend
On	peuvent
Nous	peux
Vous	prenons
Ils	prenez
Elles	peut

(b) In the dialogue on pages 79–80 there are two examples of **prendre** in the future tense (*I will take* etc.). Can you identify them?

(c) Encore un proverbe! Another proverb! Here are two versions of the same French Proverb:

Quand on veut on peut.
Vouloir c'est pouvoir.

Can you find an equivalent English proverb?

9 | UNE SI JOLIE PETITE VILLE!

Such a pretty little town!

In this unit you will learn:

■ places in a town and their location
■ more about the time
■ to plan for the near future
■ parts of the day

1 C'est à côté du commissariat

Dominique and Sarah visit the old town. They each go their own way.

Listen to the audio once, then answer these questions:

(a) What is Sarah going to do?
(b) Can it be found on the map of the town?

Listen to the audio again.

(c) What is Dominique going to do?
(d) When will they meet again? In:
    1) two hours' time   2) an hour's time   3) half an hour's time

Now read the dialogue:

Sarah	Je vais poster quelques cartes postales. Je vais essayer de trouver un bureau de poste.
Dominique	Regarde, la poste est indiquée sur le plan de la ville, là, PTT. C'est Place des Frères Lamennais. Tiens, regarde, c'est à côté du commissariat de police, en face de la cathédrale.
Sarah	Parfait, j'y vais! Et toi qu'est-ce que tu vas faire?
Dominique	Oh je ne sais pas, je vais peut-être faire un tour des remparts. On se retrouve dans une heure?
Sarah	OK! Où ça?

Dominique	Euh, au bout de la Grand' Rue, derrière la cathédrale, au coin de la rue Porcon de la Barbinais
Sarah	Au revoir! Bonne promenade!
Dominique	Salut! A tout à l'heure!

à côté de *next to*		**chacun/chacune** *each one*	
en face *opposite*		**de l'autre côté*** *on the other side*	
derrière *behind*		**·devant*** *in front of...*	
entre* *in between*			
au coin de... *at the corner of/round the corner from*		(*not in the text)	

 Link the following English phrases to the equivalent French expressions.

1) the police station
2) The post office is marked on the map.
3) look
4) I may go round the ramparts
5) What are you going to do?
6) Have a good walk!
7) Let's meet again in an hour's time.
8) Where abouts?

(a) La poste est indiquée sur le plan.
(b) Où ça?
(c) Bonne promenade!
(d) On se retrouve dans une heure.
(e) le commissariat de police
(f) regarde
(g) Qu'est-ce que tu vas faire?
(h) Je vais peut-être faire un tour des remparts.

 Vrai ou faux? Say whether the following statements are true or false.

(a) Le commissariat de police est derrière la cathédrale.
(b) La poste est indiquée sur le plan.
(c) Sarah cherche la cathédrale.
(d) Dominique va à la poste.
(e) Elles (les deux femmes) se retrouvent dans deux heures.

Comment ça marche?

1 Aller

The verb **aller** *to go* appears several times in the dialogue. In Unit 7 (page 67), you learnt that **aller** is the only verb ending in **-er** which does not follow the usual pattern. Here it is:

Aller *in the present tense*

je vais	*I go/I am going*	nous all**ons**	*we go/are going*
tu vas	*you go/are going*	vous all**ez**	*you go/are going*
il/elle/on	*he/she/one goes/*	ils /elles	*they go/are going*
va	*is going*	vo**nt**	

Aller + *a second verb in the infinitive*

This is used to indicate that an action will take place in the very near future:

Je **vais poster** quelques cartes postales.	*I am going to post a few postcards.*
Je **vais essayer** de **trouver** un bureau de poste.	*I am going to try and find a post office.*

In fact in this last example there are two verbs following **aller**, both of them in the infinitive.

Qu'est-ce que tu **vas faire**?	*What are you going to do?*
Je **vais** peut-être **faire** un tour des remparts.	*Perhaps I'll take a walk around the ramparts.*
Je **vais faire** une promenade.	*I am going to go for a walk.*

J'y vais *I am going (there)*

Y is a pronoun standing in place of a phrase beginning with **à**. When Sarah says **J'y vais** in the dialogue it is short for **Je vais à la poste**.

2 Trouver – se retrouver *to find – to meet again*

re- at the beginning of a verb indicates that the action is being done again e.g. **faire** *to do* and **refaire** *to redo/do again*.

Se retrouver is like a reflexive verb but here it involves two people. The action is reciprocal (Sarah is going to find Dominique again and Dominique is going to find Sarah).

S'embrasser *to kiss one another* is another example of a reciprocal action:

Les amants s'embrassent. *The lovers kiss.*

☑ À vous maintenant!

1 Faites des phrases

What are all the people whose names appear in column A going to do? For each sentence columns A and C remain the same. Columns B and D are jumbled. You have to find the right items from these two columns to complete each sentence. Can you find eight correct sentences? Can you say what they mean?

A	B	C	D
1) M & Mme Olivier	allons	visiter	des cartes postales
2) Tu	va	téléphoner	une promenade
3) Sarah Burgess	vas	choisir	le petit déjeuner au lit
4) Vous	vont	chercher	la vieille ville
5) Je	vont	faire	à St Malo
6) On	allez	rester	du travail
7) Les enfants	va	voir (to see)	à ton frère
8) Nous	vais	prendre	le dernier film de Spielberg

Point info

Les PTT ou LA POSTE

PTT is the old acronym for **P**oste et **T**éléphones et **T**élécommunications. Although the name changed a long time ago to **La Poste**, the acronym has remained in most older French people's vocabulary.

2 Une si jolie petite ville!

Spend a few minutes studying the diagram overleaf. There is a multitude of small French towns where you can find all the buildings, shops and institutions pictured in it. You have already learnt some of the names and therefore you only need to concentrate on the new ones.

Look at the names of all the places in the town and say which of them are referred to in the second column.

Lieu place	**C'est où?** Where is it?
1) la Place de la République	(a) C'est entre la mairie et la boucherie.
2) le Bar-Tabac du Centre (bureau de tabac) *bar-tobaconnist's*	(b) C'est derrière la poste, entre la banque et le bar-tabac.
3) l'église *the church*	(c) C'est entre le Café de la Poste et l'Office de Tourisme.

4) la pharmacie *the chemist's*

5) le Commissariat de Police

6) la Mairie *the Town Hall*
   (l'Hôtel de Ville in larger towns)

7) la bibliothèque municipale
   the public library

8) la boucherie *the butcher's*

9) l'Office de Tourisme

10) la Maison de la Presse
    the newsagent's + bookshop

11) le Café de la Poste

12) l'Hôtel-Restaurant St Jacques

13) l'Alimentation (l'épicerie)
    general food store

14) la poste

15) la boulangerie–pâtisserie
    baker's/cake shop

16) la banque *the bank*

17) la charcuterie *the delicatessen*

18) le camping municipal
    the municipal campsite

(d) C'est devant la bibliothèque et
   à côté de l'Office de Tourisme.

(e) C'est rue François Mitterand,
   derrière l'alimentation.

(f) C'est à côté de l'église, près
   du Commissariat de Police.

(g) C'est derrière le bar-tabac et à
   côté du camping municipal.

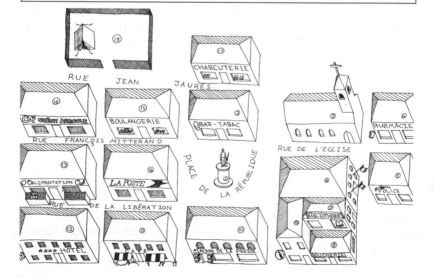

You are in **la Place de la République** when a passer-by stops you and asks you two questions. Complete the dialogue – in order to do so you need to refer to the diagram on page 88.

Passant Excusez-moi Monsieur/Madame/Mademoiselle. Pour aller au _____ s'il vous plaît?

Vous Le _____, c'est derrière la boulangerie et en face de la _____ .

Passant Merci bien! Et où est la _____ s'il vous plaît?

Vous C'est à côté de la _____municipale et en face du Commissariat de Police.

3 Qu'est-ce qu'on va faire aujourd'hui?

A family is staying in St Malo for the weekend. They are planning what they are going to do.

Listen once to the audio and answer these questions:

(a) Who would like to go either to the beach or for a boat trip down the river?

(b) Who would like to go to Mont Saint Michel?

Listen again.

(c) What would the boy like to do?

(d) Who puts a stop to the discussion?

(e) At the end of the discussion what does the boy want to know?

C'est samedi matin

Maman	Alors, soit on va à la plage et à marée basse on peut aller visiter la tombe de Chateaubriand sur le Grand Bé, ou bien on fait une excursion en bateau sur la Rance jusqu'à Dinan…
Fillette	Moi je voudrais aller au Mont Saint Michel!
Maman	Non, il y a beaucoup trop de monde au Mont Saint Michel le weekend!
Petit garçon	Moi je voudrais prendre le petit train pour visiter St Malo. C'est moins fatiguant et plus amusant!
Maman	Quel paresseux!
Papa	Bon moi aussi j'ai une idée, on va visiter le barrage de la Rance. Plus de discussion!
Petit garçon	Dis Papa et demain qu'est-ce qu'on va faire?

la marée basse *low tide*	**aujourd'hui** *today*
soit... ou bien *either... or*	**demain** *tomorrow*
beaucoup trop de monde *far*	**la marée haute*** *high tide*
too many people	(*not in the text)

 Link the following English phrases to the equivalent French expressions:

1) We go to the beach.   (a) Quel paresseux!

2) I'd like to go on the little train.   (b) une excursion en bateau

3) What a lazy boy!   (c) C'est plus amusant!

4) a boat trip   (d) On va à la plage.

5) It's not so tiring.   (e) Je voudrais prendre le petit train.

6) It's more fun.   (f) C'est moins fatiguant.

Comment ça marche?

3 The immediate future: aller + infinitive

You have already met (page 86), an easy way to talk about the future. You can use **aller** followed by another verb to refer to what will happen soon, for example in the next second, minute, hour or day, or even in the next few years in some cases:

Tu vas tomber!	*You are going to fall over!*
Il va pleuvoir	*It's going to rain.*
Nous allons faire une promenade à vélo.	*We are going to go for a bike ride.*
Avec le nouveau gouvernement tout ça va changer!	*With the new government all that is going to change!*

In most cases the time scale is implicit but to be more precise use **aujourd'hui** *today*, **demain** *tomorrow*, **après-demain** *the day after tomorrow*, **bientôt** *soon*:

Qu'est-ce qu'**on va faire** aujourd'hui?	*What are we going to do today?*
Qu'est-ce qu'**on va faire** demain?	*What are we going to do tomorrow?*

4 The immediate future: present tense

You can also use the present tense to express the immediate future:

Qu'est ce que **tu fais** cet après-midi?	*What are you doing this afternoon?*
Qu'est-ce que **vous faites** ce soir?	*What are you doing this evening?*
Ce midi **nous allons** au restaurant.	*This lunch time we are going to the restaurant.*
Cette année **nous allons** en vacances en Irlande.	*This year we are going on holiday to Ireland.*

5 Amusant *amusing/funny*, **fatiguant** *tiring*

-ant in French is equivalent to *-ing* in English:

Marcher toute la journée, c'est très fatiguant.	*Walking all day is very tiring.*
C'est un homme vraiment amusant.	*He's a really funny man.*

Amuser means *to amuse/to entertain* and the reflexive verb **s'amuser** means *to enjoy oneself*:

Les enfants s'amusent sur la plage.	*The children are enjoying themselves on the beach.*

6 Dis Papa!/Dis Maman!

These are children's expressions generally used to attract the attention of adults. **Dis/dites** are the imperative forms of **dire** *to say*:

Dis-moi la vérité.	*Tell me the truth.*
Dites-le au maire.	*Tell it to the mayor.*

Point info

■ **Chateaubriand** is a French Romantic author born in St Malo in 1768. His grave is on a tiny island or rock, **Le Grand Bé**, which can be reached from the beach at low tide

■ **Le Barrage de la Rance** or **Usine marémotrice de la Rance** is a tidal dam across the river Rance which uses the tide as a means to create electricity.

☑ À vous maintenant!

2 Le Petit Train de St Malo

Read the advert for the little train and answer the questions below.

LE PETIT TRAIN DE SAINT-MALO

INFORMATIONS RESERVATIONS GROUPES
Tél. 02 99 40 49 49 - Fax 02 99 40 44 62
BP 173 35408 SAINT-MALO

Visite touristique et commentée
de l'intra-muros et de ses alentours

Départ et arrivée : porte St-Vincent
au pied du Château
NOCTURNE JUILLET/AOUT
Durée du trajet : 30 minutes

ENGLISH GUIDED TOUR

(a) What could you expect to see if you took the little train?
(b) What happens at Porte St Vincent?
(c) Could you take a night ride all year round?

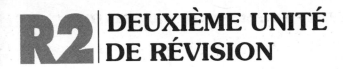

DEUXIÈME UNITÉ DE RÉVISION

◢ Grand jeu-concours

At 45 you are the managing director of a company from Rennes (Ille-et-Vilaine). You are representing your firm at an annual four-day conference in St Malo. Your firm has always favoured St Malo as a venue for this conference because of the excellent facilities and the range of activities available. You enjoy going to the swimming pool and going on your own around museums in your free time. You are staying in the conference centre hotel.

YOUR TASK:

Fill in the questionnaire on the next two pages as if you were the person described above and win the main prize in the competition.

1) What is the main prize?
2) What is the deadline for entering the competition?
3) Who are the organisers of the competition?

Grand JEU-CONCOURS
Jusqu'au 14 septembre
Bienvenue
à SAINT-MALO

Vous êtes de passage ou en vacances à SAINT-MALO, nous souhaitons mieux vous connaître, recueillir vos attentes et vos appréciations. C'est pourquoi **LA VILLE et L'OFFICE DU TOURISME** vous proposent de remplir ce questionnaire pour participer au **JEU-CONCOURS**.

Chaque semaine, GAGNEZ UN ALLER-RETOUR pour l'Angleterre pour 2 personnes et de nombreux autres lots.
VOIR AU DOS

❶ – COMMENT AVEZ-VOUS CONNU SAINT-MALO?

☐ Bouche à oreille
☐ Foires ou salons
☐ Reportages TV ou presse
☐ Guides touristiques ou Agences de voyage
☐ Office du Tourisme
☐ Excursions précédentes
☐ Déplacements professionels

❷ – FIDÉLISATION

☐ Premier séjour à Saint-Malo
☐ Visites occasionnelles à Saint-Malo
☐ Visites régulières à Saint-Malo

❸ – ACTIVITÉS PRATIQUÉES
    (*Plusieurs réponses possibles*)

☐ Culturelles   ☐ Autres : préciser
☐ Découvertes   ------------------
☐ Nautiques
☐ Sportives
☐ Animations gratuites
☐ Theramlisme
☐ Déplacements professionels et congrès

❹ – SATISFACTION :
    Êtes-vous satisfait de votre séjour à Saint-Malo ?
☐ Pas du tout   Justifier votre réponse - - - - - - - - - - - - - -
☐ Plutôt pas   -
☐ Plutôt satisfait   -
☐ Très satisfait

❺ – DURÉE DU SÉJOUR :

☐ La journée   ☐ 2 à 3 jours   ☐ 4 à 8 jours
☐ 9 à 15 jours   ☐ 16 jours et plus

❻ – MODE D'HÉBERGEMENT

☐ Hôtel   ☐ Camping-car   ☐ Camping
☐ Location meublé   ☐ Résidence secondaire ☐ Bateau
☐ Amis – Famille –   ☐ Gîtes – chambres   ☐ Famille d'accueil
    Parents   d'hôtes

❼ – ÂGE

☐ - de 25 ans   ☐ 25/34 ans   ☐ 35/44 ans
☐ 45/54 ans   ☐ 55/65 ans   ☐ + de 65 ans

❽ – ACCOMPAGNEMENT
    (*Êtes-vous venu à Saint-Malo?*)

☐ Seul   ☐ En couple
☐ En famille   ☐ Avec des amis

❾ – CATÉGORIE SOCIO-PROFESSIONNELLE

☐ Agriculteur   ☐ Chef d'entreprise,
☐ Cadre et profession libérale   commerçant, artisan
☐ Employé   ☐ Cadre moyen
☐ Retraité   ☐ Ouvrier
☐ Autres   ☐ Scolaire et étudiant

❿ – ORIGINE GÉOGRAPHIQUE

☐ Ille-et-Vilaine
☐ Autre département : |___|___| (n° du département)
☐ Étranger   (Préciser la nationalité et la région) _ _ _ _ _ _ _ _ _

Pour participer au JEU CONCOURS,
n'oubliez pas d'indiquer vos coordonnées ci-dessous :

NOM: . . . . PRÉNOM: . . . .

Adresse . . . .

Lieu d'hébergement à Saint-Malo . . . .

Tél. : . . . .

ATTENTION!

Toutes les rubriques du questionnaire doivent être remplies pour valider
votre participation au JEU CONCOURS.

DÉPOSEZ VOS BULLETINS DANS L'URNE

10 CHOISIR UN RESTAURANT
Choosing a restaurant

In this unit you will learn:

■ about eating out
■ how to express an opinion
■ about the French and their attitude towards food

 ## 1 Où est-ce qu'on mange?

Sarah and Dominique are enjoying their stay in St Malo. As well as places to visit they discuss the restaurants and other places where they can have meals.

 Listen to the audio and answer these questions:

(a) What does Dominique suggest they do for lunch?
(b) Dominique sees a small restaurant. Where is it?
(c) How much would they have to pay for mussels, chips and a glass of wine?

Now read the dialogue:

Dominique Où est-ce qu'on mange ce midi? On fait un pique-nique?
Sarah Non! Il ne fait pas assez beau. En fait on dirait qu'il va pleuvoir.
Dominique Oui je pense que tu as raison. Alors qu'est-ce qu'on fait? On prend quelque chose de rapide dans une brasserie ou bien dans une crêperie? Qu'est-ce que tu en dis?
Sarah Euh … J'ai envie de manger des moules avec des frites.
Dominique Bonne idée! Tiens regarde, il y a un petit restaurant de l'autre côté de la rue: Repas express, moules-frites plus un verre de vin 50 francs tout compris.
Sarah C'est parfait. On y va!

avoir envie de ... *to long for/to have a craving for/to feel like/to fancy ...*	**quelque chose** *something* **un verre de vin** *a glass of wine* **pleuvoir** *to rain*

Link the following English phrases to the equivalent French expressions:

1) In fact it looks as if it is going to rain.
2) What do you say to that?
3) The weather is not good enough.
4) Where are we going to eat this lunch time?
5) Shall we have a quick meal...?
6) Fifty francs all included.
7) I think you are right.
8) I fancy eating mussels with chips.

(a) Il ne fait pas assez beau.
(b) On prend un petit repas rapide?
(c) J'ai envie de manger des moules aves des frites.
(d) Je pense que tu as raison.
(e) Qu'est-ce que tu en dis?
(f) Où est-ce qu'on mange ce midi?
(g) En fait on dirait qu'il va pleuvoir.
(h) 50F tout compris.

Comment ça marche?

1 Expressing an opinion and seeking an opinion from someone

To express an opinion you can use **penser** *to think* or **croire** *to believe*:

Je pense que/ Je crois que	*I think / I believe that...*
Je pense que oui.	*I think so.*
Je crois qu'il est malade.	*I believe he's ill.*

To seek an opinion you can use **penser** and **dire** *to say*:

Qu'est-ce que tu en penses?	*What do you think (of it)?*
Q'est ce que tu en dis?	*What do you say (about it)?*

En is a pronoun which replaces whatever has just been said or suggested. Addressing someone more formally you will use **vous**:

Q'est-ce vous en dites?
Qu'est-ce que vous en pensez?

À vous maintenant!

1 La cuisine française

The following statement contains new vocabulary which is essential for slightly more complex conversations. Use the keywords, learn them and then read the text.

c'est-à-dire *that is to say*	**faire preuve de** *to demonstrate/to show*
souvent *often*	**s'agir de** *to be a matter of*
surtout *above all*	**la meilleure cuisine** *the best cooking*
lorsque/quand *when*	
partout *everywhere*	

> *En général les Français sont très chauvins, c'est-à-dire qu'ils font souvent preuve de chauvinisme, surtout lorsqu'il s'agit de ce qu'il y a de plus important: la cuisine française. Pour beaucoup de Français, c'est la meilleure cuisine du monde.*

Now answer the questions:

(a) What national trait is mentioned here?
(b) When is this particular trait mostly evident?

Listen to the audio. What do they say? Three people are arguing about the best cooking in the world.

(c) How many think that French cooking is best?
(d) What is best about it?
(e) What other countries are mentioned as possible contenders?
(f) How many speakers think that the whole issue is a matter of taste?

Point info

There are different types of eating-out places in France, apart from traditional restaurants:

Une brasserie is often a large café which sells mainly beer and serves all sorts of quick meals. They are generally very good value for money.

Une crêperie is a type of restaurant specialising in the cooking of pancakes with various types of fillings. **Crêpes** *pancakes* are a speciality from Brittany but there are now **crêperies** all over France. **Crêpes** can have a savoury or a sweet filling and therefore it is possible to have a full meal eating a savoury pancake (or two) for the main course and a sweet one for dessert.

Brittany is also famous for its sea food and **plateaux de fruits de mer** (sea food platters with all sorts of shellfish which can be shared amongst several people).

Couscous, a North African dish, is often prepared and sold on certain days in campsites or supermarkets: **couscous à emporter** *couscous to take away*. There are also many North African restaurants, especially in Paris.

The latest trend is to eat at a farm house: **Une ferme auberge.** You can eat traditional French country cooking in traditional farm houses. Sometimes they are the same farms which offer **chambres d'hôtes.**

2 Les repas dans la vie des Français

Read this passage – you will understand it all!

> *Les Français aiment manger. Ils aiment la bonne nourriture* (good food) *et les bons repas* (good meals). *Toute occasion est bonne pour faire un repas de famille ou un repas entre amis: un baptême, une communion ou une confirmation, un mariage, un résultat d'examen, un anniversaire, et évidemment Noël et surtout le premier janvier.*

Did you understand it? Now answer these questions:

(a) What do French people like?
(b) Name at least six occasions which are particularly good pretexts for a family meal or a meal with friends.

Here is some more information:

Les heures des repas *meal times*

LES REPAS	LES MOMENTS DE LA JOURNÉE
Le petit déjeuner	Le matin
Le déjeuner	À midi, entre midi et deux heures
Le goûter	L'après-midi (surtout pour les enfants)

Le dîner   Le soir, vers sept, huit heures
Le souper   Plus tard le soir (repas assez léger)

Le midi les Français mangent à la cantine, à la cafétéria, au restaurant ou bien chez eux s'ils habitent près de leur lieu de travail.

le goûter afternoon tea (nearest translation but not the same connotation) **goûter** (as a verb) to taste/to appreciate	**assez léger** fairly light **chez eux** at (their) home (Lit. at theirs) **leur lieu de travail** their place of work

Obviously everybody does not have all these meals every day but generally French people are fairly punctilious about when they eat their meals. You might find that roads are nearly empty at meal times because nearly everybody eats at the same time. Also far fewer French people have snacks or sandwiches at lunchtime.

 Here are some more questions:

(c) At what time are French people likely to have dinner in the evening?
(d) Who is **le goûter** mainly for?
(e) What is the difference between **le dîner** and **le souper**?
(f) Where do French people eat at midday?

🐾 3 Où est-ce qu'on mange ce soir?

Look at the following adverts and say which eating places best fit your requirements. (You can have more than one for each question.)

De quoi est-ce que vous avez envie?

(a) You wish to eat sea food.
(b) You would like a meal to take away.
(c) You would like a Sunday lunch.
(d) You would like a pancake meal.
(e) You would like a restaurant with a sea view.
(f) You would like to take the children out for a meal.
(g) You are waiting for the boat to Ile de Sein.
(h) You would like a restaurant open every day until late in the summer.
(i) You would like a North African meal.
(j) You would like a sea food supper with mussels and chips.

📖 4 Le goûter à la ferme

This is an advert for a farm in the heart of Brittany – **La Ferme des Monts** – near an ancient site called **La Roche aux fées** (*Fairies' Rock*)

ILLE-ET-VILAINE

Contact	Descriptif
Jacques RUPIN Les Monts 35150 PIRE SUR SEICHE Tél. 02 97 37 55 92	Au pays de la Roche aux fées, près de l'axe Rennes-Angers, venez visiter les vergers de la ferme des Monts. Vous pourrez découvrir la fabrication traditionnelle du cidre, voir la cave et le matériel utilisé hier et aujourd'hui. Ensuite vous goûterez au jus de pomme, au cidre, aux crêpes et gâteaux maison accompagnés de confitures ou gelées. Vente directe sur place. Ouvert tous les après-midis **sur réservation** du 1/05 au 15/09. Hors saison : ouvert sur RDV. Possibilité de recevoir des groupes.

You are not expected to understand every word in the advert but use the following keywords to answer the questions.

un verger	*an orchard*	**des confitures**	*jams*
la cave	*the cellar*	**des gelées**	*preserves*
hier	*yesterday/in the old days*		

(a) Name two things you could see or visit at the farm.
(b) What could you drink?
(c) What could you eat with the home-made cakes?
(d) When is the farm open for **le goûter**?
(e) What would you need to do before going there?

À vous maintenant!

2 Le souper marin

You and your friend Michel would like to go to the sea food supper at Plovan (see page 101). Listen to the audio and answer Michel's questions.

11 | LA PLUIE ET LE BEAU TEMPS!
Rain and shine!

In this unit you will learn:

- how to talk about the weather
- how to listen to a radio bulletin and read the weather forecast in the newspaper
- about the regions of France
- to express the present and the future

1 Il va faire de l'orage

Sarah et Dominique sont dans leur voiture. Elles vont visiter Dinan, une cité médiévale sur la Rance. Elles parlent de la pluie et du beau temps ...

Listen to the audio and answer these questions:

(a) When is it certainly going to rain?
(b) Why do they turn the radio on?

Listen again.

(c) The weather forecast mentions storms for at least three French regions. Can you name any of them?

Now read the dialogue.

Dominique	Tu as raison, le temps change...il fait lourd, il va faire de l'orage!
Sarah	Oui, le ciel est couvert. En tout cas il va certainement pleuvoir cet après-midi.
Dominique	Ah oui, voilà les première gouttes de pluie.
Sarah	Écoutons les prévisions météorologiques.

Elles écoutent France Inter

... et pour les jours suivants le temps lourd va persister. Il fera encore chaud et ensoleillé. L'évolution orageuse sera plus marquée sur les Pyrénées, les Alpes et sur la Corse. Dans l'ensemble de la France les températures resteront cinq degrés au-dessus des températures de saison. C'était notre bulletin météorologique de la mi-journée. Vous pourrez écouter notre prochain bulletin sur France Inter à seize heures cinquante-cinq. Et voici maintenant notre bulletin d' informations de treize heures...

Dominique	Alors c'est partout pareil en France.
Sarah	Qu'est-ce qu'on fait demain? On va dans le Finistère comme prévu?
Dominique	Oui d'accord et après cela on commencera à descendre vers Bordeaux en passant par chez moi à St Nazaire et chez mon copain à Nantes.

le temps *weather* (in the text above) but also *time*	**la mi-journée** *midday/lunchtime*
le temps est lourd *the weather is close/muggy*	**au-dessus** *above*
	au-dessous *below*
le ciel *the sky*	**pareil** *the same*
une goutte de pluie *a raindrop*	**prévoir** *to forecast/plan*
les prévisions météorologiques/	**comme prévu** *as planned*
la météo *weather forecast*	**mon copain** *my friend/boyfriend*
	ma copine *my friend/girlfriend*

Reread the dialogue and answer these questions:

(d) Will temperatures over France:
1) go up   2) go down   3) be higher than the seasonal norm
4) be very low

(e) The forecast is for:
1) today only   2) tomorrow only   3) the weekend
4) the next few days

(f) The weather bulletin was:
1) at 6am   2) just before the 1 o'clock news   3) at 4.55pm

(g) Tomorrow Dominique and Sarah:
1) plan to stay in St Malo   2) move on to Finistère
3) get to Bordeaux

(h) On their way to Bordeaux they will:
    1) visit Paris   2) stop on the way in St Nazaire
    3) stop to see Dominique's boyfriend

⚙ Comment ça marche?

French people tend to spend a lot of time talking about the weather. To discuss today's weather they use the present tense and the following structures:

1 Quel temps fait-il aujourd'hui? *What is the weather like today?*

■ **Il fait** … best translated as: *It is...*
    Il fait beau (*nice*)/ chaud (*hot*) / froid (*cold*) /lourd (*muggy*)/ du soleil (*sunny*)/ du vent (*windy*)/ du brouillard (*foggy*) / de l'orage (*stormy*)
■ **Le temps est....** *The weather is...*
    Le temps est ensoleillé (*sunny*) / nuageux (*cloudy*) / brumeux (*misty*) / pluvieux (*rainy*), orageux (*stormy*) / couvert (*overcast*)
■ **Il y a...** *There is ...*
    Il y a du vent (*wind*)/des nuages (*clouds*)/de la pluie (*rain*)/de la neige (*snow*)
■ **Il pleut** (*it's raining*) / **il neige** (*it's snowing*)

You can see how to read and understand most of the weather conditions on the map from the newspaper on pages 109–110.

2 Quel temps fera-t-il?

In conversational French you are likely to hear people using the immediate future: **il va** + infinitive:

■ **Il va faire** beau / **il va pleuvoir** (*it's going to rain*) / **il va faire** de l'orage etc...

But in more formal situations (forecasts on the radio, TV or newspapers) the verbs are mainly in the future tense:

■ Il **fera** beau (**faire** in the future tense)
■ Le temps **sera** orageux (**être** in the future tense)
■ Il y **aura** … (**avoir** in the future tense): Il y aura des **averses** (*showers*), des **éclaircies** (*bright periods*), de la **brume** (*mist*)

- Le vent **soufflera** (*the wind will blow*) (**souffler** in the future tense)

- Il **pleuvra** (*it will rain*)/il **neigera** (*it will snow*)

3 The future tense

Look at the text accompanying the map of France (see pages 109–110) and you will be able to find many more examples of verbs in the future tense.

Using verbs in the future tense is simple for most verbs ending with **-er** or **-ir**:

- When the subject is **il/elle** (*it*) use the verb (in the infinitive) + ending **-a**:
  Le soleil **brillera** *The sun will shine.* (**briller** + **-a**)

- When the subject is **ils /elles** (*they*) use the verb (in the infinitive) + ending **-ont:**

  Les températures **avoisineront** les 30 degrés *Temperatures will be close to 30 degrees.* (**avoisiner** + **ont**)

- Whatever the verb, the endings for verbs in the future are always the same:

je	**-rai**	nous	**-rons**
tu	**-ras**	vous	**-rez**
il	**-ra**	elles	**-ront**

Point info

UN PEU DE GÉOGRAPHIE

France is often referred to as **L'Hexagone** because of its shape (six sides).

Look at the map of France and the article above it (pages 109–110) 'LE TEMPS AUJOURD'HUI, RÉGION PAR RÉGION'.

For weather forecast purposes France has been divided into seven broad areas, some representing a whole region and others several regions. The towns on the map can be used as markers for you to locate these regions.

Complete the following sentences either with the name of a town or with the name of a region of France:

1) Rennes est en B_____, Nantes est dans les Pays de Loire, Rouen et _____ sont en Normandie.

2) _____ et Amiens sont dans le Nord-Picardie, Paris est en Ile de France.

3) Metz et _____ sont dans le _____, Dijon est en Bourgogne et Besançon est en Franche-Comté.

4) Poitiers est dans le _____-_____, Orléans est dans le Centre et Limoge est dans le _____

5) Toulouse est dans la région Midi-Pyrénées et _____ est dans l'Aquitaine.

6) Clermont-Ferrand est en A_____ et _____ est dans la région Rhône-Alpes.

7) Montpellier, _____ et _____ sont sur le pourtour méditerranéen et Ajaccio est en _____.

Note that **Le Midi** is used as a generic name for the South of France.

Les points cardinaux:

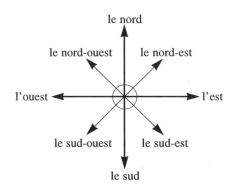

Comment ça se prononce?

le sud: you can hear the **d** at the end of the word but in **le nord** the **d** is dropped

le sud-est / le sud-ouest : are both pronounced linking the two words and the -**t** at the end of **est** and **ouest** is also pronounced: [*le sudest/le sudouest*].

le nord-est / le nord-ouest: are both pronounced linking the two words but dropping the -**d** at the end of **nord**: [*le norest / le norouest*]

Comment ça marche?

4 en, dans *and* sur

- **En** is usually used in front of the name of a region or province:
  en Bretagne   *in Brittany*
- **Dans** is used in front of a geographical area:
  dans le nord-est   *in the north-east*
- **Sur** is used in association with the name of a region mainly with reference to the weather:
  sur la Bretagne et la Normandie *over Brittany and Normandy* (see the text below)

À vous maintenant!

1 Le temps aujourd'hui

Using the weather map and text which follow say where you can find the following weather conditions for the day (in some cases it applies to more than one area):

(a) Thunderstorms from midday onwards

(b) Sunny all day

(c) Muggy in the afternoon

(d) Morning mist

(e) A light north-east wind

(f) Temperatures ranging from 30° on the coast to 35° inland

(g) Temperatures 5° above the seasonal norm

(h) Cloudy (veiled) sky in the afternoon

LE TEMPS AUJOURD'HUI, RÉGION PAR RÉGION

Bretagne, Pays de la Loire, Normandie.
Sur la Bretagne et la Normandie, le soleil brillera largement toute la journée. Sur les Pays de la Loire, le soleil sera bien présent, mais le ciel se voilera dans l'après-midi. Il fera chaud, entre 24 et 30° du nord au sud.
Nord-Picardie, Ile-de-France. Après quelques brumes matinales, le soleil

Aquitaine, Midi-Pyrénées. Dans la matinée, le temps deviendra lourd. Des ondées orageuses se produiront l'après-midi et des orages éclateront sur les Pyrénées dès la mi-journée. Les températures seront comprises entre 27 et 31°.
Auvergne, Rhône-Alpes. En Auvergne, le temps deviendra lourd l'après-midi

---

Un léger vent de nord-est soufflera. Le thermomètre indiquera entre 26 et 30° du nord au sud.

Nord-Est, Bourgogne, Franche-Comté. Le temps sera chaud et bien ensoleillé. Les températures avoisineront les 30° soit 5 degrés au-dessus des températures de saison.

Poitou-Charentes, Centre, Limousin. La matinée sera bien ensoleillée mais le temps deviendra lourd et des ondées parfois orageuses se produiront sur Poitou-Charentes et sur le Limousin. Le thermomètre atteindra souvent les 30°.

avec des risques d'ondées orageuses. Sur Rhône-Alpes, le temps sera ensoleillé. Des nuages se développeront sur les Alpes et quelques orages isolés éclateront. Le thermomètre indiquera entre 27 et 31°.

Pourtour méditerranéen, Corse. Sur le Languedoc-Roussillon, la matinée sera assez ensoleillée mais le temps deviendra lourd l'après-midi avec des ondées orageuses. Ailleurs, le soleil brillera largement. Il fera chaud entre 30° sur les côtes et 35° dans l'intérieur.

VENDREDI 15 AOUT
METEO

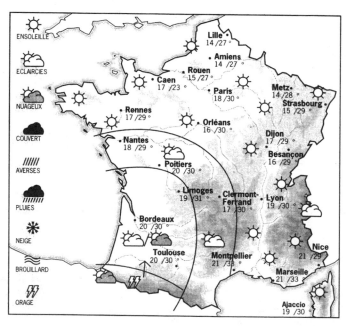

2 Où sont-ils en vacances? *Where are they on holiday?*

(a) Listen to the audio and look at the list of towns and their weather conditions. Then say where the following French people are spending their holidays.

Exemple: 'Bonjour, je m'appelle Étienne. La ville où je suis est ensoleillée et la température est entre 18 et 30 degrés'

Réponse: Étienne est à Paris.

1) Fabienne est _____ .
2) Jérôme est _____ .
3) Stéphanie est _____ .
4) Alexandre est _____ .

(b) Say what the weather is like in the towns where you are holidaying.

1) Vous êtes à Varsovie. Quel temps fait-il?
2) Vous êtes à Berlin. Quel temps fait-il?

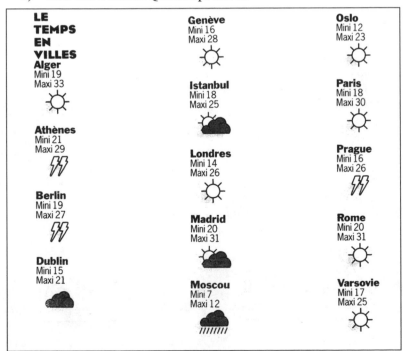

LE TEMPS EN VILLES

Alger
Mini 19
Maxi 33

Athènes
Mini 21
Maxi 29

Berlin
Mini 19
Maxi 27

Dublin
Mini 15
Maxi 21

Genève
Mini 16
Maxi 28

Istanbul
Mini 18
Maxi 25

Londres
Mini 14
Maxi 26

Madrid
Mini 20
Maxi 31

Moscou
Mini 7
Maxi 12

Oslo
Mini 12
Maxi 23

Paris
Mini 18
Maxi 30

Prague
Mini 16
Maxi 26

Rome
Mini 20
Maxi 31

Varsovie
Mini 17
Maxi 25

12 | **AU RESTAURANT**
At the restaurant

In this unit you will learn:

■ how to order a drink in a café
■ how to read a menu in a restaurant and how to order a meal
■ some information on **le Finistère**
■ how to recognise the past tense and how to express the recent past

1 Un peu de lecture

Read the paragraph below.

> *C'est le mois de juillet. Nos deux amies, Dominique et Sarah, ont passé le week-end à Quimper pour les Fêtes de Cornouaille. Aujourd'hui elles viennent de visiter des chapelles dans le Pays Bigouden. Maintenant elles sont assises à la terrasse d'un café, Place de l'Église, à Plonéour-Lanvern. Il fait chaud et elles ont très soif.*

Now answer these questions:

1) The month is:
   (a) June (b) July (c) January

2) Our two friends have spent the weekend:
   (a) in Cornwall (b) St Malo (c) in Quimper

3) They have just visited:
   (a) some chapels (b) some castles (c) some churches

4) They are now:
   (a) in the church (b) in a restaurant (c) sitting at the terrace of a café

5) The weather is:
   (a) muggy and they are tired (b) hot and they are very thirsty
   (c) cold

🔧 Comment ça marche?

1 How to talk about events which have already happened

To say something has just happened use **venir** in the present tense + **de** + verb (in the infinitive):

Elles viennent de visiter des chapelles.	*They have just visited some chapels.*
Le bateau vient d'arriver au port.	*The boat has just arrived in the port.*
Tu viens de rencontrer le président.	*You've just met the president.*

Venir on its own means *to come* e.g. Venez-vous souvent ici? *Do you come here often?*

Venir de... indicates that something has just happened or has just been done.

➤ À vous maintenant!

1 Faites des phrases

In the grid below, columns A and C remain the same. Columns B and D are jumbled.

Can you find the six correct sentences? Can you say what they mean?

A	B	C	D
1) Je	viennent	d'arriver	un bon film
2) Tu	venez	de finir	le gros lot au loto
3) Jean-Paul	viens	de gagner	St Malo
4) Nous	vient	de visiter	à Paris
5) Vous	venons	de choisir	tes examens
6) Elles	viens	de voir	un menu

Il vient de
gagner le gros
lot au loto!

🎛 Comment ça marche?

2 How to talk about events which happened recently

To say something or someone has recently completed an action use the
perfect tense. The word *perfect* here means *complete* – something has
been achieved or completed:

Elles ont passé le weekend   *They have spent the weekend*
à Quimper.   *in Quimper.*

How to form the perfect tense

■ The perfect tense is formed with **avoir** or **être** in the present tense +
another verb: **j'ai choisi** *I chose* (page 24).

Avoir and **être** are called auxiliary verbs when they are used in this way.
The verb which indicates the event or action which has been completed is
in a form called a past participle. When Jean-Paul discovers that he has
won the jackpot he says: J'ai **gagné** le gros lot. **Gagné** is the past
participle of the verb **gagner** *to win.*

In this unit you will learn how to recognise and use the perfect tense with
avoir which is the auxillary verb used with the vast majority of verbs.

Verbs which end with **-er** and those which end with **-ir** are very easy to use:

All verbs ending with **-er** in their basic form (infinitive) have a past
participle ending with **-é**.

All verbs ending with **-ir** have a past participle ending with **-i**.

visiter → visit**é**	finir → fin**i**
passer → pass**é**	choisir → chois**i**
gagner → gagn**é**	servir→ serv**i**
aller → allé (though **aller** is used with **être**)	

À vous maintenant!

2 Encore des phrases

Once again columns B and D have moved. Can you find six correct sentences in the box below and say what they mean?

A	B	C	D
1) J'	avons	écouté	des moules-frites
2) Tu	ont	fini	les infos à la radio
3) On	avez	mangé	vos cartes postales
4) Nous	a	choisi	ton travail
5) Vous	ai	posté	une cabine
6) Sarah et Dominique	as	réservé	un hôtel pas trop cher

Point info

Un peu de géographie et un peu de culture

France is divided administratively into 95 **départements**. **Le Finistère** is the furthest west, jutting into **l'Océan Atlantique**. It is one of Brittany's four **départements**. **Quimper** is the administrative capital of **Finistère** and at the heart of **la Cornouaille** (the French Cornwall).

Throughout the summer there are festivals all over Finistère and the other **départements bretons**. One of them is **les fêtes de Cornouaille** which celebrates Brittany's traditional costumes and Celtic music and always takes place the third weekend in July. Another well-known festival is **le Festival Inter-Celtique de Lorient** which takes place in Lorient

(Morbihan) in the first two weeks of August each year and is dedicated to Celtic music from all Celtic areas of Europe.

Un peu d'histoire

The part of **Finistère**, south-west of Quimper, around the towns of **Pont-L'Abbé** and **Plonéour-Lanvern** is called **le Pays Bigouden**. There are still a few women, known as Bigoudènes, who wear an extremely high lace head dress most of the time. Although many parts of France have their own traditional costumes which often include a lace head dress, **les Bigoudènes** seem to have kept the tradition of wearing their **coiffes** even to go to the market.

The historical background for such a tradition appears to find its roots in events which took place a few years prior to the French Revolution when local peasants rioted against the local nobility. As a punishment the king ordered that the steeples of their churches and chapels be decapitated. In turn the local women are said to have decided to wear the high coiffes as a sign of defiance. From then onwards they have been wearing them higher and higher.

2 Au Café de la Baie

Sarah et Dominique sont à la terrasse d'un café.

Listen to the audio once and answer these questions:

(a) When the two women order their drinks do they both order the same thing?
(b) Does Sarah order anything else?
(c) Does Dominique sound very enthusiastic about it?

Listen again.

(d) Who asks for the bill?
(e) Who is going to pay? Why?

Listen for a third time.

(f) How much is the bill?
(g) Do they leave a tip?

Now read the dialogue.

Serveur	Bonjour mesdames, qu'est ce que je vous sers?
Sarah	Alors pour moi une bière pression...et toi Dominique?
Dominique	Euh … je conduis alors je vais prendre un panaché.
Serveur	Alors une bière pression et un panaché.
Sarah	Et nous allons prendre des glaces aussi?
Serveur	Tout de suite madame, je vous apporte la carte.

Quelques minutes plus tard

Sarah	Tu prends une glace Dominique?
Dominique	Non, je suis au régime!
Sarah	Eh bien prends un sorbet, il y a moins de calories.
Serveur	Vous avez choisi?
Sarah	Oui, alors une glace à la fraise et un sorbet au citron. Et l'addition s'il vous plaît.

Un peu plus tard

Dominique	C'est moi qui paie cette fois-ci, toi tu as payé la dernière fois! C'est combien l'addition?
Sarah	Ça fait cinquante-six francs.
Dominique	Soixante avec le pourboire.

une bière	*a beer*	**quelques minutes plus tard**	
un panaché	*a shandy*	*a few minutes later*	
une glace	*an ice-cream*	**être au régime**	*to be on a diet*
l'addition	*the bill*	**cette fois-ci**	*this time*
le pourboire	*the tip*	**tout de suite**	*right away*
conduire	*to drive*	**apporter**	*to bring*

☑ Now read the dialogue and find the French equivalent for the following
sentences:

(g) I'll bring you the menu.
(h) Have a sorbet it's got less calories.
(i) A strawberry ice-cream and a lemon sorbet please.
(j) You paid last time.
(k) a few minutes later
(l) a short while later

☑ There are also two examples of the perfect tense in the dialogue. Can you
find them and say what they mean? Now find the verbs in the present and
the immediate future.

🔋 Comment ça marche?

3 C'est moi

   C'est moi qui paie cette fois-ci.   *It's me who is paying this time.*

In the dialogue, Dominique could have said **Je paie cette fois** *I am paying
this time* but for emphasis she said **C'est moi qui paie**. In English we
would probably use our voice for emphasis, stressing *I'm paying*.

Moi and other pronouns used in conversation to emphasise what is being
said can be referred to as emphatic pronouns. In some cases (**elle**, **nous**,
vous, **elles**) they are the same as subject pronouns, but the masculine
singular pronoun is **lui** and the masculine plural pronoun is **eux**:

C'est **toi** qui as gagné?	*Is it **you** that won?*
C'est **lui** qui a choisi pas moi!	*He's the one that chose not **me**!*
C'est **elle** qui conduit!	***She's** driving!*
C'est **nous** qui avons visité la Corse.	***We're** the ones who've visited Corsica!*
Ce sont **elles** qui ont passé l'été en Bretagne.	***They're** the ones who spent the summer in Britanny!* (fem. pl.)
C'est **vous** qui habitez à Marseille?	*Is it **you** that lives in Marseille?*
Ce sont **eux** qui arriveront les premiers.	*It's **them** who arrived first.* (masc. pl.)

Point info

Le tarif des consommations

There are some regulations about the price of drinks in France. These are guidelines and there are discrepancies between various places. Prices of drinks in cafés and restaurants are not in any way comparable with the price of drinks you buy in a supermarket or any other shop.

When you ask for **une bière à la pression** you can expect a 25 cl glass of draft lager. Labelled beers in bottles are more expensive. For English people tempted to ask for a pint of beer, there is obviously not such a concept in France so the best thing is to ask for **une grande bière** which means that you will probably get half a litre of beer.

**Et voilà, un coca et
un sandwich au fromage!**

3 Au restaurant

Situation: *Didier et Véronique Morin et leurs deux enfants, Armelle et Fabien passent la nuit à l'Hôtel des Voyageurs. Ils ont décidé de dîner au restaurant de l'hôtel.*

Listen once to the audio, then answer the questions.

(a) What seating arrangement does the waitress offer the family?
(b) Do they wish to have an aperitive?

Listen to the audio again.

(c) Apart from fixed price menus, what kind of menu do they ask for?
(d) Would they like to see the wine list?

Listen once more.

(e) Véro asked for a 67 F menu. Why does the waitress say that she cannot serve it?

(f) What do they order?

Now read the dialogue.

Serveuse	Bonsoir Monsieur-dame. J' ai une table pour quatre près de la fenêtre, est-ce que cela vous convient?
Didier	Oui, très bien.
Serveuse	Vous désirez prendre un apéritif?
Didier	Non non, apportez-nous le menu s'il vous plaît.
Serveuse	Vous voulez le menu à la carte?
Didier	Non, nous prendrons des menus à prix fixes. Vous avez un menu pour enfants?
Serveuse	Oui monsieur. Je vous apporte la carte des vins?
Véro	Oui merci.

Quelques minutes plus tard

Serveuse	Monsieur-dame vous avez choisi?
Véro	Alors nous allons prendre un menu à 67F, un menu à 127F, deux menus pour enfants et une bouteille de Muscadet s'il vous plaît.
Serveuse	Je suis désolée madame mais le menu à 67F est pour midi seulement.
Véro	Pas de problème, nous prendrons deux menus à 127F.

la fenêtre	*the window*	**je suis désolée**	*I am sorry*
convenir	*to suit*	**cela vous convient?**	*does it*
une bouteille	*a bottle*		*suit you?*

Point info

 ## The menu

Whether you order a meal **à la carte** or **un menu à prix fixe** the pattern of your meal is likely to be similar to the menu shown below:

une entrée / un hors d'œuvre (*a starter*)
un plat principal (*a main course*)
(either **de la viande** *meat* or **du poisson** *fish*)
du fromage (*cheese*)
un dessert

Unfortunately it is not easy to find restaurants with a vegetarian menu. If you are vegetarian (**Je suis végétarien/végétarienne**) you are likely to be offered:

> **une assiette de crudités**
> (*a plate of mixed salad*)
> **un plateau de fromages:**
> **du camembert, du gruyère, du Roquefort** (*a selection of cheeses*),
> **du fromage de chèvre** (*goat's cheese*)
> **un dessert**

When you order your meal check that the service is included in the price:

Le service est compris?

Restaurants are obliged to indicate on their menus if the prices quoted are net prices: **prix nets**.

À vous maintenant!

3 Bon appétit!

Look at the four menus which follow and listen to the audio. You have to enter in the table below what Luc and Florence have ordered. You may have to listen to the audio several times.

The last row is for you. There are gaps on the audio for you to respond to the waiter and order from the 170F menu.

	Menus (prix)	First course	Second	Cheese	Dessert
Luc					
Florence					
vous	170F	6 oysters served hot with seaweed	Grilled scallop kebab	Cheese	Strawberry ice cream

MENU À 127F

ASSIETTE DE FRUITS DE MER
PLATE OF SEAFOOD
OU
COQUILLE SAINT JACQUES À LA BRETONNE
SCALLOPS "À LA BRETONNE"
12 PALOURDES DES GLENAN FARCIES
12 STUFFED GLENAN CLAMS

BROCHETTE DE JOUE DE LOTTE À LA DIABLE
DEVIL MONKFISH KEBAB
OU
LE COQ AU VIN DU PATRON
COQ AU VIN SPECIAL
OU
CONTREFILET GRILLÉ MAÎTRE D'HÔTEL
GRILLED SIRLOIN STEAK MAÎTRE D'HÔTEL

SALADE DE SAISON

PLATEAU DE FROMAGES OU CHOIX DE DESSERTS
CHEESE PLATTER OR CHOICE OF DESSERTS

MENU À 170F

ASSIETTE DE FRUITS DE MER
PLATE OF SEAFOOD
OU
SALADE GOURMANDE AUX TROIS CANARDS
GOURMANDE THREE DUCK SALAD
OU
6 HUITRES CHAUDES AU COCKTAIL D'ALGUES
6 OYSTERS SERVED HOT WITH SEAWEED COCKTAIL

BROCHETTE DE SAINT JACQUES AU BEURRE BLANC
GRILLED SCALLOP KEBAB IN BEURRE BLANC
OU
MAGRET DE CANARD AUX AIRELLES ET AU PORTO
MAGRET OF DUCK IN PORT AND BILBERRY
OU
CHÂTEAUBRIAND AUX CINQ POIVRES
STEAK CHÂTEAUBRIAND SEASONED WITH FIVE PEPPERS

PLATEAU DE FROMAGES
CHEESE PLATTER

CHOIX DE DESSERTS
CHOICE OF DESSERT

MENU À 230 F

PLATEAU DE FRUITS DE MER
SEAFOOD PLATTER

BROCHETTE DE SAINT JACQUES GRILLÉE, BEURRE BLANC
GRILLED SCALLOP KEBAB IN WHITE BUTTER

ROGNONS DE VEAU BEAUGE AUX MORILLES
VEAL KIDNEYS IN CREAM AND MORREL SAUCE

PLATEAU DE FROMAGES
CHEESE PLATTER

FRAISES MELBA
STRAWBERRY MELBA

MENU À 285 F

PLATEAU DE FRUITS DE MER
SEAFOOD PLATTER

HOMARD BRETON À NOTRE FAÇON
BRETON LOBSTER; CHIEF'S SPEACIAL

PLATEAU DE FROMAGES
CHEESE PLATTER

DESSERT
CHOICE OF DESSERT

13 | SUR LA ROUTE
On the road

In this unit you will learn:

■ about French roads and driving in France
■ useful expressions to use in a service station
■ some car vocabulary
■ pronouns **y** and **en**

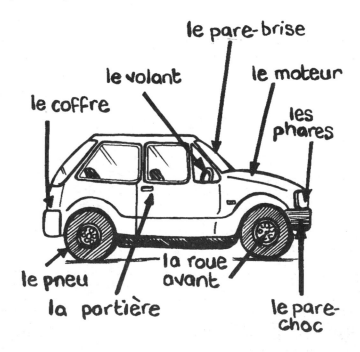

le pare-brise

le volant

le moteur

le coffre

les phares

le pneu

la roue avant

la portière

le pare-choc

La voiture de Dominique

 1 Il y a une déviation

*Sarah et Dominique sont en route pour St Nazaire où habite Dominique.
Elles sont sur la RN (route nationale) 175. C'est Sarah qui conduit.*

> # TRAVAUX SUR RN 175
> # ROUTE BARRÉE À 500M
> # RALENTISSEZ!

Listen to the audio once, and answer these questions:

(a) What's happening on the road?

(b) What is the speed limit?

Listen again:

(c) Where are they going to stop next?

(d) Is the place they are stopping at on the left or on the right?

Now read the dialogue:

Dominique   Ah zut alors! Tu as vu le panneau? La route est barrée à cinq cents mètres.

Sarah   Oui il y a une déviation.

Dominique   Il faut passer par Auray. Ralentis un peu Sarah! Regarde le panneau: 'Travaux'. La vitesse limite est de cinquante kilomètres à l'heure. En plus il y a souvent des gendarmes sur cette route!

Sarah   De toute façon il faut qu'on s'arrête à la prochaine station service parce qu'il n'y a presque plus d'essence.

Dominique   Tiens, il y en a une sur la droite, ici, tout de suite. On devrait aussi vérifier le niveau d'huile et la pression des pneus tant que nous y sommes. Prends la première pompe, là, 'sans plomb'.

Sarah   On fait le plein?

Dominique   Oui il vaut mieux.

Zut! *Drat! (mild expletive)*	**il faut...** *we must...*
en plus *what's more*	**il faut qu'on...** *it's necessary that*
de toute façon *in any case*	*we ...*
tout de suite *right here*	**il n'y a presque plus de ...**
(immediately)	*there is hardly any ...*
il vaut mieux *we'd better*	

 Link the following English phrases to the equivalent French expressions:

1) There is a diversion.
2) Did you see the road sign?
3) The road is closed in 500 metres.
4) The speed limit is 50km /h.
5) We'll have to stop.
6) We ought to check the tyre pressure.
7) Shall we fill up?
8) Slow down a bit Sarah!

(a) On devrait vérifier la pression des pneus.
(b) La vitesse limite est 50km à l'heure.
(c) On fait le plein?
(d) Ralentis un peu Sarah!
(e) Il y a une déviation.
(f) Il va falloir s'arrêter.
(g) La route est barrée à 500mètres.
(h) Tu as vu le panneau?

Comment ça marche?

1 Il faut / il faut que

The verb **falloir** *to be necessary* is only ever used in an impersonal form with subject pronoun **il**: **il faut**.

■ **Il faut** + verb in the infinitive:

Il faut conduire à droite. *You must drive on the right.*

Il faut se reposer souvent quand on conduit sur de grandes distances. *You must rest often when driving long distances.*

■ **Il faut que** + verb in a present form. As the second verb must be in the present subjunctive (see page 188) it is best to avoid this structure and use **il faut** + infinitive. However, for **-er** verbs the singular present subjunctive looks like the present tense you know:

Il faut qu'on s'arrête à la prochaine station service. *We have to stop at the next petrol station.*

Il faut que j'achète un litre d'huile. *I have to buy a litre of oil.*

2 Ne ... plus / ne ... pas / ne ... que

Il **n'**y a **plus** / il **ne** reste **plus** d'essence. *There is no petrol left.*
Il **n'**y a **presque plus** d'essence. *There is hardly any petrol left*
Il **n'**y a **pas** de station service sur cette route. *There is no service station on this road.*
Il **n'**y a pas assez d'huile. *There is not enough oil.*
Il **n'**y a **que** de l'essence super. *There is only high grade petrol.*
Il **ne** reste **qu'** un billet de cent francs. *There is only a 100F note left.*

Reminder:
Use **ne** in front of a consonant and **n'** in front of a vowel.

3 Pronouns y and en

Y is used frequently in expressions like **il y a** (*there is* or *there are*):

Tant que nous y sommes. *While we are about it.* (Lit. here **y** – here / there)

En is used with expressions of quantity and replaces a word already mentioned:

Une station service? Il y en a une sur la droite. *A service station? There is one on the right.*

(en replaces **une station service)**

Il ne reste plus de bonbons, j'en achète? *There aren't any sweets left, shall I buy some?*

(en replaces **bonbons)**

Y and **en** are used in negative sentences:

– Il reste du pain? *Is there some bread left?*
– Non, il n'y en a plus. *No there isn't any (left).*

– Tu as du lait? *Have you got some milk?*
– Non, je n'en ai pas. *No I haven't got any.*

Comment ça se prononce?

■ **Il n'y en a** may seem difficult to pronounce but all the sounds roll into one [*ilniena*].

For **i** (like the *mi* and *ti* in English) your lips are straight but taut.

■ **Zut!** Getting your **u** right is essential to sound at all French. You may need to practise in front of a mirror in order to get the correct position for your lips which should be tightly rounded, as though you are going to whistle. Now try to say **ee** - the result will be a French **u**!

Try saying i ... u ... i ...u ... i ... u several times, alternately stretching your lips and then pursing them.

À vous maintenant!

1 Il manque toujours quelque chose! *There is always something missing!*

Link the first part of each sentence to the correct ending from the second column. You need to use all the information contained in **Comment ça marche**? page 126.

1) Il n'y a plus d'essence, il faut	(a) en remettre*.
2) Il ne reste que cinquante francs, il faut	(b) j'en achète.
3) Je n'ai plus d'argent, il faut que	(c) trouver une station service.
4) Il n'y a pas assez de café, il faut que	(d) je trouve du travail.
5) On n'a plus de fromage, il faut qu'	(e) trouver une banque.
6) Il n'y a plus d'huile dans le moteur, il faut	(f) on en achète.

Note that there are two possible ways of ending sentences 1 and 6.

* **mettre** *to put* and **remettre** *to put more / again*

2 Qu'est ce qu'elles doivent faire?

Look back at the dialogue on page 125. What is the third thing that Sarah and Dominique must do when they get to the petrol station?

1) Faire le plein d'essence
2) Vérifier le niveau d'huile
3) …

 3 À la station service

Choisissez la bonne pompe et le carburant qui convient à votre voiture.

Attention! Si vous avez un moteur diesel il faut mettre du gazole. La plupart des voitures modernes utilisent de l'essence sans plomb *(lead-free petrol).*

Listen to the audio and say which car each person is driving: **A**, **B** or **C**.

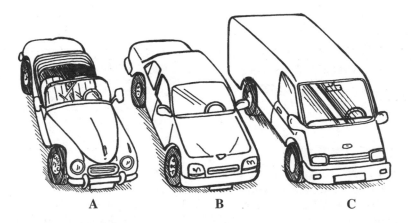

A   B   C

1) La première personne conduit la voiture_____.
2) La deuxième personne conduit la voiture_____.
3) La troisième personne conduit la voiture_____.

Filling up

Petrol *Essence*		**Leaded 4 star** *Super*	
Leaded 2 star *Ordinaire*		**Unleaded** *Sans plomb*	
Leaded 3 star *93 octane*		**Diesel** *Gazole*	

Listen to the audio again.

4) What do each of the three drivers ask for.

Point info

Roulez à droite

The main thing not to forget if you are a British driver arriving in France is that you have to drive on the right-hand side. There are signs when coming out of the port or off the Shuttle.

ROULEZ À DROITE	**CONDUISEZ À DROITE**

TOURISTES BRITANNIQUES N'OUBLIEZ PAS DE ROULER À DROITE!

N'oubliez pas!

Don't forget!

La priorité à droite

There is one particular rule to remember on French roads. It is known as **priorité à droite** (*priority to the right*). It means that cars have to let vehicles coming from the right go first. This does not apply if you are on a **route prioritaire** (*a main road*). Smaller roads intersecting with the main ones have signs telling drivers to stop at the white line. It is important to check for signs indicating on which kind of road you are driving.

In small towns, street intersections often have **priorité à droite** and most drivers use their rights mercilessly. Many road accidents are due to this particular rule.

On most roads you are told if you do not have priority:

> # ATTENTION!
> ## VOUS N'AVEZ PAS LA PRIORITÉ

Les routes

There are several kinds of roads in France:

A: Autoroute (a motorway; many motorways have a toll : **route à péage**)

E: Route Européenne (the same road as **A** but with a different number: the motorway from Dunkerque to Lille is the **A25** and also the **E 42**)

N: Route Nationale (e.g. the **RN 175**, equivalent to a British 'A' road)

D: Route départementale (maintained by the Département)

C: Route communale (municipal road maintained by the locality; not shown on 1/200 000 road maps.)

> **Opération Bison Futé** is the code name for a police and national safety exercise which takes place any time there are major holidays (14 July and 15 August). Drivers are given advice via the radio and more police are out on the roads.

À vous maintenant!

4 Quelle route?

Look at the map of the North of France.

Find the numbers for the following roads:

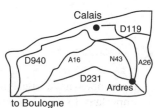

(a) The A road going from Boulogne to Calais.
(b) The N road going from Calais towards Ardres.
(c) The D road from Boulogne to Calais via the coast.

2 Les panneaux de la signalisation routière

The following table from **La prévention routière** shows the four kinds of road signs which are used on French roads.

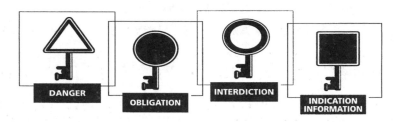

> La signalisation routière est une forme de langage très simple;
> elle peut être comprise par tous.
>
> Il suffit d'en connaître **les clefs**
>
> ■ La **FORME** permet de reconnaître facilement un panneau.
>
> ■ La **COULEUR** précise la nature exacte du panneau :
>
> **ROUGE = interdiction, BLEU = obligation.**
>
> ■ Un **SYMBOLE** facilement identifiable lui donne un
> sens précis.
>
> ■ Enfin, une **BARRE OBLIQUE** sur un panneau signifiera toujours
> la fin d'une interdiction, d'une obligation ou d'une indication.
>
> Ces quelques clefs suffisent à comprendre la signification de la
> plupart des panneaux routiers.

les principales couleurs

blanc/blanche	white	
bleu/bleue	blue	
noir/noire	black	
vert/verte	green	
orange	orange	
rouge	red	
rose	pink	

*Words for colours can be nouns or adjectives. As adjectives they change according to the gender (unless they end with an **-e**) and number of the noun they are linked to.*

obligation *mandatory*
interdiction *strictly forbidden*

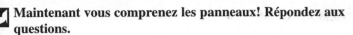

Maintenant vous comprenez les panneaux! Répondez aux questions.

(a) What does it mean when there is a sign with an oblique line across ?
(b) Which colour indicates that you have to do something?
(c) Which colour sign indicates that something is forbidden?
(d) Which colour and shape gives you some information?

Un peu de lecture

In the box below tick only those sentences which reflect what is written in the two paragraphs accompanying these two road signs.

ZONES A VITESSE LIMITÉE

De nombreuses agglomérations ont vu la création de zones de circulation à vitesse limitée, dites "Zones 30", à l'intérieur desquelles la vitesse des véhicules est réduite à 30 km/h. En l'absence de panneau, rappelez-vous qu'en agglomération, vous ne devez pas dépasser 50 km/h.

STATION DE GONFLAGE

Cette signalisation annonce une station de gonflage qui vous permettra de vérifier la pression de vos pneus (sans oublier la roue de secours!). Faites-le au moins une fois par mois et surtout avant un départ en vacances. Attention, la pression se vérifie sur un pneu froid ou ayant roulé moins de 15 km. En cas de mesure à chaud, il ne faut pas enlever de pression. N'oubliez pas que la profondeur des rainures ne doit pas être inférieure à 1,6 mm.

1) Don't forget to check the spare wheel.	
2) Most built-up areas do not have speed limit road signs.	
3) If there is no speed limit sign in a built-up area the maximum speed is 50km per hour.	
4) Check your tyre pressure when your tyres are cold.	
5) Many built-up areas have ramps to slow down traffic.	
6) Check your tyre pressure before going on holidays.	
7) Check your tyres when you have driven less than 15km.	
8) Ask someone to measure the grooves in your tyres.	
9) Check your tyres at least once a month.	
10) Many built-up areas have 30km per hour speed limit signs.	

Point info

Quels embouteillages sur les routes!

Un autocar   **des voitures**   **un camion**

When travelling in France during the summer it is important to remember two dates which can mean chaos on the roads – 14 July and 15 August. These are both bank holidays and people tend to take a few days off around them. For example if 14 July is on a Thursday most people are likely to take the Friday off. This practice is known as **faire le pont** *to do the bridge*. Special traffic measures are put in place to prevent accidents and excessive traffic jams at busy times (see **Opération Bison Futé** page 131).

> **embouteillages**   *bottle necks*
> **bouchons**   *bottlenecks* (Lit. *corks*)

3 Les informations: un weekend meutrier sur les routes françaises

 On the audio you will hear a news bulletin following a particularly bad weekend on French roads.

> **tué** *killed*   **meutrier** *murderous*
> **blessé** *hurt*

You will need to listen to the audio several times in order to fill in the grid. Listen to all the news in the first place and then listen separately to each accident report.

Accidents	Type of vehicles involved in the accident	Place where accident occured	Number of people killed	Number of people injured
1				
2				
3				

Once you have listened to the news you may read the article below, reporting one of the accidents mentioned on the radio. Use the information to help you fill in the grid.

FAITS DIVERS

Accident mortel sur la Route Nationale 10
Un camion sort d'un chemin privé devant un autocar bilan:
8 morts, 24 blessés

Comment l'accident s'est-il produit?

Un accident grave a fait huit morts et vingt-quatre blessés dans la nuit de mardi à mercredi, sur une section dangereuse de la Route Nationale 10 au sud de Bordeaux. Un autocar portugais a percuté un camion qui sortait d'un chemin privé devant l'autocar. Les deux chauffeurs portugais ont été tués. Le chauffeur du camion a été blessé.

Point info

Informations supplémentaires

If you are not used to driving in France, you need to be able to read these signs in order to drive safely.

Signs on other cars

Conduite accompagnée is the equivalent of a red learner's L, compulsory when people are learning to drive under supervision in a private car.

A red **A** at the back of a car indicates that the driver has passed the driving test less than two years ago.
A stands for **apprentissage** *apprenticeship*.

And on the roads, especially on Routes Nationales and Autoroutes there is a constant dialogue between **La prévention routière** (*accident prevention department*) and drivers.

À vous maintenant!

5 Qu'est-ce que ça veut dire?

Use the **Mots-Clefs** to work out what the signs opposite mean.

un créneau de dépassement *overtaking lane*		**le pied**	*foot*
		briser	*to break (an object)*
le frein moteur	*engine brake*	**la vie**	*life*

What do they mean?

1
**Votre sécurité.
Créneau de
dépassement
dans 3
minutes**

2
**La vie est
fragile. Ne la
brisez pas!**

3
**Trop Vite!
90
Levez le pied**

4
**Merci de votre
prudence
Bonne route!**

5
**Utilisez
votre
frein
moteur**

6
Merci de ralentir

7
Cédez le passage

Now match each of the signs above to its message below.

a)	You are going too fast! The speed limit is 90 kilometres per hour so be sensible, take your foot of the accelerator.
b)	You are not on a priority road so let traffic coming from the right go first.
c)	Thank you for slowing down.
d)	Thank you for being careful. Have a good journey!
e)	You are going down a steep road. Use a low gear to slow down.
f)	Think about safety. Don't overtake now when in three minutes' time you can use the overtaking lane.
g)	Life is fragile. Don't break it!

14 | ON CHERCHE UN APPARTEMENT
Looking for a flat

In this unit you will learn:
- about housing in France
- about looking for a flat to rent
- how to enquire about a flat on the telephone
- more about pronouns
- adjectives ending with **-al**

1 L'appartement de Dominique

			Porte d'entrée	
				Escaliers

Bureau | Salle de bains | Toilettes | Cuisine

Couloir

Chambre | Salle de séjour | Coin salle à manger

↑
Fenêtre

Balcon

L'appartement de Dominique

Dominique Périer
5 Avenue de la Vieille Ville
St NAZAIRE 44600

Look at the plan of Dominique's flat opposite and listen to the audio. Then answer these questions:

(a) On which floor is Dominique's flat?
(b) Is there a lift?
(c) Does she like her flat? Why or why not? (Give one reason)

Listen again.

(d) Why is Dominique out of breath?
(e) What does Sarah say is as good as aerobics?

Listen for a third time.

(f) Who decorated Dominique's flat?
(g) What can they just about see when leaning out of the window?

Now read the dialogue.

Dominique	Je te préviens, mon appartement est au quatrième étage et il n'y a pas d'ascenseur dans l'immeuble.
Sarah	Tu devrais déménager alors!
Dominique	Non! Je l'adore mon appartement! Je le loue pour presque rien, il y a une vue magnifique sur les anciens chantiers navals de St Nazaire, et puis mes voisins sont tranquilles. Ouf! Nous y sommes! Je suis à bout de souffle.
Sarah	Ne te plains pas ma vieille! Monter et descendre les escaliers c'est aussi bien que de faire de l'aérobic, tu sais!
Dominique	Zut! Je ne trouve pas mes clefs. Ah si les voilà!
Sarah	Oh la, la, quel bel appartement! C'est toi qui l'a décoré?
Dominique	Euh ... oui, plus ou moins, avec l'aide de mon copain.
Sarah	Tu me fais visiter?
Dominique	Allons-y pour le tour du propriétaire: voici la salle de séjour avec le coin salle à manger, sans oublier le balcon. Ici c'est la cuisine et au bout du couloir il y a ma chambre, et mon bureau: tu vas dormir là, sur le canapé. Ici à gauche il y a la salle de bains et les toilettes.

Sarah   Il me plaît ton appartement. Bon, je m'installe!
Dominique Tiens, ouvre la fenêtre. Viens voir, en se penchant on
                      aperçoit la mer! Tu la vois?

> **je te préviens**   *I am warning you (**prévenir** to warn)*
> **déménager**   *to move (house)*
> **louer**   *to rent*
> **les voisins**   *the neighbours*
> **à bout de souffle**   *breathless*
> **un copain**   *a friend/boyfriend*
> **une copine**   *a friend/girlfriend*
> **le tour du propriétaire**   *the tour of the property*
> **le propriétaire**   *the owner*
> **la propriété**   *the property*

 Now link the following English phrases to the equivalent French expressions.

1) There is no lift in the building.   (a) Ouvre la fenêtre.
2) I rent it for next to nothing.   (b) la salle de séjour
3) going up and down stairs   (c) Ici c'est la cuisine.
4) with my friend's help   (d) Tu vas dormir sur le sofa.
5) the living room   (e) Je le loue pour presque rien.
6) Here is the kitchen.   (f) En se penchant on aperçoit la mer.
7) You are going to sleep   (g) monter et descendre les escaliers
   on the sofa.   (h) Il n'y a pas d'ascenseur dans
8) When you lean out you   l'immeuble.
   can just about see the sea   i) Viens voir.
9) Don't complain old thing!   j) Ne te plains pas ma vieille.
10) Open the window.   k) avec l'aide de mon copain
11) Come and see.

Comment ça marche?

1 Les pronoms: l'/le/la/les

You already know these four pronouns, which are used to replace nouns.

In the dialogue on page 139 there are five examples of these pronouns. The first is:

Je l'adore mon appartement!   *I love (it) my flat!*

l' replaces **appartement**. This is an example where the pronoun is used first, in anticipation of the noun which comes next. It is used in spoken French to emphasise a point.

Remember that with pronouns and articles the -e is dropped in front of a vowel: **J'adore mon appart!** (**appart** is short for **appartement**). When the pronoun **le** is placed directly in front of the verb, the -e of **je** is reinstated and the -e of **le** is dropped instead: **je l'adore**. The same process applies with pronoun **la**.

À **vous de les reconnaître** *Your turn to recognise them*

1) Can you find the four other pronouns used in the dialogue above?
2) Say which nouns they replace.

2 Les pronoms: me, te, lui, nous, vous, leur

At this point you need to be able to recognise these pronouns rather than use them yourself.

Tu **me** fais visiter?	*Can you show **me** round?*
Il **me** plaît ton appartement.	*I like **it**. Lit. It pleases me your flat.*

These pronouns are used in front of verbs. You have already met some of them in reflexive verbs but here their function is slightly different. They are used to target the recipient of an action, as for example in **faire visiter sa maison à quelqu'un** *to show one's home to somebody*:

Faire visiter à ...

tu **me** fais visiter	*you show **me** round*
je **te** fais visiter	*I show **you** (to one person, familiar)*
je **lui** fais visiter	*I show **him** or **her***
tu **nous** fais visiter	*you show **us***
je **vous** fais visiter	*I show **you** (to more than one person or one person you address formally)*
tu **leur** fais visiter	*you show **them***

A slightly different set of pronouns applies with a verb like **prévenir**. **Prévenir quelqu'un** means *to warn someone/to inform someone in advance of an event*.

If the verb is followed by **à** (**faire visiter à**) the above pronouns are used. However, if the verb is not followed by **à** (**prévenir**), **l'**, **le**, **la**, **les** are used for *him*, *her*, *it them*.

Compare the two examples:

Je préviens Sarah. *I warn Sarah.* Je **la** préviens.
Je fais visiter **à** Sarah. *I show Sarah round.* Je **lui** fais visiter.

Here are more examples of pronouns with **prévenir**:

Tu **me** préviens s'il pleut n'est-ce pas? *You'll let me know if it rains won't you?*
Je **la** préviens. *I am warning her.*
Je **le** préviens. *I am warning him.*
Je préviens **mes parents** de notre arrivée. Je **les** préviens. *I'm letting my parents know about our arrival. I'm letting them know.*

For more about these pronouns see the table on page 303.

3 adjectives ending in **-al**

In the masculine form most adjectives ending in **-al** have a plural form ending in **-aux**:

un repas normal *a normal meal*   des repas normaux *normal meals*

In the feminine form all adjectives ending in **-al** take an **-e**, with a plural form ending in **-ales**:

une vie normale   *a normal life*   des vies normales *normal lives*

But there are a few exceptions which you need to know about: in the dialogue above Dominique says that her flat has a fantastic view over the old shipyards:

Il y a une vue magnifique sur les anciens chantiers **navals**.

Naval is one of the extremely rare adjectives ending in **-al** which have a plural form with **-s**:

un chantier naval   des chantiers navals

Another example:

un accident fatal   des accidents fatals

Comment ça se prononce?

When **c** becomes **ç**

The verb **apercevoir** (*to perceive/to catch a glimpse*) is one of the many verbs which changes **c** to **ç** in order to keep to an original [*s*] sound. This is necessary if the letter **c** is followed by **a/o/u** when it would normally have a [*k*] sound. To keep to the [*s*] sound the letter **c** becomes **ç**:

J'aperçois une amie là-bas.   *I can see a friend over there.*
Nous **apercevons** les montagnes.   *We can see the mountains.*
J'ai **aperçu** la Tour Eiffel.   *I spotted the Eiffel Tower.*

With other verbs this change does not always occur for the same part of the verb:

Nous **commençons** à apprendre   *We are beginning to learn English.*
  l'anglais.
Nous **recevons** des amis pour dîner.   *We are having friends for dinner.*
Il **reçoit** une récompense.   *He gets a reward.*

À vous maintenant!

1 Comment déménager sans soucis

Read the article overleaf and the twenty questions on moving home:

Tick the correct answers only.

(a) *Why are you moving?*

1 You are moving because you have got a new job.
2 You are moving because your family needs more space.
3 You have found the house of your dreams.

(b) *How are you going to manage it?*

4 It is simpler to do the lot yourself, with the help of your children.
5 Your friends can help.
6 You have to hire a van.
7 You have to make sandwiches for your friends.
8 You need lots of milk cartons.
9 You need to collect lots of cardboard boxes.

COMMENT
déménager
SANS SOUCIS

Vous avez trouvé la maison de vos rêves ? Votre petite famille aspire à un peu plus d'espace ? Bref, vous devez déménager.

Pour déménager, la solution la plus simple reste de faire appel aux copains. On amasse les cartons, on loue une camionnette, on prépare des sandwichs et le tour est joué! Oui mais voilà, tout le monde n'a pas des amis disponibles. A fortiori quand on habite au dernier étage sans ascenseur ou quand le piano à queue pèse trois tonnes! Dans certaines situations, mieux vaut faire appel à des pros.

(c) *What problems are you likely to face?*

10   You have no friends available for the task.
11   Your friends are a little bit careless.
12   Your friends are not strong enough.
13   Your front door is too narrow.
14   You live on the top floor.
15   Your washing machine weighs a ton.
16   You have a grand piano.
17   There is no lift.

(d) *What should you do if in doubt?*

18 Decide not to move.
19 Leave the piano in your old flat.
20 Call a professional removal firm.

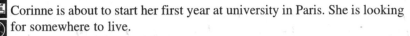# 2 Où loger?

Corinne is about to start her first year at university in Paris. She is looking for somewhere to live.

Listen to the audio once and answer these questions:

(a) Who is Corinne speaking to?
(b) What did Corinne fail to get?

Listen a second time.

(c) What does Corinne want to do?
(d) She says that all she needs is a table, two chairs and a bed. How is she going to pay for it?

Now read the dialogue.

Corinne Allô Maman, c'est Corinne. Je téléphone pour te dire que je n'ai pas obtenu de chambre à la cité universitaire. Je crois que je vais chercher un studio à louer ou bien un appart avec une ou deux copines.

Maman Un studio! Mais c'est beaucoup trop cher! Et puis il faudrait le meubler!

Corinne Bien sûr mais je vais travailler pendant les vacances pour acheter des meubles. J'ai besoin d'une table, deux chaises et un lit ou un sofa, c'est tout!

Maman Non, il n'en est pas question! Alors tu m'écoutes: il serait beaucoup plus simple de prendre une chambre meublée chez des particuliers, dans une famille. Cherche dans les petites annonces dans le journal demain.

Corinne OK! Je regarderai dans le journal, en cherchant bien j'arriverai à trouver un studio pas cher!

des meubles *furniture*	
meubler *to furnish*	
une chambre meublée	*a furnished room*

Link the following English phrases to their French equivalent:

1) I am going to look for a studio to rent.
2) I need a table, two chairs and a bed.
3) I am going to work.
4) It's out of the question.
5) I shall look in the newspaper.
6) by looking thoroughly

(a) Je vais travailler.
(b) en cherchant bien
(c) Je regarderai dans le journal.
(d) Je vais chercher un studio à louer.
(e) Il n'en est pas question.
(f) J'ai besoin d'une table, deux chaises et un lit.

Comment ça marche?

4 En

You already know about the present participle of a verb: **-ant** in French is equivalent to **-ing** in English (see page 92).

When used with **en** *when/while* it is a verb form referred to as a gerund in English:

En se penchant par la fenêtre on aperçoit la mer.
Leaning out of the window one can see the sea.
en cherchant bien
looking thoroughly

Sometimes present participle in French is not translated by a gerund in English:

Ils sifflent **en travaillant**.
They whistle while they work.
Corinne fait ses devoirs **en écoutant** de la musique.
Corinne does her homework whilst she listens to music.

Point info

L'immobilier

If you are looking for a flat or a house to rent you can search for it in any newspaper under **annonces immobilières** or you can go to an estate agent, **une agence immobilière. L'immobilier** literally refers to what cannot be moved as opposed to **le mobilier,** another word for furniture.

There are three indicators to give you an idea of the size of places to rent or buy, whether it is a flat or a house (**une maison**): The letter **T** followed by a number indicates the number of people the place is designed to accommodate: **T1/T2/T3/T4/T5**. Some adverts indicate the number of rooms (**le nombre de pièces: 2P / 3P etc.**). The number of rooms indicated includes all types of rooms except the kitchen and the bathroom. Finally there is always a figure (25m², 50m², etc.) which relates to the measurements of the place in square metres and which will answer the question: **Il fait combien de mètres carrés?**

You also need to understand a vast number of abbreviations and vocabulary. The following table should help.

M°	métro *tube station* (this applies to Paris, Lyon and Marseille)
12è.	douzième arrondissement (Paris district number – 20 districts in all)
2è. étg/der. étg	deuxième étage/dernier étage
c.c./ch.comp	charges comprises *charges included*
sdb/wc	salle de bains/wc (pronounced *les double v c* or *wouataire*)
cuis.équip.	cuisine équipée
asc.	ascenseur
ch.perso.	chambre personnelle
10m² env.	10 m² environ *approximately*
ref.nf	refait neuf *newly-decorated*
chauff.élec.	chauffage électrique
rép	répondeur automatique *answerphone*

3 Corinne cherche un studio à paris

Corinne a découpé des petites annonces dans des journaux. Elle n'a pas l'intention de prendre une chambre chez des particuliers. Elle cherche un petit appartement à partager avec une copine ou bien un petit studio pas cher. Elle a 2700F par mois pour payer son loyer.

Maisons & appartements

Particuliers

301.50F la parution
de 5 lignes
Tél.: 01.44.78.39.51

Studios Location

a) 14è. M° PLAISANCE Studio
    20m² Refait à neuf, 3è, étage
    2.800FccJP2L01.43.35.15.40

b) ☐ 19è.CITE de la MUSIQUE
    Studio meublé sympa
    imm. très calme, pour 1 an
    ou moins, loyer 2.640F cc.
    Gilles 01.40.17.15.35

c) ☐ Paris 3è. Particulier loue
    petit 2 P., 25m², wc, bains,
    3.200F cc. visite sur place lundi
    1er septembre de 12h à 14h
    4, RUE BLONDEL. 01.40.60.10.50

d) ☐ 18è.M° Marx-Dormoy
    studio 18m², tbe. coin cuisine
    s. de bains, 2è. et dern. étg.
    clair, calme sur cour. Chauff.
    élec. 2.250Fcc. 01.40.37.71.21

e) ☐ NATION - Studio 25m²
    clair, calme, 1er. étg. sur cour,
    salle de bains, wc, kitchenette,
    2.900Fcc. Direct propriétaire
    01.48.60.60.15

f) ☐ 20è. Pyrénées - Gd. studio
    40m², 6è. étg. asc. beaucoup
    de charme, poutres, ref. nf. cuis.
    équip. vue dégagée, ds. imm.
    PdT.4.000Fcc 01.43.61.49.37

g) ☐ 2è M° Strasbourg St-Denis
    Studio 27m², séjour + vraie
    cuis., sdb.libre le 1er octobre
    2.990F charges et chauffage
    compris - 01.48.02.40.10

h) ☐ 3è. M° Fille du Calvaire
    STUDIO MEUBLE
    3.000F ch. comprises
    Tél.: 01.43.65.75.57

Partages

i) ☐ **20è. M° JOURDAIN**
    100M² Meublé sympa, sdb. +
    chambre perso. 3.500Fcc.
    Tél.: 01.43.65.80.15

j) ☐ 9e. Place Clichy Part. grd
    appart. 120m² Chbre. 2.600F.
    C.C. Tél.: 01.42.70.60.50

2 Pièces Location

k) ☐ **M° LOUIS BLANC**
    2 Pièces 45m², cuisine équipée
    nombreux rangements,
    Libre de suite
    Tél. 01.43.59.39.32

 Look at the adverts Corinne has cut out from the newspaper and answer the following questions:

1) How many studios, flat shares or small flats are within her price range?

2) Which ad is about a furnished studio flat for rent for at least a year?

3) Which ads should she call if she wants to move in immediately or no later than 1 October?

4) How much could she pay for a room in a large flat?

5) Which studio flat is on the 3rd floor and has recently been decorated?

À vous maintenant!

2 Un coup de téléphone

You want to rent a studio flat in Paris. You have decided to phone about advert b) from the page opposite.

There are very few details about the studio so you need to ask a few questions.

The telephone conversation below is incomplete. The **propriétaire's** lines are in the correct place. Your lines have been jumbled up. You can find all your responses in the box.

Propriétaire	Allô, j'écoute!	
1) **Vous**	…	
Propriétaire	Oui, c'est bien cela.	
2) **Vous**	…	
Propriétaire	C'est au sixième.	
3) **Vous**	…	
Propriétaire	Euh, non mais monter et descendre les escaliers est excellent pour la santé!	
4) **Vous**	…	
Propriétaire	Non, le chauffage est électrique.	
5) **Vous**	…	
Propriétaire	Oui il y a une cuisine moderne toute équipée.	
6) **Vous**	…	
Propriétaire	C'est bien cela. Vous pouvez visiter aujourd'hui?	
7) **Vous**	…	

(a)	Il y a un ascenseur?
(b)	Je viendrais cet après-midi si vous êtes disponible.
(c)	C'est bien 2600F toutes charges comprises?
(d)	Il y a une cuisine?
(e)	J'ai vu une annonce pour un studio dans *Libé*. C'est bien ici?
(f)	Il y a le chauffage central?
(g)	C'est à quel étage?

Now listen to the whole dialogue and check your answers.

15 | **DANS LES GRANDES SURFACES**

Shopping centres

In this unit you will learn:
■ about shopping in hypermarkets
■ about buying clothes
■ how to make comparisons, say something is better or worse
■ how to find a bargain
■ demonstrative pronouns: **celui-ci**, **celui-là**, etc.

1 Rien dans le frigo

 Dominique has come home to an empty fridge. The two friends decide to go shopping. They go to one of the many out-of-town supermarkets.

Listen once to the audio, then answer these questions:

(a) Name four items on Dominique's list.
(b) Who are the tins for?
(c) Who looks after him when Dominique is away?

Listen again.

(d) Name three items on Sarah's list.
(e) Who is the wine for?

Listen for a third time.

(f) Dominique noticed that there were sales in the clothes and shoes department. What attracted their attention?
(g) Do they buy anything?
(h) Which colour suits Dominique best?

Listen again for the last time.

(i) Which department do they go to?

Dominique	Je n'ai plus rien dans le frigo. Il faut que j'achète de tout.
Sarah	N'oublie pas que tu as fait une liste ce matin.
Dominique	Ah oui, ma liste ... je l'ai. Alors lait, fromage, yaourts, beurre, pain, poisson, fruits et légumes, liquide lave-vaisselle, sans oublier des boîtes pour Papaguéno!
Sarah	Pour qui?
Dominique	Papaguéno? C'est mon chat. Ma voisine s'en occupe quand je pars en voyage.
Sarah	Eh bien moi j'ai besoin d'une pellicule pour mon appareil photo, des piles pour ma torche et puis une bonne bouteille de vin blanc pour boire avec le poisson et un gâteau de pâtisserie pour le dessert.
Dominique	Tu as vu, il y a des soldes de vêtements et de chaussures.
Sarah	J'aime beaucoup ces chaussures - il n'y en a qu'une paire. C'est quelle pointure?
Dominique	C'est du trente-huit.
Sarah	Dommage, je chausse du trente-neuf!
Dominique	Regarde, il n'est pas mal ce pull! Et celui-ci est encore mieux!
Sarah	Oui mais j'ai vu meilleure qualité! Et puis le vert te va mieux que le bleu ... Ah non pas le rouge, c'est encore pire!
Dominique	Oh la la, tu es agaçante, tu as toujours raison! Allez viens, on va au rayon poissonnerie acheter du poisson. J'espère qu'ils ne vendent pas de poisson rouge sinon on ne mangera rien ce soir!

---

le frigo short for **réfrigérateur**
 the fridge
des boîtes short for **des boîtes de**
 conserve *tins*
Une pellicule pour appareil
 photo *a film for a camera*
des vêtements et des
 chaussures *clothes and shoes*

le rayon poissonnerie *the fish counter*
un pull short for **un pullover**
la taille *size* (for clothes)
la pointure *size* (for shoes)
agaçante *annoying*
un poisson rouge *a gold fish*

Link the following English phrases to the equivalent French expressions.

1) I have nothing left in the fridge.
2) washing-up liquid
3) My neighbour looks after him.
4) to drink with the fish
5) There are sales on.
6) Pity, I take size 39.
7) Green suits you better than blue.
8) otherwise we won't eat anything tonight

(a) Dommage, je chausse du trente-neuf.
(b) pour boire avec le poisson
(c) Il y a des soldes.
(d) Le vert te va mieux que le bleu.
(e) Je n'ai plus rien dans le frigo.
(f) du liquide lave-vaisselle
(g) sinon on ne mangera rien ce soir
(h) Ma voisine s'en occupe.

 Dominique plaisante. At the end of the dialogue Dominique makes a joke which would be meaningless in translation. Why is it a joke in French and not in English?

On va à quel rayon pour nos provisions? Look at the map opposite of the supermarket where Dominique and Sarah are now. Listen to the dialogue again and say which departments they go to (take their shopping lists into account). Tick the department numbers below.

1)   2)   3)   4)   5)   6)   7)   8)   9)   10)

11)   12)   13)   14)   15)   16)   17)   18)   19)   20)

21)   22)   23)   24)   25)   26)   27)   28)   29)   30)

31)   32)   33)   34)   35)   36)   37)   38)   39)   40)

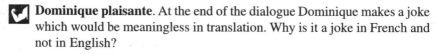

Comment ça marche?

1 En

There is a further example of **en** in the dialogue:

C'est mon chat. Ma voisine s'en occupe.
It's my cat. My neighbour looks after it.

Here **en** replaces **de mon chat**. (Ma voisine s'occupe **de mon chat**.)

■ **S'occuper de** *to mind/to look after/to take care of*:

Elle s'occupe **de ma maison**. Elle s'**en** occupe.

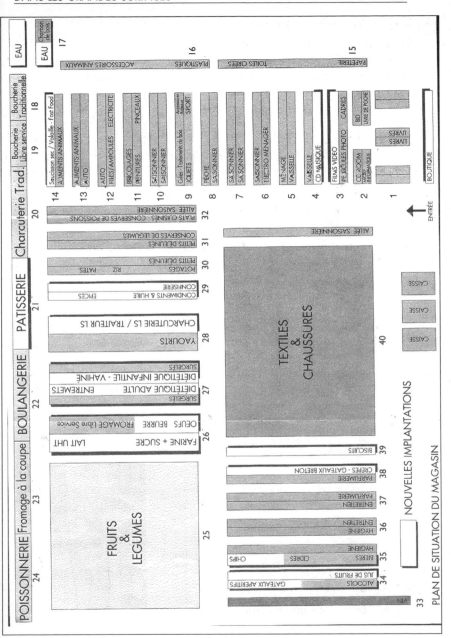

PLAN DE SITUATION DU MAGASIN

NOUVELLES IMPLANTATIONS

2 Making comparisons

Plus/plus ... que

You have already met **plus** ... **que** *more ... than* and **moins** ... **que** *less ... than*: You can use **plus** ... **que** with almost all adjectives:

C'est **plus cher qu**'à Continent.   *It's more expensive than at*
                                           Continent.

Plus ... que can also be used with adverbs:

Tu marches **plus vite que** moi.   *You walk faster than me.*

Meilleur(e)(s)/mieux

Plus and **plus** ... **que** cannot be used with the adjectives **bon(s)/bonne(s)** *good* **meilleur(e)(s)** *better* is used instead:

Les glaces à la fraise sont **meilleures**   *Strawberry icecreams are better*
(que les glaces à la vanille).   *(than vanilla icecreams).*
Le climat est **meilleur** dans le   *The climate is better in the*
Midi de la France.   *south of France.*

Meilleur can also be used as a superlative: *the best!*

– Les vins français sont **les**   – *French wines are the best*
meilleurs vins du monde.   *wines in the world.*

– Les vins allemands, les vins   – *German wines, Italian wines...*
italiens ... sont bons aussi.   *are good too.*

– Oui mais les français sont   *Yes but French ones are the best!*
les meilleurs!

La championne olympique de   *The Olympic swimming champion*
natation c'est **la meilleure**   *is the best swimmer in the world.*
nageuse du monde.

Plus and **plus** ... **que** cannot be used with the adverb **bien** *good/well*. **Mieux** *better* is used instead:

Le bleu te va bien.   *Blue suits you* (Lit. *Blue goes*
                                            well with you.)

Le vert te va mieux (que le   *Green suits you better (than red).*
rouge).

Plus mauvais(e)(s) (pire) and plus mal (pis)

Although **plus** and **plus...que** can be used with the adjective
mauvais(e)(s) *bad* and the adverb **mal** *badly*, you may come across their
alternative forms: **pire** and **pis**. **Pis** is not commonly used in comparisons,
but you will often hear the expression **Tant pis!** *Too bad!* (lit. *So much the
worse!*)

Il est **mauvais** ce vin! Pouah!

Celui-ci est encore **plus mauvais**!   *This one is even worse!*
Celui-ci est encore **pire**!

Marc conduit **plus mal**   *Marc drives worse than
que son frère.   his brother.*

3 Demonstrative pronouns

You can use demonstrative pronouns when you need to refer to something
which is present at the time of the conversation:

(masc.sing.)	**Celui-ci**	*this one* ⎫	**Celui-là**	*that one* ⎫	
(fem.sing.)	**Celle-ci**		**Celle-là**		
(fem.pl.)	**Celles-ci**	*these ones* ⎫	**Celles-là**	*those ones* ⎫	
(masc.pl.)	**Ceux-ci**		**Ceux-là**		

◤ À vous maintenant!

1 Trouvez les phrases correctes

Choose the correct ending for each of the sentences below.

1)	Ce poisson a l'air frais	(a)	mais celles-ci sont meilleures.
2)	Cet artichaut est gros	(b)	mais celui-ci sent encore meilleur.
3)	Ces pommes sont bonnes	(c)	mais celle-ci est meilleure.
4)	Ce melon sent bon	(d)	mais ceux-ci sont meilleurs.
5)	Ces gâteaux sont bons	(e)	mais celui-ci a l'air plus frais.
6)	Cette bière est bonne	(f)	mais celui-ci est encore plus gros.

Point info

Les grandes surfaces

All French towns have out-of-town shopping centres with a vast range of
supermarkets and hypermarkets (Auchan, Carrefour, Continent, Géant,
Leclerc, Mammouth, etc.). They are generally referred to as **grandes
surfaces** because of the large space they occupy. Some have up to thirty
checkouts (**caisses**) and have a policy of employing young people on roller
skates to help with customer service. Most of them are located in large
shopping arcades, with a whole range of smaller shops, boutiques of all
sorts and restaurants. In addition to the permanent shopping area, they
frequently have seasonal products at competitive prices under a large
marquee (**Sous Chapiteau**): wines in the autumn, Chrysanthemum for All
Saints Day on First November, oysters for Christmas and the New Year,
bedding and furniture in the spring and camping equipment in the summer.

They all compete with one another by having promotional offers
(**Promotions**), sales (**Soldes**), the bargains of the day (**Affaire du Jour**),
special offers (**Offres Spéciales**). Once or twice in the year all the shops
in an area all have sales on at the same time (**Grande Braderie** or **Foire
aux Soldes**). They all advertise in the local press and have slogans like:
Guerre sur les Prix (*War on Prices*), **Prix Fous** (*Crazy prices*) or **Prix
Défi** (*Price challenge*).

All **grandes surfaces** have **Un Point/Espace Environnement** for
recycling glass and plastic bottles.

✔ À vous maintenant!

📖 2 Prix Fous!

Look at the adverts from local papers where local shops have advertised their bargains.

« L'AFFAIRE DU JOUR!! »
A ne pas manquer. »

OFFRE VALABLE DU 1er AU 3 AOÛT
(le 3 août pour les magasins ouverts le dimanche matin)

NECTARINE BLANCHE

origine France
catégorie 1, calibre B

6F,50

le kg

CHEZ STOC, UN CLIENT C'EST SACRÉ

stoc
SUPERMARCHÉ

FOUESNANT — 4, rue de Kernevéleck
CONCARNEAU — 17, quai Carnot
LE GUILVINEC — 1, rue des Moulins
MORLAIX — Rue de Brest
CARANTEC — Kérouguelen
PLOUGUERNEAU — Douar Nevez

A

PRIX FOUS ...

D

AUJOURD'HUI MERCREDI 6 AOÛT
DERNIER JOUR
FOIRE AUX SOLDES
à **PONT-L'ABBÉ**
C'est à côté
U.D.C.P.

Par autorisation préfectorale du 30 avril 97

PROMO LITERIE
SOUS CHAPITEAU
GRANDES MARQUES
monsieur meuble
nous sommes bien ensemble!
Route de Quimper
PONT-L'ABBÉ

E

B

SOLDES
DERNIERS JOURS
MEUBLES L. Bilien
15, rue du Général-De Gaulle
29750 LOCTUDY
Ancien élève de l'école Boulle

C

AURAY • CENTRE-VILLE
MARDI 12 - MERCREDI 13 AOÛT
GRANDE BRADERIE
Organisation : Auray Préférence
et Rugby Auray Club
CRÉDIT AGRICOLE DU MORBIHAN

OFFRE SPÉCIALE
MOTEUR 135 CV 2L V6 MERCURY
Prix catalogue : 83.000 F
Vendu **51.000F**
hors pose
BREST NAUTIC
Port du Moulin-Blanc - BREST
02.98.41.43.70

F

Answer these questions:

(a) What is the bargain of the day at STOC?
(b) How long will it last?
(c) What day of the week is 3 August?
(d) Where and when in Auray is the Grande Braderie taking place?
(e) What is 'Monsieur Meuble' selling **Sous Chapiteau**? (Clue: first three letters of LITERIE)
(f) How much would one save at Brest Nautic?
(g) When does **La Foire Aux Soldes** end in Pont-L'Abbé?
(h) What is in the sales at 15 rue du Général de Gaulle?

2 Au rayon charcuterie

Madame Rouzeau has a long list of delicatessen products she wants to buy: Bayonne ham, garlic sausage, farmhouse pâté, Greek mushrooms, scallops.

Listen to the dialogue as many times as necessary so you can identify everything on Madame Rouzeau's shopping list.

In the grid below fill in the quantity required for each item:

Bayonne ham	
Garlic sausage	
Farmhouse pâté	
Greek mushrooms	
Scallops	

Now read the dialogue and check your answers.

Vendeuse	Soixante-quinze? C'est à qui le tour?
Madame R	C'est à moi. Mettez-moi six tranches de jambon de Bayonne s'il vous plaît.
Vendeuse	Ça vous va comme cela?
Mme R	Oui, c'est bien.
Vendeuse	Et avec ça?
Mme R	Alors il me faut douze tranches de saucisson à l'ail, ... deux cent cinquante grammes de pâté de campagne, ...

deux cents grammes de champignons à la grecque, ...
et quatre coquilles St Jacques.

Vendeuse   Et avec cela?

Mme R   Ça sera tout merci!

Vendeuse   Voilà Madame, bonne journée.

Dans les paniers de Madame Rouzeau il y a des fruits et des légumes frais. Look in Madame Rouzeau's basket, and then try the puzzle overleaf.

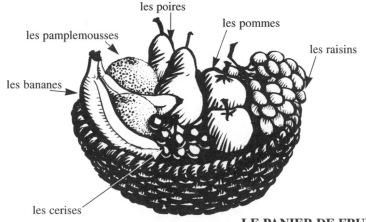

les poires

les pommes

les pamplemousses

les raisins

les bananes

les cerises

**LE PANIER DE FRUITS
DE MADAME ROUZEAU**

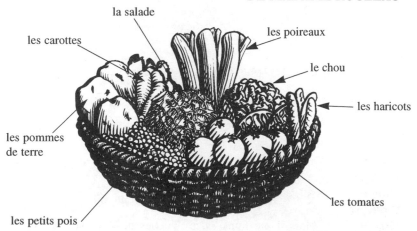

la salade

les poireaux

les carottes

le chou

les haricots

les pommes
de terre

les tomates

les petits pois

**LE PANIER DE LÉGUMES
DE MADAME ROUZEAU**

Find the names of fruit and vegetables hidden in the grid.

P	A	C	C	D	M	N	G	H	I	L	P	K
A	D	S	E	A	P	O	M	M	E	S	O	D
M	S	Q	R	D	S	A	Y	E	E	G	M	H
P	E	T	I	T	S	P	O	I	S	K	M	K
L	R	G	S	F	T	Y	M	S	E	L	E	H
E	A	P	E	B	A	N	A	N	E	S	S	A
M	I	O	S	D	C	E	T	A	P	A	D	R
O	S	I	Z	A	H	R	E	T	O	L	E	I
U	I	R	C	V	O	B	S	M	I	A	T	C
S	N	E	R	H	U	S	G	D	R	D	E	O
S	C	A	R	O	T	T	E	S	E	E	R	T
E	T	U	Y	U	H	N	F	D	S	V	R	S
S	F	X	J	V	B	C	A	S	W	R	E	M

 # À vous maintenant!

3 Le quiz sur les produits surgelés

There are two words in French for frozen products: **produits surgelés** and **produits congelés**, both from **geler** *to freeze*.

Surgelé refers to the industrial type of freezing at very low temperatures (-50°C). **Congelé** refers to home freezing (–18°C).

With just a few **mots-clefs** you should be able to attempt the quiz found in a Carrefour guide about frozen food.

sans sel *without salt*	**un milliard** *a billion*
la récolte *picking*	**chez soi** *at home*
suivre *to follow*	**entraîne des pertes** *leads to losses*

Don't forget **V**: Vrai **F**: Faux

Bonne chance!

QUIZ?

TESTEZ VOTRE CULTURE "SURGELÉS"

		V	F
1	Les produits surgelés nature sont sans sel ajouté	❏	❏
2	Il faut 1,5 kg de petits pois frais pour faire un kilo de petits pois surgelés	❏	❏
3	Il existe 30 espèces de poissons au rayon "surgelés"	❏	❏
4	Les légumes sont surgelés dans les heures qui suivent la récolte	❏	❏
5	Les Français ont consommé un milliard 600 millions de portions de frites en une année	❏	❏
6	Tous les réfrigérateurs sont conçus pour congeler des produits chez soi	❏	❏
7	La surgélation entraîne des pertes de vitamines et minéraux	❏	❏
8	On trouve tout au rayon "surgelés": de l'entrée au dessert, du petit déjeuner au dîner!	❏	❏

Point info

Les cartes de crédit

French credit cards are no longer swipe cards but **carte à puces** (*silicone chip cards*). Customers are handed a key pad instrument and they enter their own code at the cash desk. You may see a notice advising customers not to key in their code in full sight of other customers:

> *Frappez votre code à l'abri des regards indiscrets*

Other non-French credit cards are still accepted however.

16 À LA MAISON DU PEUPLE

At the community centre

In this unit you will learn:

■ a little about multi-ethnic France
■ about young people and out of school activities
■ about tackling racism
■ the perfect tense with **être**

1 Je suis animateur

As planned Dominique and Sarah are on their way to Dominique's parents in Bordeaux but on the way they stop for one night at Dominique's boyfriend in Nantes.

Le copain de Dominique s'appelle Gildas Marrec. Il est Directeur de la Maison du Peuple dans un quartier populaire de Nantes.

Listen to the audio once, then answer the questions:

1) Who is Djamel?
   (a) Gildas' brother   (b) a colleague   (c) a neighbour
2) Djamel works
   (a) with adults   (b) in a college   (c) with young people
3) What kind of activities does he supervise?

Listen to the audio again.

4) Where did Djamel and some young people travel to?
5) How long did they stay there?
6) How many young people and how many adults went on the journey?

Listen for the last time to the audio

7) Where did some young people stay?
8) Who did they all meet?

Now read the dialogue.

Gildas	Salut! Vous avez fait un bon voyage?
Dominique	Oui, très bien. Gildas je te présente Sarah.
Sarah	Enchantée!
Gildas	Enchanté! Dominique m'a beaucoup parlé de vous. Je vous présente Djamel, un collègue de travail. Djamel, Dominique, ma copine et Sarah, une amie à elle.
Sarah	(*à Djamel*) Vous travaillez avec des jeunes aussi?
Djamel	Oui, je suis animateur, c'est-à-dire que j'encadre des jeunes dans de nombreuses activités en dehors du collège.
Sarah	Quel genre d'activités?
Djamel	Oh un peu de tout: du sport, de la photo, de la musique et même des voyages. Nous avons beaucoup de jeunes maghrébins dans le quartier. Ils n'ont pas grand'chose à faire, à part regarder la télé. Là on vient de rentrer d'un voyage au Maroc.
Gildas	Djamel est formidable avec les gamins.
Dominique	Combien sont allés au Maroc?
Djamel	Dix-huit et on était trois animateurs. On est resté trois semaines. Certains sont restés dans leurs familles.
Sarah	Ils ont rencontré des jeunes marocains?
Djamel	Oui, bien sûr. Ils ont tous fait énormément de découvertes.

---

un animateur (une animatrice)   *someone organising activities, youth worker* (the full name for this profession is **animateur socio-culturel**)
encadrer   *to provide a framework for activities* (**un cadre**: *a frame, support*. In a work context it also means *a manager*)
des jeunes maghrébins   *young people with North African origins*
le quartier   *the district/the area*

Link the following English phrases to the equivalent French expressions.

1) Dominique has told me lots of things about you
2) Do you work with young people too?
3) a bit of everything
4) There aren't many things for them to do.

(a) Djamel est formidable avec les gamins.
(b) On est resté trois semaines.
(c) Ils ont rencontré des jeunes marocains.
(d) Certains sont restés avec leur famille.

5) Djamel is fantastic with kids.
6) We stayed three weeks.
7) Some stayed with their own family.
8) They met young Moroccans.

(e) un peu de tout
(f) Vous travaillez avec des jeunes aussi?
(g) Ils n'ont pas grand'chose à faire.
(h) Dominique m'a beaucoup parlé de vous.

Comment ça marche?

1 The perfect tense with être

Look back at Unit 12 page 115 where you met the perfect tense with **avoir**. Since then you have come across many examples of verbs which are formed with **avoir** in the perfect tense.

There are fewer verbs which form the perfect tense with **être** and they function slightly differently from those with **avoir**. They are closer to adjectives and in fact the past participle varies according to the gender and number of the subject in the same way that some adjectives do:

Elle est fatiguée (adjective) *She is tired*

fatiguée ends with an **-e** for feminine because it is she who is tired.

Elle est allée (past participle) en ville. *She went to town.*

allée also ends with **-e** because it is she who went.

The thirteen verbs with être

There are only thirteen frequently used verbs which form the perfect tense with **être**:

aller *to go*	**allé**	naître *to be born*	**né**
arriver *to arrive*	**arrivé**	partir *to leave*	**parti**
descendre *to go down*	**descendu**	rester *to stay*	**resté**
devenir *to become*	**devenu**	sortir *to go out*	**sorti**
entrer *to enter*	**entré**	tomber *to fall*	**tombé**
monter *to go up*	**monté**	venir *to come*	**venu**
mourir *to die*	**mort**		

Study carefully the examples below, paying particular attention to the spelling of the past participle:

- Je suis **allée** à la banque. (a woman speaking)
- Tu es **arrivé** en retard ce matin, Pierre! (someone speaking to a young boy)
- Sophie est **devenue** très sage. (*very well-behaved*)
- Mathieu est **entré** à l'université.
- Nous sommes **descendus** de voiture (m.pl. – more than one man or a man and a woman)
- Nous sommes **entrées** à la Samaritaine (f.pl. – more than one woman speaking)
- Vous êtes **né** à Paris, Maurice? (addressing one male only)
- Vous êtes **partis** sans moi les garçons! (m.pl.)
- Ils sont **morts** dans un accident de voiture (Dodi and Diana)
- Elles sont **venues** à pied (f.pl.) (*They walked here.*)

How to remember the verbs with être

The following story is a mnemonic device which you can use to remember easily those thirteen verbs: It is Henri's story who was born in Marseille, went to Paris, went up the Eiffel Tower, went up to the second floor stayed there half an hour, came down, came out, went to see la Seine, fell in it and died:

Henri est **né** à Marseille. À l'âge de trente ans il est **venu** à Paris. Il est **allé** à la Tour Eiffel. Il est **entré**. Il est **monté** jusqu'au deuxième étage. Il est **resté** là une demi-heure. Il est **descendu**. Il est **sorti**. Il est **allé** au bord de la Seine. Malheureusement il est **tombé** et il est **mort**.

You may write the story of Henri's twin sister, Henriette: Henriette est **née** à Marseille ...

If you want to write a different version with Henri and Henriette both involved, its starts: Henri et Henriette sont **nés** à Marseille ... (One masculine + one feminine = masculine plural in French grammar rules).

Reflexive verbs with être

In addition to these specific thirteen verbs, all reflexive verbs form the perfect tense with **être**. When they are not reflexive they form the perfect tense with **avoir**.

Exemples: **couper** *to cut*, past participle **coupé**

- Caroline **a coupé** du pain avec un couteau. (perfect tense with **avoir**) *she cut the bread with a knife* BUT

■ Caroline **s'est coupée** avec un couteau. (perfect tense with **être**)
She cut herself with a knife. (Reflexive verb has extra -**e** on past
participle because Caroline is feminine).

☑ À vous maintenant!

1 Faites six phrases correctes

Find six correct sentences and say what they mean

1) Djamel est l'animateur qui s'	(a)	sont allés au Maroc.
2) Sarah et Dominique	(b)	êtes parti avec un groupe de jeunes?
3) Je	(c)	est occupé du voyage.
4) Les jeunes	(d)	est resté trois semaines au Maroc.
5) Vous	(e)	sont arrivées chez Gildas.
6) Le groupe	(f)	suis montè(e) à la Tour Eiffel.

2 À votre tour de poser des questions

It's your turn to ask questions – you are being told what to say.

You are speaking to Adidja, Djamel's friend, who is also **animatrice socio-culturelle**.

(a) **Vous** *Ask her if she also went to Morocco with the group.*
Adidja Oui, j'y suis allée.
(b) **Vous** *Ask her how many young people went to Morocco.*
Adidja Dix-huit. Huit filles et dix garçons.
(c) **Vous** *Ask her how long they stayed.*
Adidja Nous sommes restés trois semaines.
(d) **Vous** *Ask her if they met young Moroccans.*
Adidja Oui beaucoup. C'était formidable.

If you are satisfied with your questions you can now listen to the audio.

Point info

All French towns have places such as **centres socio-culturels, Maisons des Jeunes, Maisons du Peuple** or **Maisons de Quartier**. These centres are normally run by **la municipalité** (*the Council*) and do not only cater for young people. There are usually cultural and leisure activities for various groups of people at various times of the day. They can vary in terms of the facilities they offer but most of them have their own premises, sports halls, art rooms, games rooms, etc. They do not normally share buildings or facilities with schools. The role of the **animateur socio-culturel** is to provide a place for leisure and social purposes and also for education but clearly distinct from the school system. With many French school children on a four day week* now, the role of **animateurs socio-culturels** is vital although attendance at these centres is not compulsory. Part of the task includes tackling racism in a constructive way.

In the dialogue (page 163) Djamel refers to **jeunes maghrébins**: young people fom the **Maghreb**, the area of North Africa which covers **la Tunisie** *Tunisia*, **l'Algérie** *Algeria* and **le Maroc**. These countries were at one time French colonies. Most young people of Arabic origin were born in France but they live with a dual culture which is not always understood or accepted. Young Arabs are often pejoratively called **les beurs** or **les harkis** (born from North African parents – second generation people). In the 1980s young French people became aware of racial problems and under the leadership of a young black man called **Harlem Désir** started a movement called **SOS Racisme**, with a slogan **'Touche pas à mon pote!'** (*Don't touch my mate!*) and an open hand as a symbol.

* The reason why more and more French schools operate a four day week is that traditionally Wednesday is a day off school used for various activities or for private study. Saturday, from being a full school-day, has become over the years morning only. But under parental pressure many schools are no longer time-tabling lessons at all on Saturdays. French children are still having to work hard, each of their four days can be a nine-hour day in school, seven hours of lessons and a heavy homework programme.

2 Je suis né en France

Sarah continues the conversation with Djamel.

Listen to the audio and answer the questions.

(a) What question does Sarah ask Djamel?
(b) Where was he born?
(c) Who did he go to Morocco with?
(d) How many times have they been there?

Listen again.

(e) Which language does Djamel speak at home?
(f) How many languages can he speak?

Now read the dialogue.

Sarah   Et vous, c'est la première fois que vous êtes allé au Maroc?
Djamel Non, non, je suis né en France mais avec mes parents et mes sœurs nous y sommes allés une dizaine de fois.
Sarah   Vous parlez l'arabe alors?
Djamel Bien sûr, on parle l'arabe à la maison. Je pense que c'est enrichissant d'avoir une double culture. Je parle trois langues: le français, l'arabe et l'anglais. Je me sens ouvert et tolérant.

 # À vous maintenant!

3 Un sondage d'opinion

Lisez les résultats de l'enquête du *Nouvel Observateur*. Est-ce que la France mérite la réputation d'être le pays des droits de l'homme? *Does France deserve its reputation as the country of human rights?*

SONDAGE

«Le Nouvel Observateur» vient de publier une enquête sur la façon dont les Français d'origine étrangère jugent la France. Voici ce qu'ils répondent à deux des questions.

– Est-ce que vous avez été personnellement victime de propos ou de comportements racistes?

Oui	65%
Non	32%
Ne se prononcent pas	3%

– Pensez-vous que la réputation de la France comme pays d'accueil et pays des droits de l'homme est tout à fait justifiée, assez justifiée, peu justifiée, ou pas du tout justifiée?

Tout à fait et assez justifiée	50%
Peu et pas du tout justifiée	48%
Ne se prononcent pas	2%

---

une enquête	an investigation	des comportements	attitudes
étranger/étrangère	foreign	accueil	welcome
des propos	remark/utterance		

Now link the English phrases to the French expressions.

1) No opinion
2) Little justified
3) Fully justified
4) Fairly justified
5) Not at all justified

(a) Tout à fait justifiée
(b) Assez justifiée
(c) Ne se prononcent pas
(d) Pas du tout justifiée
(e) Peu justifiée

4 Combien de Français?

Look at the results of the opinion poll (opposite) and answer the questions verbally only.

Reminder: **20% se dit 'vingt pour cent'**

Combien de Français d'origine étrangère :

(a) pensent que la réputation de la France est justifiée?
(b) pensent que la réputation de la France n'est pas justifiée?
(c) ont été victimes de racisme?
(d) n'ont pas été victimes de racisme?

5 Noir et blanc

Noir et blanc: Cantona et Karembeu

Eric Cantona, aspirant-acteur, et Christian Karembeu, défenseur de l'équipe de Gênes, ont décidé d'échanger leur couleur de peau. Cantona s'est maquillé en noir et Karembeu en blanc à l'occasion du tournage d'un documentaire sur la lutte contre la discrimination raciale, dans le cadre de l'année contre le racisme.

Les deux footballeurs seront encore sous les feux de l'actualité le 12 octobre prochain quand trois équipes participeront à un match placé sous le signe de l'amitié, de la solidarité et de la lutte contre le racisme au stade Santiago Barnabeu, le terrain du Real Madrid. Les plus grands joueurs de football du monde dont Cantona, Weah et Maradonna prendront part à cette manifestation. ■

You are not expected to understand every single word of this article but do try to get the gist of it. The questions overleaf should help a little.

(a) Is Cantona playing much football?

(b) What is he aspiring to do?

(c) Who is Christian Karembeu?

(d) What did the two agree to do in front of the cameras?

(e) Why?

(f) Where will they be playing on 12 October?

(g) What kind of match will it be? Why has it been organised?

(h) Who else will be playing?

(i) You may have to guess a few new words. See whether you can find the following:

1) their skin colour   4) the greatest players in the world

2) a team   5) would-be actor

3) the limelight   6) sign of friendship and solidarity

(j) **Mots cachés**

Ten words from the above article are hidden in the grid. In English they mean:

footballers, players, solidarity, against, team, year, new, world, friendship, fight, defender, skin

F	N	A	U	B	M	J	A	K	L	Y	P
C	O	N	T	R	E	T	M	O	N	D	E
S	U	O	R	E	D	F	I	G	H	H	A
O	V	S	T	E	L	U	T	T	E	G	U
L	E	Q	U	B	F	M	I	Y	M	F	V
I	A	S	A	Z	A	C	E	B	M	U	E
D	U	A	D	G	B	L	W	A	E	I	O
A	N	N	E	E	W	S	L	A	E	D	G
R	S	T	U	V	J	O	U	E	U	R	S
I	T	D	E	F	E	N	S	E	U	R	J
T	A	E	Y	Q	U	I	O	P	N	R	M
E	Q	U	I	P	E	X	A	Z	F	R	S

La voiture idéale

Neuf personnes (ou couples) avec des goûts bien individuels

Look at the cars below. In the second column of the grid indicate which car is most likely to belong to each of the nine people described. The third and fourth columns are jumbled. Choose where these people are mostly likely to live and what is likely to be their favourite eating place.

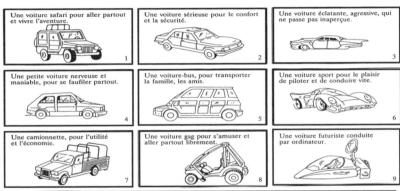

1. Une voiture safari pour aller partout et vivre l'aventure.

2. Une voiture sérieuse pour le confort et la sécurité.

3. Une voiture éclatante, agressive, qui ne passe pas inaperçue.

4. Une petite voiture nerveuse et maniable, pour se faufiler partout.

5. Une voiture-bus, pour transporter la famille, les amis.

6. Une voiture sport pour le plaisir de piloter et de conduire vite.

7. Une camionnette, pour l'utilité et l'économie.

8. Une voiture gag pour s'amuser et aller partout librement.

9. Une voiture futuriste conduite par ordinateur.

Neuf caractères très différents	La voiture de leurs rêves	Où habitent-ils?	Où mangent-ils?/ qu'est-ce qu'ils aiment?
1) André Morin a trente-cinq ans, célibataire. Il vient d'être nommé Directeur d'une grande banque parisienne. Il aime la vitesse, les avions, le ski, le ski nautique, etc. Quelle est la voiture de ses rêves?		a) À Lyon dans une grande maison avec une piscine et un grand jardin.	j) Ils adorent les pique-niques à la campagne.
2) Gérard Duigou a tout juste dix-huit ans. Il aime la mer, la plage et s'amuser avec ses copains. Quelle sera sa première voiture?		b) Une petite maison dans la campagne pas loin de Toulouse	k) Elle aime surtout les bons couscous de sa mère.

3) M. et Mme Dumas ont cinq enfants. Ils vont souvent chez leurs parents dans le Midi. Quelle voiture viennent-ils d'acheter?	c) Dans une grande propriété à Deauville.	l) À la cantine universitaire.
4) Jean-Yves et Florence Beaumont habitent à Toulouse où ils sont tous les deux enseignants dans un collège. Ils adorent passer leurs week-ends à explorer les Pyrénées. Leur rêve est d'aller en Afrique. Quelle est leur voiture?	d) Dans un élégant appartement du seizième arrondissement de Paris.	m) Chez Maxime ou à la Tour d'Argent, les deux restaurants les plus chers de Paris.
5) Etienne Vaillant a habité à Grenoble toute sa vie. Il est maintenant chercheur à l'université de Grenoble où il travaille sur un prototype de voiture pour l'an 2000.	e) Dans un studio avec vue sur le vieux port.	n) À MacDonald's aussi souvent que possible!
6) Bernard Fargeon est fermier. Il a une ferme d'élevage de poulets dans le Finistère. Il y a cinq ans il a acheté un véhicule pratique pour transporter la nourriture pour la volaille et aussi pour transporter sa mère qui est Bigoudène.	f) Il partage un appartement avec des copains.	o) Chez Maxime ou à la Tour d'Argent, les deux restaurants les plus chers de Paris.
7) Olivier Dubois est le PDG (Président Directeur Général) d'une chaîne d'hypermarchés. Il aime le confort, le luxe et tout ce qui est solide. Quelle voiture a-t-il choisi?	g) Il habite toujours chez ses parents. Sa chambre a un décor de science-fiction.	p) Dans les restaurants chics du quartier de l'Opéra Garnier.
8) Laurent Dubois, le fils de M. Dubois ne travaille pas mais avec l'argent de son père il s'est acheté une vieille Cadillac rouge, remise à neuf.	h) Une ferme dans un village sur la Baie d'Audierne.	q) Une soupe bien chaude après une longue promenade en montagne.
9) Adidja Ahmed est docteur à Marseille. Elle a choisi une petite voiture rapide et pratique pour aller visiter ses patients. Quelle est sa voiture?	i) Il habite à Paris avec son amie qui est chanteuse à l'Opéra.	r) Il aime un bon poulet rôti cuit à la ferme.

17 | ON CHERCHE DU TRAVAIL
Looking for work

In this unit you will learn

■ to talk about jobs and professions
■ to look for jobs in the newspapers
■ one more way to express the past: the imperfect tense

1 Mon père était professeur

Dominique et Sarah sont arrivées chez les parents de Dominique, Monsieur et Madame Périer, à Pessac, une ville près de Bordeaux.

Listen once to the audio and answer these questions:

(a) What does M. Périer think of Sarah's French?
(b) What does Dominique say about it?
(c) Who spoke French at home when Sarah was a child?

Listen again.

(d) What happened to Sarah's father?
(e) How long ago was that?
(f) How is Sarah's mother?

Listen one more time.

(g) Why does Mme Périer interrupt her husband?
(h) What is she going to show Sarah?
(i) How long ago did M. et Mme Périer retire?

Now read the dialogue.

M. Périer   Mais vous parlez bien le français Sarah.
Dominique   Sarah est bilingue, Papa!
Sarah   C'est-à-dire que ma mère est française et elle m'a appris le français dès toute petite et le français était la première langue à la maison.

M. Périer	Ah bon! Et qu'est-ce qu'ils font vos parents?
Sarah	Mes parents étaient tous les deux professeurs de langues. Mon père était professeur d'allemand mais il est mort d'un cancer il y a cinq ans. Il parlait couramment le français et l'allemand.
Mme Périer	Je suis désolée. Votre maman va bien?
Sarah	Oui, oui, elle enseigne toujours le français dans une école à Londres.
M. Périer	Et vous, qu'est-ce que vous faites comme profession?
Sarah	Je suis éditrice dans une maison d'édition.
M.Périer	Ah, c'est un métier très intéressant! Dites-moi …
Mme Périer	Voyons François, tu vas fatiguer Sarah avec toutes tes questions. Je vais vous montrer votre chambre.

Un peu plus tard

Sarah	Quelle belle maison! Qu'est-ce qu'ils font tes parents?
Dominique	Oh ils sont en retraite depuis deux ans. Ma mère travaillait en tant que pharmacienne dans une grande pharmacie de Bordeaux et mon père était viticulteur.

apprendre *to learn* but also *to teach someone something*	**être en retraite** *to be retired*
dès *since*	**couramment** *fluently*
dès que *as soon as*	**maison d'édition** *publishing company*
enseigner *to teach (as a job)*	

In the grid below only the first row is completed correctly. Place the correct profession by each name and also its correct translation. Tick the names of thoses who are still working.

Noms	profession/métier	profession/job
Dominique	Prof de Philo	*Philosophy teacher*
Sarah	Professeur de français	*Wine grower*
Mme Périer	Viticulteur	*French teacher*
M. Périer	Editrice	*Pharmacist*
Mr. Burgess	Pharmacienne	*German teacher*
Mrs. Burgess	Professeur d'allemand	*Editor*

🗝 Comment ça marche?

1 Talking about professions

On page 28 you learnt that there is no article in front of the name of a profession. This applies with the following structure only: subject + **être** + name of profession:

Elle était pharmacienne.	*She used to be a pharmacist*
Elle est Ministre de	*She is the Minister for*
l'Environnement.	*the Environment.*
Il est ingénieur.	*He is an engineer.*
Je suis professeur d'allemand.	*I am a German teacher.*

But in other structures the article is necessary:

J'avais horreur de **la** prof de maths. *I couldn't stand the maths teacher.*

Professeur is always a masculine word, except in pupils' vocabulary at school when the abbreviation '**prof**' is commonly used. When among school pupils you are likely to hear : '**Chouette! On a la prof' d'anglais de l'année dernière**' or **Le prof de physique est vache avec nous!**

Chouette!	*Cool! Great! Brill!* (Lit. *owl*) (slang)	**Vache**	*nasty* (Lit. *cow*) (slang)

2 Apprendre et enseigner

■ Enseigner: *to teach* (e.g. in a school):
J'enseigne l'espagnol dans un lycée *I teach Spanish in an upper secondary school.*

■ Apprendre *to learn*:
J'apprends la musique. *I am learning music.*

■ Apprendre quelque chose à quelqu'un *to teach someone something:*
Mon professeur m'apprend à jouer du piano. *My teacher teaches me to play the piano.*
Ma mère a appris à lire à tous ses enfants. *My mother taught all her children to read.*

3 One more way to express the past: the imperfect tense

The various past tenses of verbs offer a range of nuances for what happened in the past. The perfect and the imperfect are often used in the same sentence to express when one event occurred in relation to another event.

How to form the imperfect

To form the imperfect tense you need to learn the following endings. They apply to all verbs without exception:

je	**-ais**	nous	**-ions**
tu	**-ais**	vous	**-iez**
il/elle	**-ait**	ils/elles	**-aient**

The four verbs below should provide you with a pattern for all other verbs in the imperfect.

Subject pronouns	**être**	**parler**	**finir**	**prendre**
je/j'	étais	parlais	finissais	prenais
tu	étais	parlais	finissais	prenais
il/elle/on	était	parlait	finissait	prenait
nous	étions	parlions	finissions	prenions
vous	étiez	parliez	finissiez	preniez
ils/elles	étaient	parlaient	finissaient	prenaient

When to use the imperfect tense:

1) When an action which was continuous or relatively lengthy is interrupted by a shorter one expressed by the perfect:

J'étais aux Etats-Unis quand **j'ai appris** la mort de mon père. *I was in the US when I learnt of my father's death.* (both events took place in the past but being in the US is longer than the few seconds it took to hear the news)

Nous sommes arrivées au moment où **il prenait** sa douche. *We arrived just as he was taking his shower.* (taking a shower is relatively longer than the action of arriving somewhere)

Les jeunes filles travaillaient au café quand **la bombe a explosé.** *The girls were working in the café when the bomb went off.*

2) When reminiscing, talking about and describing how things used to be and referring to events which occurred repeatedly in the past.

Quand **j'étais** petite **je passais** toutes mes vacances en France. *When I was little I used to spend all my holiday in France.*

Nous allions chez notre grand-mère en Provence. *We used to go to my grandmother in Provence.*

Nos grand-parents s'occupaient bien de nous. *Our grand-parents took good care of us.*

Nous travaillions dans les champs tous les étés. *We used to work in the fields every summer.*

Nous prenions le goûter tous les après- midi. **On mangeait** des confitures délicieuses. *We had tea every afternoon. We ate delicious jams.*

À vous maintenant!

1 Qu'est-ce que vous faisiez quand vous étiez jeune?

Answer with the verbs in the imperfect tense.

Start your answers with **Je / J'**:

(a) danser

(b) skier

(c) faire du basket

(d) aller à la pêche

(e) faire de la planche
à roulettes

(f) jouer du piano

Comment ça se prononce?

In Unit 14 on page 143 you were given a few examples of verbs where **c** became **ç** in order to keep the same sound. A similar process takes place in the imperfect tense with verbs ending in **-cer** and verbs ending in **-ger.**

■ **Commencer** *to begin*: **je commençais** , **elle commençait, ils commençaient**

These are all pronounced the same way. With **nous commencions** and **vous commenciez** the cedilla disappears again because it is not required: **c** followed by **i** sounds [*s*].

■ **Manger** *to eat*, **nager** *to swim*

In order to keep the sound [*je*] verbs ending with **-ger** keep the **e** after the **g**:

Je nageais, elle nageait, ils nageaient

The **-e** disappears with **nous nagions** and **vous nagiez** because **g+i** has a [*je*] sound.

 # 2 À l'A.N.P.E.

Three unemployed young people are outside the **Agence Nationale pour l'Emploi**, (the employment agency) known as **l'A.N.P.E** (pronounced by spelling out each of the letters of the acronym).

Listen to the audio once, then answer these questions:

(a) What kind of apprenticeship does Raphaël want to do?
(b) What does Youssef say about his brother?
(c) What does his brother do now?

Listen again.

(d) According to Youssef what can't his brother do any longer?
(e) At what time does he start work in the morning?
(f) Where does Lætitia say she would like to work?

Now read the dialogue.

Raphaël	Salut, vous venez avec moi?
Lætitia	Où ça?
Raphaël	A l'A.N.P.E.?
Lætitia	Qu'est-ce que tu vas faire?
Raphaël	Je voudrais des renseignements sur l'apprentissage.

Lætitia	Un apprentissage pour faire quoi?
Raphaël	Je ne sais pas moi, je vais demander ce qu'on peut faire.
Youssef	Mon frère Rashid, il était apprenti-boulanger.
Lætitia	Ah oui? Et maintenant qu'est-ce qu'il fait? Des croissants?
Raphaël	Arrête un moment Lætitia!
Youssef	Maintenant mon frère a un vrai boulot chez un boulanger. L'inconvénient, avant il aimait bien sortir en boîte et tout et maintenant il ne peut plus parce qu'il commence à travailler à cinq heures du matin.
Lætitia	Bon alors vous venez? On y va à l'A.N.P.E. mais pas pour devenir apprenti boulanger! Moi j'aimerais bien travailler dans une pharmacie ou quelque chose comme ça. Alors tu viens Youssef, on va aider Raphaël à choisir son apprentissage.
Raphaël	Ah, non, elle me casse les pieds celle-là! Tu n'as qu'à en choisir un pour toi d'apprentissage!

un apprentissage *apprenticeship*	**elle me casse les pieds** *she's annoying me (Lit. she is breaking my feet) (slang)*
un boulot *a job (slang)*	
sortir en boîte *to go to a club (slang)*	

Link the following English phrases to the equivalent French expressions:

1) Are you coming with me?
2) My brother used to be an apprentice.
3) He starts work at five in the morning.
4) What does he do now?
5) something like that
6) We are going to help Raphaël choose.

a) Il commence à travailler à cinq heures du matin.
b) quelque chose comme ça
c) Et maintenant qu'est-ce qu'il fait?
d) Vous venez avec moi?
e) On va aider Raphaël à choisir.
f) Mon frère était apprenti.

◖◗ Comment ça se prononce?

Because some words tend to be linked up together, you may frequently hear utterances which are not exactly grammatically correct but which are used in every day conversation:

> Tu n'as qu'à en choisir un pour toi ! *You'd better choose one.* Lit. *You only have to choose one for yourself.*

The structure is: **ne** + **avoir** +**que** + **à** but in every day language the **ne** disappears, even in public talk by most eminent people (on TV, radio etc.).

This is high on the list of language used to give advice, for making suggestions in all sorts of circumstances but especially when people suggest what the government should be doing:

Ils n'ont qu'à… *all they need to do*… becomes **ils ont qu'à** … [*isonka*]

Tu n'as qu'à … *all you need to do*… becomes **T'as qu'à** …. [*taka*]

Il n'y a qu'à … *all there is to do*… becomes **y a qu'à...** [*yaka*]

You may even see YACKA used as the name of bars or cafés, places where people put the world right!

| BAR - TABAC |
| LE YACKA |

Point info

L'emploi

Le chômage *unemployment* is still high in France. Over three million people are out of work (**au chômage**) and the trend could get worse in the 21st century. **L'Agence Nationale pour l'Emploi** *the National Employment Agency* was created in 1967 and its work is needed more than ever. All sorts of measures have been put in place to get young people on to the work market.

The return to **l'apprentissage des métiers** *apprenticeship* is seen as a positive move. It is under strict control with compulsory courses and a three-way contract (between the young person, the management of the firm and the **Centre de Formation d'Apprentis** *training centre*. Apprentices are paid the national minimal wage, **Le SMIC** (**Salaire Minimum Interprofessionnel de Croissance**). The contract is rigorous and aimed at providing young people with the same conditions of service as those available to full-time workers.

3 Le contrat d'apprentissage

The text below is an excerpt from an apprentice's contract.

Read it and then answer the questions on page 182. You are not expected to understand every word of the text.

LE CONTRAT D'APPRENTISSAGE

LE CONTENU DU CONTRAT

Le contrat d'apprentissage est un contrat de travail de type particulier qui permet au jeune d'acquérir une qualification professionnelle sanctionnée par un diplôme technologique ou professionnel, ou un titre homologué. Ce type de contrat associe une formation en entreprise et des enseignements dans un Centre de Formation d'Apprentis (CFA).

SIGNATAIRES Le contrat d'apprentissage est signé entre l'employeur, l'apprenti et le C.F.A. Il concerne tous les employeurs et tous les jeunes de 16 à moins de 26 ans.

DURÉE La durée d'un contrat d'apprentissage est en général de 2 ans. Elle peut être portée à 3 ans ou réduite à 1 an en fonction du métier, de la qualification préparée et du niveau initial de l'apprenti.

PÉRIODE D'ESSAI Les deux premiers mois constituent une période d'essai pendant laquelle le contrat peut être rompu.

CONGÉS ● L'apprenti bénéficie d'un congé annuel de 5 semaines.

● Au même titre que les autres salariées, l'apprentie peut bénéficier d'un congé maternité (6 semaines avant la date présumée de l'accouchement et 10 semaines après).

● Des congés pour événements familiaux sont également accordés, à savoir :
4 jours pour le mariage de l'apprenti,
3 jours pour la naissance de l'enfant de l'apprenti,
2 jours pour le décès du conjoint ou d'un enfant de l'apprenti,
1 jour pour le décès du père ou de la mère de l'apprenti.

TEMPS DE FORMATION Sur son temps de travail, le jeune suit une formation générale et technologique dans un centre de formation. La durée varie en fonction de la formation choisie (entre 1 à 2 semaines par mois).

1) How old do you have to be to sign the contract?
2) How long is the apprenticeship for ?
3) Can it be lengthened or shortened?
4) How long is the trial period?
5) What can happen during that time?
6) How many weeks holiday does an apprentice have?
7) How much maternity leave does a young woman get?
8) How many days off do apprentices get:
   (a) to get married?
   (b) for the birth of a child?
9) What kind of course does the apprentice have to attend?
10) What proportion of the time has to be spent on a course?

l'employeur employer	**une période d'essai** trial period
en fonction du métier	**rompu** broken
according to the job	**pendant laquelle** during which
durée duration	

À vous maintenant!

2 À l'A.N.P.E. II

You have decided to choose an apprenticeship. Tell the A.N.P.E. employee
which category of work interests you.

Look at the list opposite, then listen to the audio to hear your questions.

Exemple:

Looking at the list, you think you are interested in the building trade:
Employé de l'A.N.P.E.   Quels genres de métiers vous intéressent?
(a) **Vous**   Je m'intéresse surtout aux métiers du bâtiment.
Employé   Quels genres de métiers vous intéresse?
(b) **Vous**   *Say you are interested in catering.*
Employé   Qu'est-ce qui vous intéresse?
(c) **Vous**   *Say you are interested in photography.*
Employé   Qu'est-ce qui vous intéresse?
(d) **Vous**   *Say you are interested in the food industry.*

Employé	Quels genres de métiers vous intéressent?
(e) **Vous**	*Say you are interested in jobs to do with health.*
Employé	A quoi vous vous intéressez?
(f) **Vous**	*Say you are interested in the clothes industry.*

Métiers du bâtiment ....

Métiers de la chaudronnerie et de la métallerie ....

Métiers de bouche...

Métiers de l'hôtellerie et de la restauration.......................................

Métiers de la santé et des soins personnels.............................

Métiers de l'hygiène et de l'environnement ....

Métiers de l'habillement ....

Métiers de la photographie et des industries graphiques................

Métiers du commerce et de la distribution ....

Métiers du secrétariat et de la comptabilité......................................

Métiers du secteur agricole ....

Métiers de la pierre ....

3 Où chercher du travail? *Where to look for work?*

Dans les petites annonces dans les journaux, sur l'internet et avec votre Minitel

Look at the adverts on the next page and answer the questions.

http://www.liberation.com

PROFILS NET

1

Toutes les annonces
d'offres d'emploi
parues dans Libération *depuis*
quinze jours. *Dès aujourd'hui*
vous pouvez y répondre
instantanément *en laissant votre CV.*

OPPORTUNITES

Des formations,
des voyages, des services,
des produits

2

NOTRE OBJECTIF :

VOUS FORMER À L'INFORMATIQUE DE GESTION

Nous vous proposons une formation de 1200 heures à l'informatique, dans le cadre d'un contrat de qualification.

Dynamique, motivé, âgé de moins de 26 ans, vous êtes diplômé de mathématiques, physique, chimie, sciences économiques, gestion..., l'informatique vous intéresse et vous souhaitez en faire votre métier.

Alors n'hésitez plus, prenez contact avec nous, nous nous ferons un plaisir de vous présenter notre structure et nos projets de développement.

Etes-vous prêt à travailler à l'étranger?

Alors consultez sur
3617 TO WORK*,
nos centaines
d'annonces classées
* *"Travailler" en anglais*

3617 TO WORK
SNPC - 3,48 F/minute

3

2000 OFFRES D'EMPLOI
36.17 PLEIN EMPLOI

3,48 F la mn

4

EMPLOIS OFFRES

COMMERCIAL VENTES

Sté LVG, vins de Bordeaux, recrute **2 VENDEURS** sur votre secteur, clientèle particuliers exclusivement, sur rendez-vous, profil, contact, convivialité, poste stable, débutants acceptés. Formation assurée. Tél. 02.99.51.66.51, pour rendez-vous, de 9 h à 17 h, sauf samedi.

EMPLOIS DU COMMERCE

Discothèque Finistère-Sud cherche **PORTIER.** Tél. 02.98.60.15.71

METIERS DE BOUCHE

Recherche **PATISSIER** sérieux, sachant travailler seul, Pont-de-Buis. Tél. 02.98.79.01.17

HOTELLERIE RESTAURATION

SERVEUSE, 2 ans expérience, recherche emploi **RESTAURATION** tradition nelle ou gastronomique, région Brest ou Quimper. Tél. 02.38.61.07.10

APPRENTISSAGE

Recherche **APPRENTI(E) VENDEUR9SE)en charcuterie-traiteur.** Super U, Plestin-les-GrΩeves. Tél. 02.96.51.19.21

GENS DE MAISON

LAVAL: recherche employée de maison, **temps plein**, logée, nourrie, pour s'occuper de deux enfants et entretien maison. 02.908.17.16.25

Recherche DAME pour contrat temps plein, dans appartement centre **QUIMPER**, garde bébé, ménage, repassage. Tél. 02.98.66.31.15

EMPLOIS DEMANDES

ADMINISTRATION COMPTABILITÉ

FEMME, 48 ans, avec expérience, cherche emploi temps partiel, **SECRETARIAT, COMPTABILITÉ** ou **COMMERCE**, secteur Quimperlé ou environs. Tél. 02.98.75.15.14

TECHNIQUE PRODUCTION

ELECTRICIEN possédant CAP électroménager, bon bricoleur, expérience homme d'entretien, cherche **EMPLOI**, pour toutes propositions, tél. 02.98.17.19.15

Avec le Minitel (voir **Point info**)

(a) If you were using your Minitel to look up jobs, how much would you pay every minute?

(b) Are you prepared to work abroad? What do you need to do?

Sur l'internet

On the Internet, the national newspaper *Libération* has a site which you may wish to look up.

(c) What can you find on the Internet?

(d) What if the advert is one week old, can you still find it?

(e) How and when can you answer the job adverts?

Dans les journaux locaux

(f) Can you name three jobs which are advertised in the local paper?

(g) Can you give three types of jobs people are looking for?

If you wanted to be trained in information technology for management purposes what profile would be required?

(h) How old would you have to be?

(i) Which qualities would you have to demonstrate?

(j) Which background would you need?

Point info

Le Minitel

Le Minitel is a kind of electronic, interactive telephone directory which was introduced on a large scale in France in the 1980s. The Minitel is also available at the post office. Many French people are now switching to the Internet and the days of the Minitel may be numbered.

18 | **ON PREND LE T.G.V**
Catching the high-speed train

In this unit you will learn:

■ about travelling by rail, and how to buy a ticket
■ all about **la SNCF** and **le TGV**
■ more verbs in the imperfect tense
■ the subjunctive

1 Vous prenez le TGV?

Sarah has spent a week visiting Bordeaux and **Les Landes** (vast pine forests south of Bordeaux). *She is now planning to travel back to London via Paris.*

Listen to the audio once through and answer these questions.

(a) Why is Sarah leaving the Périers?
(b) Name two things, which according to Dominique, Sarah is starting to know well?
(c) What does Sarah think of the area?

Listen again.

(d) Where is Sarah going tomorrow?
(e) How is she getting there?
(f) How long will it take?

Listen for a third time.

(g) How long did it used to take when Monsieur Périer was a student?
(h) What could Sarah use the Minitel for?

Listen one more time.

(i)   At what time is Sarah leaving tomorrow?

(j)   Who is meeting Sarah on arrival?

Now read the dialogue.

M. Périer   Alors Sarah, vous nous quittez déjà?

Dominique   C'est vrai, la semaine a passé très vite! Sarah commence à bien connaître Bordeaux et les Landes, les vins de la région ...

Sarah   Oui, j'adore votre région mais il faut que je rentre à Londres, je reprends le travail lundi et j'ai promis à ma sœur de passer quelques jours chez elle à Paris.

M. Périer   Vous prenez le TGV?

Sarah   Oui, c'est très rapide.

Mme Périer Ça prend combien de temps maintenant pour monter à Paris?

Sarah   Ça dépend des trains mais en choisissant bien c'est faisable en trois heures.

M. Périer   Incroyable! On n'arrête pas le progrès! Savez-vous que lorsque j'étais jeune j'étais étudiant à Paris alors je prenais souvent le train pour rentrer. Cela prenait douze heures, sinon plus!

Dominique   Eh oui le progrès! Au fait Sarah, tu as réservé ta place dans le TGV? Tu pourrais le faire par Minitel.

Sarah   Non, je te remercie mais je préfère tout bonnement acheter mon billet à la gare. De toute façon on devait aller à Bordeaux cet après-midi, non?

Dominique   Oui bien sûr, c'est comme tu veux. À quelle heure tu pars demain?

Sarah   Je ne sais pas encore mais probablement entre quinze et seize heures: ma sœur viendra me chercher à Montparnasse après le travail, je pensais lui donner rendez-vous vers dix-neuf heures, dix-neuf heures quinze environ.

le TGV: Train à Grande Vitesse	**sinon plus** *if not more*
high-speed train	**la gare** *the station*
tout bonnement/tout	**lorsque** *when*
simplement *very simply*	

Link the following English phrases to the equivalent French expressions.

1) Well then Sarah are you leaving us already?

2) Sarah is starting to know Bordeaux well.

3) I am going back to work on Monday.

4) Incredible! Progress never stops!

5) I used to be a student.

6) I often took the train to get home.

7) We were going to go to Bordeaux this afternoon, weren't we?

8) I thought I would arrange to meet her around 7 pm.

(a) Je reprends le travail lundi.

(b) J'étais étudiant.

(c) Je prenais souvent le train pour rentrer.

(d) Eh bien Sarah vous nous quittez déjà?

(e) Je pensais lui donner rendez-vous vers 7h.

(f) Sarah commence à bien connaître Bordeaux.

g) Incroyable! On n'arrête pas le progrès.

h) On devait aller à Bordeaux cet après-midi, non?

Comment ça marche?

1 Prepositions + infinitive

You already know that when two verbs follow one another the second one is in the infinitive form:

On **devait aller** à Bordeaux.

Verbs following a preposition are also in the infinitive (prepositions are words which have a constant spelling, they are placed in front of nouns or pronouns or in front of verbs). The following prepositions are frequently used in front of verbs in the infinitive: **à** *at*, **de** *to*, *of*, **pour** *for/in order to*, **sans** *without*:

pour monter à Paris	*in order to get to Paris*
sans arrêter	*without stopping*
J'ai essayé **de ranger**.	*I tried to tidy up.*

2 The subjunctive

The subjunctive is a verb form which is commonly used in French. In fact you have already come across it on page 126 in sentences starting with **il faut que**. The subjunctive is a verb form which has its own range of past tenses although the present tense of the subjunctive is the most used of all. This course will only provide you with examples of the present subjunctive and a few examples of the past form with **avoir** and **être**, as you are not likely to meet other forms when you hear spoken French.

The subjunctive is usually preceded by a verb + **que**. However, there are many verbs with **que** which are not followed by the subjunctive. So this alone is not a guide to whether or not you should use the subjunctive. Instead, look at the meaning of the sentence. The subjunctive is mainly used to express necessity, possibility, doubt, regrets, wishes, fear. The subjunctive is automatically used after the following expressions:

- Necessity: **Il faut que** je rentre à Londres.
  It is necessary that I should go back to London.

- Possibility: **Il est possible que** je rentre à Londres la semaine prochaine.
  There is a possibility that I shall return to London next week.

- Doubt: **Je doute que** je rentre à Londres avant dimanche.
  I doubt that I shall be going back to London before Sunday.

- Regrets: **Je regrette qu**'elle rentre déjà à Londres.
  I am sorry that she is already going back to London.

- Wishes: **Je veux qu**'elle rentre à Londres immédiatement.
  I want her to go back to London immediately.

- Fear **J'ai peur qu**'elle rentre à Londres sans moi.
  I am afraid that she may return to London without me.

The ending pattern is similar for all verbs in the present subjunctive except for **avoir** and **être**.

Verb endings of the present subjunctive	
je **-e**	nous **-ions** (**-yons** for **avoir** and **être**)
tu **-es**	vous -iez (**-yez** for **avoir** and **être**)
elle **-e**	ils **-ent**

Prendre *to take*

que je prenne	que nous prenions
que tu prennes	que vous preniez
qu'elle prenne	qu'ils prennent

Sometimes the subjunctive can be avoided by omitting **que** and using **de** + infinitive:

> Il est possible **que je rentre** à Paris la semaine prochaine. (subjunctive)
> Il est possible **de rentrer** à Paris la semaine prochaine. (infinitive after preposition **de**)

However the sense may be slightly changed.

When you feel ready to use the subjunctive you will find that your French has a slightly more authentic ring to it.

Comment ça se prononce?

■ C'est faisable. *It's feasible/do-able*

Here, **-ai-** has a neutral sound similar to the **e** of **je** [*je*].

■ **On n'arrête** pas le progrès. **On arrête** la voiture.

There is no difference in sound between the two highlighted phrases. But the listener knows that the first example is a negative sentence because of **pas** after the verb.

À vous maintenant!

1 Quel temps? *Which tense?*

See whether you can identify which tenses are being used in the following examples. Match the sentence with the correct tense.

Examples found in first dialogue	tenses (jumbled)
1) tu as réservé ta place?	a) present subjunctive
2) je te remercie	b) perfect tense
3) je prenais souvent le train	c) present indicative
4) il faut que je rentre à Londres	d) imperfect
5) ma sœur viendra me chercher	e) conditional
6) tu pourrais le faire par Minitel	f) future

2 Ça prend combien de temps …?

The map below was produced by **la SNCF** (Société Nationale des Chemins de fer Français) for the 1998 World Cup. How long does each journey from Paris take?

Look at the map, listen to the audio, and answer the questions that you hear.

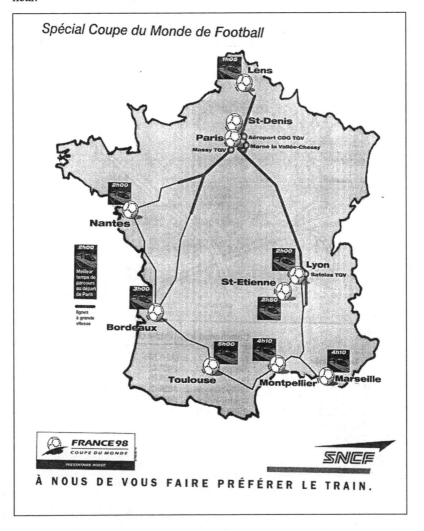

Point info

Le TGV (Train à Grande Vitesse)

The TGV links all major French towns to Paris. It travels at 300 kilometres per hour.

All seats have to be booked. Your ticket is issued to you for a specific journey at a specific time and a specific seat and your ticket cannot be used on a different train. When you buy your ticket the price includes the reservation. On all journeys longer than one hour you can order in advance your breakfast or your lunch which will be served to you at your seat. This service is only available in first class carriages. There is a buffet car in all TGVs.

Les Gares de Paris

Gare Saint Lazare; la première des gares parisiennes – <u>English Version</u>

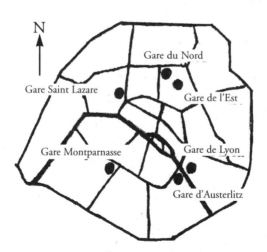

<u>Gare d'Austerlitz</u> | <u>Gare de l'Est</u> | <u>Gare de Lyon</u>
<u>Gare Montparnasse</u> | <u>Gare du Nord</u> | <u>Gare Saint Lazare</u>

Starting or ending your journey in Paris? There are six main line stations which can take you to any corner of France. There are also links (**liaisons**) to airports and other major TGV stations around Paris. For instance if you are going to Disneyland your station is Marne la Vallée Chessy.

Look at the map of Paris opposite with the six main railway stations:

From the **Gare Montparnasse** you can go west (Altlantic coast, Brittany, south-west France and Spain).

From the **Gare St Lazare** you can get to Normandy.

From the **Gare du Nord** you can get to the north of France and Belgium.

From the **Gare de l'Est** you can reach the east of France and Germany.

From the **Gare de Lyon** you can go to the south-east of France, the Mediterranean and Italy.

From the **Gare d'Austerlitz** you can reach places in central France.

2 Au guichet de la gare

Sarah and Dominique are at the ticket office at Bordeaux railway station. There are other customers in front of them.

Listen to/Read the dialogue, and answer these questions.

(a) How long does it take to go from Bordeaux to Poitiers?
(b) What kind of tickets do the old couple want? Single or return?
(c) Which day of the week do they wish to travel?

Listen/Read again and answer these questions.

(d) One train leaves Bordeaux at 8.26. At what time does it arrive in Poitiers?
(e) Which train do they choose in the end?
(f) What is the advantage of taking this particular train?

Listen/Read once more.

(g) Do they need to reserve their return tickets now?
(h) What does Sarah decide to do?

Un vieux monsieur et une vieille dame sont juste devant Sarah au guichet.

Vieille dame	Nous allons à Poitiers, ça prend combien de temps avec le TGV?
Employée de la SNCF	Voyons, une heure trois quarts environ madame. Vous voulez réserver?
Vieux monsieur	Deux billets s'il vous plaît.
Employée	Deux billets simples ou deux aller-retours?
Vieille dame	Deux billets aller-retours, s'il vous plaît.
Employée	Quel jour désirez-vous voyager?
Vieille dame	Lucien, nous partons demain n'est-ce pas?
Vieux monsieur	Mais non Simone nous allons à Poitiers jeudi, c'est-à-dire après demain.
Employée	Jeudi? Vous prendrez le train de quelle heure?
Vieille dame	À quelle heure y-a-t-il un train dans la matinée?
Employée	Alors jeudi ... il y a un train qui part de Bordeaux à 8.26 et qui arrive à Poitiers à 10.09. Le suivant est à 10.37 et il arrive à 12.32, et finalement il y a un TGV à 11.59 qui arrive à Poitiers à 13.50.
Vieille dame	Dans ce cas nous prendrons celui de 10.37 et nous arriverons chez ma fille pour le déjeuner ...
Employée	Et pour le retour?
Vieux monsieur	C'est-à-dire ... nous ne savons pas encore..
Employée	Ce n'est pas nécessaire de réserver votre retour maintenant, vous pourrez le faire plus tard. Vous avez votre carte Vermeil?
Vieux monsieur	Simone, c'est toi qui a les cartes Vermeil?
Vieille dame	Je ne sais pas où je les ai mises ... attendez, il faut que je réfléchisse.
Sarah à Dominique	Tu avais raison, je vais réserver mon billet à la billetterie automatique.

le suivant   *the next one* (verb **suivre** *to follow*)
la carte Vermeil   *SNCF concession card for old age pensioners*
réfléchir   *to reflect/to think back*
la billetterie automatique   *the ticket machine*

Les réservations

Link the following English phrases to the equivalent French expressions:

1) Would you like to make a reservation?
2) Which day would you like to travel?
3) We are leaving tomorrow aren't we?
4) We'll get to my daughter in time for lunch.
5) We don't know yet.
6) Wait I have to think.
7) I don't know where I put them.
8) You were right.

(a) Nous ne savons pas encore.
(b) Nous partons demain, n'est-ce-pas?
(c) Attendez, il faut que je réfléchisse.
(d) Vous voulez réserver?
(e) Quel jour désirez-vous voyager?
(f) Je ne sais pas où je les ai mises.
(g) Tu avais raison.
(h) Nous arriverons chez ma fille pour le déjeuner.

À vous maintenant!

3 Vous réservez un billet pour Paris Montparnasse

Arcachon → Bordeaux → Paris / Ile de France

PRIX

| 1 3 1 | 2 | 1 | TGV vert: toutes les réductions (minimum 15%) sont calculées sur le prix normal de niveau | Pour connaître le prix de votre billet, consultez - Si vous voyagez en 1ʳᵉ classe la page 46 - Si vous voyagez en 2ᵉ classe la page 47 | TGV ne circulant pas ce jour-là |

Nº du TGV		8402	8404	8410	8410	8412	7850	8414	7860(1)	8518	8420	8420	8526	8528
Restauration												(4)		
Arcachon	D						a	b	b	b	b			b	b
Facture	D						a	b	b	b	b			b	b
Bordeaux	D	4.59	6.01		6.08	6.42	6.46	7.05	7.59	8.22		8.26	10.37	10.44
Libourne	D	5.18			6.27			7.26						
Angoulême	D	6.03		7.10	7.10			8.11	8.58		9.25	9.25	11.44	
Ruffec	D			e					c		c	e	e	
Poitiers	D	6.47		7.55	7.55		8.28	8.56	9.43		10.09	10.09	12.32	
Châtellerault	D	7.04		8.12	8.12						10.25	10.25		
Saint-Pierre-des-Corps	D						9.08	9.37	10.23		10.54	10.54		
Massy TGV	D						9.58		11.13					
Marne la Vallée Chessy	D						10.34		11.53					
Aéroport Ch.de Gaulle TGV	D						10.49		12.06					
Paris-Montparnasse 1-2	D	8.20	9.00	9.30	9.30	9.40		10.35		11.25	11.50	11.50	14.05	13.50

HORAIRES

You are at the ticket office in Bordeaux station. You are travelling tomorrow. You want to reserve a single ticket on the TGV. You want to get to Paris by mid-morning. Look at the train time-table on the previous page and decide which train you need to catch.

Listen to the audio and respond to the employee's questions.

a) **Vous**   *Say you would like to reserve a ticket to Paris.*
Employée   Vous voyagez aujourd'hui?
b) **Vous**   *Say no, you are travelling tomorrow.*
Employée   Vous prenez le train de quelle heure?
c) **Vous**   *Say the time of your train.*
Employée   Vous prenez un billet aller-retour?
d) **Vous**   *Say no, you would like a single. Ask the price of the ticket.*

🔊 Comment ça marche?

There are two words for each of the following parts of the day and also for the year:

un jour	une journée	*a day*
un matin	une matinée	*a morning*
un soir	une soirée	*an evening*
un an	une année	*a year*

■ Note that **une nuitée** is sometimes found in poetry (otherwise obsolete).

There is only a slight difference in meaning between the two forms and indeed that difference is not translatable in English. **Un jour**, **un matin**, **un soir**, **un an** are more likely to describe a portion of time defined by the calendar or the clock (objective connotation). **Une journée**, **une matinée**, **une soirée**, **une année** have a social connotation and are more likely to express the time experienced by individuals (more subjective):

Nous partirons dans trois jours.   *We'll leave in three days time.*
Nous avons passé une excellente   *We spent an excellent day at the*
  journée au bord de la mer.   *seaside.*

Il passe un an à Paris.	*He is spending one year in Paris.*
Bonne année tout le monde!	*Have a good year everyone!*

It is important to understand the subtle difference between the two sets of words but in some cases either word can be used according to the emphasis given by the speaker.

À vous maintenant!

4 Choisissez le bon mot

For each sentence choose one of the two words in brackets to fill the gaps.

(a) Nous avons passé _____ magnifique chez nos amis. (un soir/une soirée)
(b) Dans trois _____ il aura cinquante ans. (ans/années)
(c) Il y a sept _____ dans une semaine. (jours/journées)
(d) Mon frère a onze _____ de moins que moi. (ans/années)

3 Les points de vente et les billetteries automatiques

Read the information on the next page about buying tickets. It can be found on the Internet (search engines **Yahoo France** or **Ecila**).

Vrai ou faux? Having read the information on where to buy tickets and how to use automatic ticket machines say whether the following statements are true or false (**vrai** ou **faux**):

(a) You cannot buy your tickets more than two months in advance at the ticket office.
(b) All stations have a special ticket office for advance booking.
(c) At the ticket machine you can only buy your ticket 61 days in advance of travelling.
(d) If you use the ticket machine you can use up to 100F in coins.
(e) You won't get any change.
(f) You can use your credit card for any journey.
(g) You can get your meal reservation from the machine too.

SNCF – Les points de vente

Accueil Grandes Lignes

Guide du voyageur

Les points de vente HABITUELS

LES POINTS DE VENTE

Tous les billets sont vendus dans les gares, les boutiques SNCF et les agences de voyages.

Achetez-les à l'avance, ils sont valables 2 mois.

Que vous prépariez votre voyage ou soyez en instance de départ, tous les guichets délivrent, en principe, l'ensemble des prestations.

Certaines grandes gares disposent de guichets vous permettant de préparer votre voyage à l'écart des flux de départs immédiats.

LES BILLETTERIES AUTOMATIQUES

Ce sont des guichets en libre service qui vous permettent d'acheter un billet pour un trajet en France ou à destination de l'étranger (principales relations):

• de 61 jours à quelques minutes avant votre départ (sauf train autre que TGV avec réservation)
• avec ou sans réservation
• avec supplément éventuellement.

Vous pouvez également y réserver vos titres repas ou y retirer vos commandes passées par Minitel ou téléphone.

Comme moyen de paiement, la billetterie automatique accepte à partir de 15F les cartes Bleues, Visa françaises ou étrangères, Eurocard/Mastercard, American Express et Diner's Club International.

La billetterie automatique accepte les pièces jusqu'à un montant total de 100 F et rend la monnaie.

La billetterie automatique vous permet d'éviter les files d'attentes aux guichets.

Mots cachés

Find twenty words or expressions hidden in the grid. They all relate to train journeys and buying and booking tickets.

```
A   R   R   I   V   E   E   S   A   R   T   Y   U   C   V   B   M   B   T   A
Z   E   F   G   H   N   M   K   L   O   S   E   R   S   T   A   Z   C   V   L
D   S   I   M   P   L   E   F   S   D   F   G   H   O   R   A   I   R   E   L
R   E   W   A   S   V   B   G   N   M   J   D   E   P   A   R   T   S   V   E
G   R   A   N   D   E   S   L   I   G   N   E   S   D   I   A   S   W   B   R
T   V   S   A   F   T   F   E   D   D   T   Y   U   I   N   G   S   A   N   -
F   A   A   W   E   G   A   H   F   E   S   V   O   Y   A   G   E   G   D   R
V   T   S   S   D   G   U   J   I   U   Y   T   R   D   G   F   A   O   F   E
B   I   L   L   E   T   T   E   R   I   E   S   F   F   R   D   X   N   G   T
C   O   F   F   G   U   I   K   L   Y   F   D   F   G   A   S   C   R   T   O
V   N   D   U   W   R   M   D   G   T   R   R   M   I   N   I   T   E   L   U
N   E   E   J   E   G   A   R   E   S   F   F   F   U   D   B   F   S   Y   R
G   U   I   C   H   E   T   F   Z   A   G   F   G   K   E   J   G   T   U   A
M   F   D   H   A   B   I   L   L   E   T   D   U   Y   V   K   H   A   E   E
O   G   F   N   S   S   Q   H   G   L   K   N   S   I   T   I   U   J   A   I
P   B   H   F   S   A   U   K   E   R   K   G   K   F   T   T   H   R   D   O
V   A   L   A   B   L   E   L   K   L   H   U   U   D   E   R   T   A   F   U
N   P   O   I   N   T   S   D   E   V   E   N   T   E   S   D   S   N   C   F
F   H   W   E   T   G   G   U   I   T   H   U   T   D   S   E   F   T   G   Y
G   S   D   M   O   N   T   P   A   R   N   A   S   S   E   S   R   S   E   A
```

Hidden words in translation:

arrivals, departures, name for French railway company, high-speed train, ticket machines, ticket office, Minitel, main lines, timetable, single, return, ticket, station, name of a Paris station, buffet car, valid, travel, booking, sales outlet, automatic.

19 | À l'HÔPITAL
At the hospital

In this unit you will learn:

■ more about public transport
■ how to use a public phone box
■ what to say at the hospital if you have to go in for a minor injury
■ indirect object pronouns
■ more about the subjunctive

 1 Sarah téléphone à sa sœur

Read this short passage and the SNCF leaflet **L'horaire garanti** opposite.

Le train de Bordeaux arrive à Montparnasse à dix-neuf heures quinze, avec dix minutes de retard. Sarah descend, mais ne voit pas sa sœur sur le quai. Elle attend quelques moments puis elle décide de téléphoner chez sa sœur. Elle trouve des téléphones dans la salle des pas perdus. Elle a une télécarte dans son sac.

Did you understand? Then answer these questions!

(a) At what time does Sarah's train arrive in Paris?
(b) What was the scheduled arrival time? Will Sarah get any compensation? (see opposite: **L'horaire garanti**)
(c) Can she see her sister on the platform?
(d) What does she decide to do after a few moments?
(e) What has she got in her bag?

la salle des pas perdus   *the departure or arrival hall in a station*
   Lit. *the room/the hall of the lost steps* (**un pas**: *a step*)
la salle d'attente   *the waiting room (in a hospital or at the dentist)*

■ La SNCF s'engage ....

> **ET TOUJOURS : L'HORAIRE GARANTI**
>
> Depuis le 1er septembre 1996, la SNCF s'engage à offrir une compensation **dès qu'un train Grandes Lignes est en retard d'au moins 30 minutes.**
> Cette compensation représente :
> - 25% du prix du billet du trajet concerné lorsque votre retard à destination est de 30 minutes à 1 heure,
> - 50% du prix du trajet si le retard est supérieur à 1 heure.
>
> Elle est réalisée sous forme de bons d'achat trains ("bons Voyage").
> Pour en bénéficier, il est nécessaire d'avoir acquitté et effectué un parcours d'au moins 100 kilomètres en train Grandes Lignes.

2 Allô!

Sarah parle au téléphone à son beau-frère, Guillaume. *Sarah speaks to her brother-in-law.*

You may need to look at the key words before you answer the questions.

Listen to/Read the dialogue and answer the questions.

(a) How many units has Sarah got on her telephone card?
(b) What is the telephone number that Sarah has just dialled?

Listen/Read again.

(c) Where is Marie-Claire?
(d) How did she cut herself?
(e) Does Guillaume think it is serious?

Listen/Read one more time.

(f) Who are Ariane and Pierre?
(g) What does Guillaume suggest Sarah should do?
(h) Is it because Sarah does not know her way round the métro?

emmener *to take someone/ something somewhere*	**un point de suture** *a stitch (medical)*
rejoindre *to rejoin/to meet someone somewhere*	**une piqûre** *an injection/insect bite*

Sarah	Ça va, j'ai quinze unités. Alors ... zéro un, quarante-huit, zéro cinq, trente-neuf, seize. Bon ça sonne! Allô!
Guillaume	Allô oui?
Sarah	Guillaume, ici Sarah. Tu sais où est ...
Guillaume	Ah Sarah! Encore heureux que tu aies téléphoné! J'étais inquiet ...
Sarah	Qu'est-ce qu'il se passe?
Guillaume	Marie-Claire a eu un petit accident, elle est aux urgences à l'hôpital.
Sarah	Quoi? Qu'est-ce qu'il lui est arrivé?
Guillaume	Rien de grave ... elle s'est coupée en ouvrant une boîte pour le chat. La voisine l'a emmenée à l'hôpital.
Sarah	Tu veux que j'aille la rejoindre à l'hôpital?
Guillaume	Non, non elle ne devrait pas être longtemps ... juste quelques points de suture et une piqûre anti-tétanique, c'est tout!
Sarah	Et les enfants? Où sont Ariane et Pierre?
Guillaume	Ici, avec moi. Ecoute ... je suis désolé ... prends un taxi.
Sarah	Non! Je connais bien le trajet en métro: je vais jusqu'à Châtelet, je change et je prends la direction Château de Vincennes et je descends à Nation.
Guillaume	Oui, c'est cela mais si tu as beaucoup de bagages un taxi sera plus pratique.
Sarah	Bon d'accord, j'arrive!

 Link the following English phrases to the equivalent French expressions.

1) I was worried.
2) What is happening?
3) What happened to her?
4) nothing serious
5) She cut herself.
6) The neighbour has taken her to hospital.
7) She should not be long.
8) I get out at Nation.

(a) Elle ne devrait pas être longtemps.
(b) Elle s'est coupée.
(c) La voisine l'a emmenée à l'hôpital.
(d) J'étais inquiet.
(e) Qu'est-ce qu'il lui est arrivé?
(f) Je descends à Nation.
(g) Qu'est-ce qu'il se passe?
(h) Rien de grave.

▐ Comment ça marche?

1 Indirect object pronouns

You have already come across the whole range of pronouns but there are still some complexities which need to be explained. In the dialogue Sarah says:

Qu'est-ce qu'il **lui** est arrivé?   *What has happened to **her/him**?*

The model for the structure in this particular example is:

Il est arrivé quelque chose **à quelqu'un**.	*Something has happened **to someone**.*
Qu'est-ce qu'il est arrivé à Marie-Claire?	*What has happened to Marie-Claire?*

When the object (here **Marie-Claire**) is linked to the verb by a preposition (here **à**), this object is called an indirect object. When a personal pronoun (here **lui**) is used to replace the indirect object it is referred to as an indirect object pronoun. The plural form of **lui** is **leur**. The other object pronouns (**me, te, nous, vous**) are the same whether the object is direct or indirect.

This can be more easily demonstrated in simpler examples, using the present tense:

Je donne les fleurs **à ma mère**.	*I give the flowers **to my mother**.*
Je donne les chocolats **à mes parents**.	*I give the chocolates **to my parents**.*

In both examples there are two objects after **donne** and it is possible to use two pronouns side by side to replace them but, taking one thing at a time, **à ma mère** is replaced by **lui** and **à mes parents** is replaced by **leur**:

Je **lui** donne les fleurs.	*I give **her** the flowers.*
Je **leur** donne les chocolats.	*I give **them** the chocolates.*

Other examples:

J'ai réservé une place **pour ma mère**.	*I've reserved a place **for my mother**.*
Je **lui** ai réservé une place.	*I've reserved **her** a place.*
Tu as écrit **à tes parents**?	*Have you written to **your parents**?*
Non, je ne **leur** ai pas écrit.	*No, I haven't written **to them**.*

2 Emphatic pronouns

These are generally used after a preposition: **à** *at*, **avec** *with*, **de** *from/of*, **dans** *in*, **chez** *at*, **pour** *for/in order to*, **sans** *without*, **sous** *under*, **sur** *on/on top of*:

Il est parti sans **moi**. *He left without **me**.*

(sans **moi**, sans **toi**, sans **lui**, sans **elle**, sans **nous**, sans **vous**, sans **elles**, sans **eux**)

3 More examples of the subjunctive

There are two examples in the dialogue. Did you find them?

Tu veux que j'aille la rejoindre à l'hôpital?
Would you like me to meet her at the hospital?
(The verb is **aller**.)

Encore heureux que tu aies téléphoné!
Just as well you phoned!

In the second example the verb is in the past subjunctive, formed with **avoir** in the present subjunctive and the past participle of **téléphoner**.

Three essential verbs in the present subjunctive

	ALLER	**AVOIR**	**ETRE**
Il faut que	j'aille	j'aie	je sois
Il faut que	tu ailles	tu aies	tu sois
Il faut que	elle aille	elle ait	elle soit
Il faut que	nous allions	nous ayons	nous soyons
Il faut que	vous alliez	vous ayez	vous soyez
Il faut que	ils aillent	ils aient	ils soient

À vous maintenant!

1 Vous passez beaucoup trop de temps au téléphone!

You have been telephoning all the people named in the box on the same day. Listen to the audio and fill in the grid. Say at what time you phoned them all. Remember to use the correct pronoun. A written example is provided for you (first line of the grid).

Names	Questions on the cassette	Your answer
(a) Nadine (11.30)	A quelle heure avez-vous téléphoné à Nadine?	Je **lui** ai téléphoné à onze heures trente.
(b) Mathieu (12.00)		
(c) Chantal et Marc (17.15)		
(d) Votre sœur (18.45)		
(e) Vos parents (20.10)		
(f) Votre fiancé(e) (22.45)		

Point info

Tout sur la télécarte et l'appel téléphonique en cabines publiques

Although you can always find plenty of telephone boxes in Paris and towns in general, it is not always easy to find one when travelling around in the country. There are still a few coin-operated telephone boxes but they are disappearing rapidly. It is always useful to be equipped with **une télécarte 50 unités ou 120 unités**.

Ever since **télécartes** were introduced **France Télécom** have been encouraging firms to use both sides of the card for publicity purposes. Many firms use them to advertise their products and sometimes they are used by the government – as can be seen at the back of the second card on the next page. This was used to inform people about the addition to telephone numbers of two extra digits for all parts of France, from 01 to 05, according to the areas indicated on the map. People collect cards which have no credit left and put them in télécartes albums, just like with stamp collecting.

À vous maintenant!

2 Les télécartes

Look at the writing on the two telephone cards on page 206, then answer the questions.

(a) Which of the two cards is sponsored by a superstore company?
(b) Which season is mentioned on card A?
(c) If you are calling anywhere in France how many digits do you need to dial if you are calling from within France?
(d) What are the first two figures you have to dial for Corsica?
(e) What are the first two figures for Paris?
(f) What if the card is not sealed?

3 Comment se servir de la télécarte?

To call Britain from France you need to dial 00 44 and then the number you wish to call, omitting the 0 at the front of the number. First make sure that you understand the instructions which appear on the liquid crystal display. They are not translated into English.

Find out what the instructions mean by linking the English translations to the French commands. Instructions 9) and 10) in the English column apply when you have asked someone to ring you back at the call box.

1) Lift up the receiver.	**A) VOTRE CRÉDIT EST ÉPUISÉ**
2) Insert your card or dial a free number.	**B) RETIREZ VOTRE CARTE**
3) Be patient.	**C) APPEL ARRIVÉ**
4) You have 0025 units.	**D) RACCROCHEZ**
5) Number you have called.	**E) RACCROCHEZ EN FIN DE COMMUNICATION**
6) Your credit is used up.	**F) NUMÉRO APPELÉ**
7) Remove your card.	**G) DÉCROCHEZ**
8) Hang up the receiver.	**H) CRÉDIT 0025 UNITÉ(S)**
9) Your call has arrived.	**I) PATIENTEZ**
10) Hang up at the end of your call.	**J) INTRODUIRE VOTRE CARTE OU FAIRE NUMÉRO LIBRE**

Comment ça se prononce?

la, là, l'a, l'as: all four sound the same *la, la, la, la* but they all mean something different.

la   Definite article: **la** voisine *the neighbour*

là   An adverb: Marie-Claire n' est pas **là** (means *there* but frequently used to mean *here*)

l'a   Pronoun **le** or **la** in front of verb **avoir**: La voisine **l'a** emmenée à l'hôpital. *The neighbour took her to the hospital.*

l'as Same as above but with **avoir** in the second person singular: Tu **l'as** vue? *Have you seen her?*

📖 3 À l'hôpital

C'est le mois d'août. A l'Hôpital d' Arcachon il y a beaucoup de personnes avec des maux et blessures en tous genres qui attendent de voir un docteur.

Look at the pictures and the **Mots-clef** on the next page to find out more about parts of the body and what aches and injuries people have.

Il s'est cassé la jambe en jouant au football

LES PARTIES DU CORPS

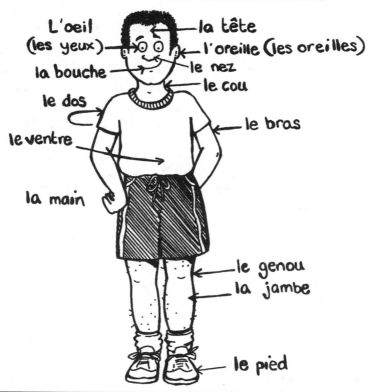

J'ai mal à la tête	*I have a headache*
J'ai mal au ventre	*I have a stomach ache*
Je me suis coupé	*I cut myself*
Je me suis brûlé	*I burnt myself*
Je suis blessée	*I am injured*
J'ai une insolation	*I have a sun stroke*
J'ai pris un coup de soleil	*I have got sunburnt*
J'ai de la fièvre	*I have got a high temperature*
J'ai du mal à respirer	*I can't breathe properly*

Les maux et les blessures *aches and injuries*

Listen on the audio to the eight young people at the hospital casualty department. They speak in the order listed in the grid, but what's wrong has got mixed up. Link their names to what they say is wrong with them. You may need to stop the audio after each person speaks and listen to it several times. Try to write just a word or two in French in the first column next to the name of each patient to say what's wrong with them.

Qu'est ce qui ne va pas?	Noms	What's wrong?
	1) Marie-José	a) infected mosqito bites
	2) Alain	b) toothache
	3) Adrienne	c) a burnt hand with an iron
	4) Benoît	d) headache
	5) Elise	e) hurt knees falling off bike
	6) Julien	f) probably a broken arm
	7) Cécile	g) a backache
	8) Didier	h) a cut foot walking on a broken bottle

J'ai mal au ventre

Still at Arcachon hospital a doctor is now seeing to a little girl called Magalie Dumas.

Listen to/Read the dialogue and answer these questions:

(a) Is Magalie still crying?
(b) Where does it hurt?
(c) What is her temperature? Is it very high?

Listen/Read again.

(d) What is Magalie's mother worried about?
(e) What did she have for lunch?

Listen/Read once more.

(f) What meal did she last eat?
(g) When was she sick?
(h) What does the Doctor say should happen tonight?

pleurer	*to cry*	**vomir**	*to vomit*
montrer	*to show*	**garder**	*to keep*

Dr Lebrun	C'est bien Magalie, tu ne pleures plus, tu es une grande fille. Alors montre-moi où ça fait mal.
Magalie	Là. Oh! Oh! J'ai mal au ventre.
Dr Lebrun	Ça fait mal quand je touche ici?
Magalie	Non. Aïe! Ici ça fait très mal!
Dr Lebrun	Elle a un peu de température 38°2.
Madame Dumas	Vous croyez que c'est une crise d'appendicite Docteur?
Dr Lebrun	Non, je ne pense pas. Est-ce qu'elle a mangé ce midi?
Madame Dumas	Non, elle n'a rien mangé depuis le petit déjeuner. Elle a vomi vers dix heures ce matin.
Dr Lebrun	Nous allons la garder en observation cette nuit. Si tout va bien elle pourra sortir demain matin.

 Now link the following English phrases to the equivalent French expressions.

1) You are not crying anymore.
2) Show me where it hurts.
3) She has a bit of a temperature.
4) She has eaten nothing since breakfast.
5) We are going to keep her tonight for observation.
6) She was sick at about 10am.

a) Montre-moi où ça fait mal?
b) Elle a vomi vers dix heures.
c) Tu ne pleures plus.
d) Elle a un peu de température.
e) Elle n'a rien mangé depuis le petit déjeuner.
f) Nous allons la garder en observation cette nuit.

Point info

La pharmacie

For many French people **la pharmacie** is the first port of call in case of a minor injury or illness. **La Sécurité Sociale**, which is the equivalent of the National Health Service, is organised differently in France. When you go to your doctor you pay the full price of the visit, and at the chemist you pay the full price of the medicine, **les médicaments,** and then you fill in a form to claim re-imbursement. There are many people who cannot afford to pay up-front for treatment and medicine and go to the pharmacist instead.

Pharmacists are mostly helpful and advise people to go to their doctor if there is any doubt. Apart from advising people on minor ailments they also offer help with checking wild mushrooms, especially in small country towns.

◀ À vous maintenant!

4 Tout savoir sur le mal de dos

Look at the poster below and answer the questions.

C.H.U. (Centre Hospitalo-Universitaire) means *Hospital*.

PLONEOUR-LANVERN

TOUT SAVOIR SUR LE MAL DE DOS

———— RÉUNION - DÉBAT ————

Animée par le Docteur FRIAT, Médecin
Service de rééducation fonctionnelle du C.H.U. de BREST

MERCREDI 19 MARS 1997, à 20H30
Salle Polyvalente, Plonéour-Lanvern
CAMPAGNE DE PRÉVENTION MENÉE PAR:

Mutualité
Sociale Agricole
Finistère

GROUPAMA
BRETAGNE

Le Télégramme

(a) When is there a meeting at Plonéour-Lanvern?
(b) Who is leading the debate?
(c) What is the debate about?
(d) Where is the meeting taking place?
(e) Where does Dr Friat normally work?

20 | ON PREND LE MÉTRO
Catching the metro

In this unit you will learn:
■ what to say if you need to apologise
■ everything you need to know about the Paris métro
■ more on the perfect tense

 ## 1 Je te prie de m'excuser

 C'est mercredi matin. Marie-Claire est en congé de maladie. Elle bavarde avec sa sœur. Les enfants sont toujours en vacances. Sarah leur a promis de les emmener au zoo du Bois de Boulogne.

Listen to the audio several times, and then fill in the boxes. You'll need to pause the audio several times when you hear the information required to fill in the boxes: what is Sarah doing or what will she be doing at each point in time? All this information is hidden in the chatting (**bavardage**) between the two sisters.

Calendar of events	What is Sarah doing/planning to do? Who with?
(a) Wednesday a.m.	
(b) Wednesday p.m.	
(c) Saturday p.m.	
(d) Sunday lunch time	
(e) Sunday 6.00 p.m.	
(f) Sunday 6.22 p.m.	
(g) Monday a.m.	

bouger *to move*		**se débrouiller** *to manage*
s'inquiéter *to worry*		**être bête** *to be silly*
prévenir *to inform/to warn*		

Now read the dialogue.

Sarah   Bonjour grande sœur, ça va mieux?

Marie-Claire   Oh écoute, je te prie de m'excuser pour hier soir!

Sarah   Mais tu n'y pouvais rien! Ce n'est pas de ta faute!

Marie-Claire   Non mais tout de même, je suis désolée!

Sarah   Ce que tu es bête! Ne t'inquiète pas pour cela! De toute façon je me suis bien débrouillée! Tu ne m'as pas dit si tu allais mieux.

Marie-Claire   Oui, ça va un peu mieux. On m'a fait six points de suture mais ça me fait encore mal quand je bouge la main. Je vais prendre trois jours de congé de maladie et je reprendrai le travail lundi matin. Au fait, tu restes jusqu'à quand?

Sarah   Jusqu'à dimanche soir. Il faudra que je sois à Paris-Nord à dix-huit heures pour enregistrer mon billet pour l'Eurostar de dix-huit heures vingt-deux. Moi aussi je reprends le travail lundi matin. Au fait Tante Eliane sait que je suis à Paris?

Marie-Claire   Oui, je l'ai prévenue. Elle nous invite tous à déjeuner dimanche midi. Je regrette mais je n'ai pas pu faire autrement.

Sarah   Non, cela ne fait rien, au contraire, je ne l'ai pas vue depuis Noël l'année dernière, ça me fera plaisir de la revoir.

Ariane   Maman, Tante Sarah a promis de nous emmener au zoo cet après-midi.

Pierre   Et puis aussi on va faire une grande balade dans le Bois de Boulogne et si on a le temps on s'arrêtera à Châtelet et on ira sur les quais voir les magasins d'animaux.

Marie-Claire   Eh bien dites-donc, vous en avez de la chance! Eh bien samedi soir on ira tous au cinéma.

Now link the following English phrases to the equivalent French expressions.

1) How silly you are!   (a) Elle nous invite tous à déjeuner.

2) In any case I managed!   (b) pour enregistrer mon billet pour l'Eurostar

3) I am feeling a bit better.
4) I am going to take three days of sick leave
5) to register my ticket for Eurostar
6) She is inviting us all for lunch.
7) I shall be pleased to see her again.
8) We are going to go for a big walk.

(c) Ce que tu es bête!
(d) Ça me fera plaisir de la revoir.
(e) De toute façon je me suis bien débrouillée!
f) On va faire une grande balade.
g) Ça va un peu mieux.
h) Je vais prendre trois jours de congé de maladie.

 # Comment ça marche?

1 How to apologise and how to respond to an apology

Most of the expressions used here are from the dialogue above so that you can see how they fit in context.

Excuses: *Apologies*

Je vous prie de m'excuser.
(a bit formal but not unusual in polite conversations) *Please excuse me.*
Excuse-moi/Excusez-moi. *Excuse me.* (more matter of fact)

Je suis désolé(e)/Désolé(e)!
I am sorry/Sorry!

Je regrette mais ...
I am sorry but ...

Je n'ai pas pu faire autrement.
I could not do anything different.

Je vous demande pardon.
Please forgive me.
(e.g. asking forgiveness when walking in front of someone)

Vous pardonnez!/Pardonnez!
'scuse! (matter of fact, bordering to rude – much is in the tone)

Réponses/Réactions: *Responses*

Most of the responses apply to any of the apologies listed on the left.

Ne t'inquiète pas! *Don't worry about it!*
Ne vous inquiétez pas! *Don't worry about it!*
Ce n'est pas grave! *Nothing serious!*

Cela/ça ne fait rien! ⎫ *It*
ça n'a pas d'importance! ⎬ *doesn't*
Peu importe! ⎭ *matter!*

N'y pense/pensez plus! *Forget it!*
Ce n'est pas de ta/votre faute.
It's not your fault.

Ne vous en faites pas. *Don't worry.*
Il n'y a pas de mal! *There is no harm!*

Je vous en prie. *Go ahead/ don't mind me.*

☑ À vous maintenant!

1 Répondre aux excuses

Say how you would respond to the following. There is more than one answer in each situation.

(a) Someone bumps into you in the tube and says: **Oh excusez-moi!**
Vous:

(b) Someone breaks a vase in your house (not a collection item): **Oh je suis désolé, j'ai cassé le vase!**
Vous:

(c) Someone phoning you on their mobile phone (**un portable**) to let you know they are late: **Je regrette, je vais être en retard d'une heure. Je vous fais attendre …**
Vous:

(d) Someone saying why they were late (a problem at home): **Je n'ai pas pu faire autrement, il y avait un problème à la maison, alors …**
Vous:

☷ Comment ça marche?

Note that if you are more interested in learning spoken French or background information about France you need not spend too much time on this section.

The perfect tense and agreement with the direct object

As usual there are several examples of the perfect tense in the dialogue:

dire *to say*:

    Tu ne m'**as** pas **dit**   *You did not tell me*

promettre *to promise*:

    Tante Sarah nous a promis.   *Aunt Sarah promised us.*

prévenir *to inform*:

    Je l'ai prévenue.   *I have informed her (Tante Eliane).*

Have you noticed the difference between the two spellings of the past participle **prévenu**?

You might need to go back to page 164 to remind yourself about the difference between verbs with **être** with the perfect tense and those with **avoir**.

With **être** (including reflexive verbs) the number and the gender of the subject affect the ending of the past participle:

> Marie-Claire est **allée** à l'hôpital. (**allé** gains an -e because Marie-Claire is feminine).

> Les Dupont sont **partis** en Espagne. (**parti** gains an -s because there is more than one Dupont in the family).

With verbs with **avoir** in the perfect tense there is no agreement between the subject and the past participle of the verb. If the subject is feminine or plural it does not affect the ending of the past participle:

> Elle a **vu** sa tante à Noël.   *She saw her aunt at Christmas.*

But:

> Elle **l'**a vue.   *She saw her.*

When a direct object (**sa tante/l'**) is placed before the verb, however, the past participle must 'agree' with the object i.e. it gains an -**e** if the object is feminine, an -**s** if it is plural and -**es** if it is feminine plural.

In the last example, a direct object pronoun (**l'**) is used instead of the direct object (**sa tante**).

In the example, the direct object pronoun precedes the past participle which consequently gains an -**e** in agreement (**vue**).

In this next example, as **Marie-Claire** (the direct object of the sentence) follows the verbs, there is no agreement between the object and the verb:

> La voisine a **emmené**   *The neighbour took*
>   Marie-Claire à l'hôpital.   *Marie-Claire to the hospital.*

But in the following example, the object does agree with the verb because as a direct object pronoun it precedes the past participle. Thus **emmené** gains an -**e** to agree with **l'** (standing for **Marie-Claire**):

> La voisine **l'**a emmenée.   *The neighbour took her.*

The explanation above is only important for those learners who wish to understand the spelling of the language and learn to write French correctly. Orally, of course, there is no difference at all between **emmené** and **emmenée** or **prévenu** and **prévenue**.

However, in some cases agreement of the past participle does make a difference to the sound of a verb:

J'ai **mis la carte postale** dans la boîte à lettres.	*I put the postcard in the post box.*
Je **l'**ai **mise** dans la boîte à lettres.	*I put it in the post box.*
Nous avons **pris les clefs de la voiture**.	*We took the car keys.*
Nous **les** avons **prises**.	*We took them.*

Mis sounds [*mi*] and **mise** sounds [*miz*]; **pris** sounds [*pri*] and **prises** sounds [*priz*].

Try to identify other examples in the next dialogue and the next units.

Point info

Les quais de la Seine

In the Dialogue Sarah has promised Ariane and Pierre that if they have time they will stop **sur les quais** to go and have a look at pet shops. **Les quais de la Seine**, the river banks throughout the centre of Paris, are amongst the city's most interesting places, with hundreds of little wooden boxes which open as stalls where people sell old books, maps, stamps postcards, etc. One of the most interesting **quais** is on the right bank of the **Seine** between **Châtelet** and **Pont-Neuf**. On one side there are **les bouquinistes** with their bookstalls and on the side of the buildings there is a multitude of pet shops with wonderful birds, cats, dogs and more exotic animals, next to flowers and seed shops selling a large variety of bulbs and seeds of all sorts.

2 Acheter des tickets

Sarah, Ariane et Pierre sont en route pour leur promenade. Ils sont à la station de métro Nation. Ils se dirigent vers le guichet.

Listen to/Read the dialogue and answer these questions.

(a) Does Sarah need to get tickets for the children?
(b) What kind of tickets have they got?
(c) Who says that Sarah is a child?

Listen/Read again.

(d) Why does Sarah say to the children she wants to think for a minute?

(e) What does she get in the end?

Listen/Read once more.

(f) Which **direction** will they take to go back?

(g) Why do the children choose les Sablons as the station where they want to get off?

demi-tarif	half-fare
un carnet de tickets	a book of tickets (10)
une station de métro	a tube station
une gare R.E.R./une gare S.N.C.F.	an RER or SNCF strain station
un changement	connection (on métro or railway line)

Sarah	Attendez les gamins! Il faut que j'achète des tickets.
Ariane	On en a, nous, des tickets.
Sarah	Ah oui? Bon très bien mais ce sont des tickets demi-tarifs pour les enfants et moi je ne suis plus une enfant!
Ariane et Pierre	Si, tu es une enfant!
Sarah	Eh bien voilà! Je vous remercie les petits! Sérieusement, est-ce que je prends une carte ou un carnet? Laissez-moi réfléchir une minute.
	…
Sarah	Pardon madame, c'est combien la carte Mobilis, Zone 1 et 2?
Employée	Cela dépend où vous allez et combien de voyages differents vous allez faire …
Sarah	Ah oui, je vois. Je vais prendre un carnet de tickets s'il vous plaît.
Ariane	Moi, je sais quelle ligne il faut prendre, c'est la ligne 1, en direction de la Grande Arche de La Défense. C'est facile, il n'y a même pas de changements.
Pierre	Et pour rentrer c'est la direction Porte de Vincennes. A quelle station on descend?
Sarah	On a le choix entre la Porte Maillot et les Sablons. C'est plus ou moins la même distance pour le zoo. Si on descend aux Sablons on peut prendre le petit train du Bois de Boulogne.
Ariane et Pierre	Les Sablons!

Link the following English phrases to the French equivalent expressions.

1) Kids, wait!

2) I am no longer a child.

3) Do I get a travel card or a book of tickets?

4) I know which line we have to take.

5) At which station do we get off?

6) It's more or less the same distance to the zoo.

(a) A quelle station on descend?

(b) Moi, je sais quelle ligne il faut prendre.

(c) Attendez les gamins!

(d) C'est plus ou moins la même distance pour le zoo.

(e) Je ne suis plus une enfant

(f) Est-ce que j'achète une carte ou un carnet?

Point info

Les transports parisiens

La Grande Arche de la Défense is a métro station named after the monument it leads to. **La Grande Arche** is President Mitterand's legacy to Paris. It is a tall futuristic building built under Mitterand between 1983 and 1989. It is spectacular in itself for its view over Paris and l'Ile-de-France but also because of its location which symbolically lines it up with l'Avenue de la Grande Armée and les Champs-Elysées and therefore with L'Arc de Triomphe and L'Obélisque de Louxor, Place de la Concorde.

Travelling around Paris you can use the bus or the métro which are run by la **R.A.T.P. (Réseau Autonome des Transports Parisiens)** and **le R.E.R. (Réseau Express Régional)** a train service which serves the Parisian suburbs of l'Ile-de-France.

Les titres de transports is the official name for tickets. In normal usage there are two separate words for ticket in French: **un billet (de train)** and **un ticket de bus/de métro**. Paris commuters have a range of season tickets which they can use but for visitors there are three options: the individual ticket (not economical, unless you only have one journey to make) , **un carnet de tickets** with ten tickets and finally **la carte Mobilis** which is a day travel card with options for all zones. Within Paris you can use just one ticket for any journey, whether you have two stops or twenty on your journey; the cost is the same. You can also use one of your tickets for the cablecar in Montmartre, **le Funiculaire de Montmartre**.

À vous maintenant!

 2 Vous vous déplacez de temps en temps

 pour les touristes

A   Paris Visite:
C'est la carte idéale pour voyager à volonté sur tous les réseaux
de transports urbains d'Ile-de-France dans la limite des zones
choisies pendant 1, 2, 3 ou 5 jours.
Une carte pour voyager malin : pas de perte de temps, les
enfants de 4 à moins de 12 ans paient moitié prix, accès à la
1re classe en RER et sur les trains Ile-de-France.
Elle n'a que des avantages : 14 partenaires proposent
réductions, offres exceptionnelles, en exclusivité.

En vente également

B   Carte Musées et Monuments
Un laissez-passer de 1,3 ou 5 jours pour visiter 70 musées et
monuments de la région Ile-de-France.

C   Passeport Disneyland® Paris
En même temps que votre titre de transport, vous pouvez
acheter votre passeport Disneyland Paris dans toutes les gares
RER de la RATP (sauf Marne-la-Vallée/Chessy), les principales
stations de métro, les Agences Commerciales RATP, les terminus
bus de la Gare de Lyon et de la Place d'Italie, le Carrousel
du Louvre et les points RATP de l'aéroport Roissy
Charles-de-Gaulle.

D   Télécarte
Vendue dans les stations de métro et les gares de RER.

Look at the leaflet and answer the questions.

(a) Which of the four cards advertised on the leaflet is a Paris transport card?
(b) What are each of the other three cards?
(c) Where can you buy your Passport for Disneyland Paris?
(d) Where can't you buy one?
(e) Which card has a half-fare tarif for children aged between 4 and 12?
(f) Can you buy une Carte Musées et Monuments for one day? For
     six days?

Points de vente et mode de paiment

Now look at the second leaflet below, and answer these questions.

(g) Make a list of all the places where you can buy Mobilis, Tickets, Ticket jeunes.

(h) How much do you need to spend before you can pay your fare with a credit card?

Vous vous déplacez de temps en temps

Mobilis: un seul ticket pour toute une journée.

Pendant une journée entière, Mobilis vous ouvre l'accès aux réseaux RATP, SNCF Ile-de-France, APTR et ADATRIF (à l'exception des dessertes aéroportuaires). Muni de votre carte nominative et d'un coupon valable pour une journée, vous pouvez, à votre gré, combiner les trajets et vous déplacer dans les zones géographiques que vous avez choisies.
Economique, Mobilis propose un tarif forfaitaire en fonction des zones sélectionnées.

Zones de validité	Tarifs Mobilis
Zones 1–2	30 F
Zones 1–3	40 F
Zones 1–4	50 F
Zones 1–5	70 F
Zones 1–6	90 F
Zones 1–7	100 F
Zones 1–8	110 F

Ticket Jeunes se déplacer partout le samedi, le dimanche ou un jour férié.

Pour tous les titulaires de la Carte Jeunes (française ou étrangère), le Ticket Jeunes permet de se déplacer partout pendant toute une journée, le samedi, le dimanche ou un jour férié. Le Ticket Jeunes est nominatif et permet de circuler en 2e classe sur les réseaux RATP (sauf Orlyval), SNCF Ile-de-France, APTR et ADATRIF dans la limite des zones choisies.

Zones de validité	Tarifs Ticket Jeunes
Zones 1–3	20F
Zones 1–5	40 F
Zones 1–8	60 F

Points de vente Mobilis, Tickets, Ticket Jeunes:
- Toutes les stations de métro, gares RER.
- Terminus des lignes de bus.
- Commerces et bureaux de tabac signalés par le visuel RATP.
- Distributeurs automatiques pour les tickets.

Vous vous déplacez de temps en temps

Ticket ou Carnet pour un ou plusieurs déplacements dans Paris et Ile-de-France.

Un ticket pour un seul voyage, c'est idéal pour un déplacement occasionnel. Il peut être vendu soit en carnet.

Dans le métro, et dans le RER à l'intérieur de Paris, un seul ticket suffit quelles que soient les correspondances effectuées et la longueur de votre parcours.

Dans le RER en banlieue, le tarif varie selon la longueur de votre parcours.

Dans le bus à l'intérieur de Paris, un ticket permet un seul trajet, sans correspondance, quelle que soit la longueur du parcours (sauf sur les lignes PC, Balabus et Noctambus).

Pour les lignes PC et Balabus, le tarif est fonction du nombre de sections parcourues.

Pour les Noctambus, une tarification spéciale est appliquée.

Dans le bus et le tram, en banlieue et pour tout trajet incluant un parcours hors des limites de Paris, un ou plusieurs tickets sont nécessaires selon le nombre de sections parcourues.

Dans le Funiculaire de Montmartre, un ticket permet d'effeutuer un seul trajet (montée ou descente), sans correspondance possible avec le métro ou le bus.

	Plein tarif		Demi-tarif	
Tickets	2ᵉ cl.	1ʳᵉ cl.	2ᵉ cl.	1ʳᵉ cl.
A l'unité	8 F	12 F		
Carnet de 10 tickets	48 F	72 F	24 F	36 F
RER Paris-banlieue (jusqu'à)	38 F	57 F	19 F	28,50 F

Noctambus*	**trajet simple**	**2 trajets consécutifs avec correspondance à Châtelet**
	3 tickets à 8 F chaque	4 tickets à 8 F chaque

* Tarification susceptible de changer au 2 septembre 1997

Modes de paiement:
Dans l'ensemble des points de vente RATP: stations de métro, gares de RER et terminus des lignes de bus, les titres de transport peuvent être réglés par chèque ou carte bancaire à partir de 45 francs.

☑ Les jeunes et l'emploi

Read carefully this short newspaper article about three young students.

1 Étudiantes stagiaires

VIE QUOTIDIENNE

«Il ne suffit pas de cocher des cases»

Étudiants stagiaires

Que faisiez-vous du 28 août au 25 octobre ? Et bien, pendant que certains profitaient encore de leurs dernières semaines de vacances, Jenny, Maria et Nathalie bossaient. Etudiantes en maîtrise A.G.E. (traduisez Administration et Gestion d'Entreprise), elles ont effectué durant huit semaines un stage non rémunéré à la Caisse d'Allocations Familiales (CAF) de Brest. Premier contact avec le monde du travail.

elles bossaient *they worked*	**cocher des cases** *to tick boxes*
bosser *to work (slang)*	(as in multiple choice questions)

Now answer these questions.

(a) What did the three students do from 28 August to 25 October?
(b) What is their area of study?
(c) Were they paid for their work?
(d) Was the work experience carried out in term time?
(e) What did this type of work do for them in terms of experience?

2 La chasse aux jobs

Read the article below about the search for a part-time job. Then turn to the grid opposite and fill in the jobs in the order in which they appear in the article. The contents of the grid are jumbled so match each list of points with the correct job category and the correct heading. (Don't worry if you can't understand it all – just try to get the gist of the article.)

La chasse aux jobs

Maigres bourses ou parents compréhensifs ne suffisent plus à subvenir à vos besoins ? La chasse aux jobs est ouverte toute l'année. La concurrence est rude et mieux vaut se pointer devant votre employeur avec une bonne dose de motivation et une idée précise de ce que vous voulez. Conseils et idées en vrac.

Fast-foods et caféterias

C'est payé tout juste le SMIC et les pourboires sont interdits. Cadences infernales, patrons omniprésents et cuisines aseptisées. Les grandes chaînes recrutent également assez régulièrement et le rythme y est légèrement plus supportable. Pour postuler, présentez-vous directement dans chaque restaurant (mais pas au moment du rush) ou envoyez lettre de candidature et CV avec photo. Un conseil : écumez les centres commerciaux. Il est rare qu'ils ne contiennent pas un ou deux points de restauration. Pour les emplois de serveur(se), les jobs sont mieux payés en général, pourboires aidant.

Télémarketing et sondages

Les horaires sont très modulables. Il vous suffit de faire preuve d'amabilité au téléphone et de ne pas être allergique à la répétition. Les sociétés de télémarketing préfèrent que le premier contact s'établisse par téléphone. Un excellent moyen pour elles de mesurer vos capacités et d'opérer une première sélection.

Distribution de prospectus

Lisez les journaux gratuits pour trouver une annonce. Avoir le pied solide et posséder une voiture sont deux atouts. L'étudiant est payé au nombre de journaux ou tracts distribués.

**Pensez aussi aux grandes surfaces, parkings,
gardiennages, livraisons à domicile…**

3 main job categories (List them in the order they appear in the article)	Requirements to secure a job	Advantages (if any)	Inconveniences (if any)
1)	(a) • Flexitime	(b) • Large fast food firms recruit regularly • Serving jobs are better paid • Tips allowed	(c) • Go and introduce yourself directly • Send a letter of application + CV • Check all the shopping centres
2)	(d) • Only paid minimum wage • Tips are not allowed • Fast rhythm of work • Bosses always present	(e) • Paid according to number of newspapers or leaflets distributed	(f) • Good if you have two assets: solid feet and a car
3)	(g) • Selection over the telephone • Need a good telephone manner	(h) • Read the free press for job adverts	(i) • Very repetitive job

21 | SI ON GAGNAIT LE GROS LOT ...
If we won the jackpot ...

In this unit you will learn:

■ about some places to visit in Paris
■ how to discuss where to go and what to visit
■ how to express what you would like to do if you had more time and
  money (the conditional tense)

1 On pourrait sortir

*C'est vendredi matin. Marie-Claire est toujours en congé de maladie mais
elle se sent beaucoup mieux. Sarah et Marie-Claire font des projets pour
la journée. Les deux sœurs s'entendent très bien.*

Listen to/Read the dialogue. Sarah and her sister are chatting about places
they might be going to and about what they might do when they get there.
Tick only what they have agreed to do.

(a) to go to the Louvre
(b) to go to the Musée d'Orsay
(c) to go and see the Impressionist paintings
(d) to go to the Bazar de l'Hôtel de Ville
(e) to go to the Samaritaine
(f) to go for a cup of tea

Listen/Read again and answer these questions.

(g) Considering that Marie-Claire is still on sick leave, why do the two
    young women decide to go out?
(h) What does Marie-Claire wish for?

Sarah	Toi ça va mieux, cela se voit! Tu es de meilleure humeur ce matin! Si tu allais mieux on pourrait peut-être sortir.
Marie-Claire	Oui je me sens beaucoup mieux et puis les gosses sont chez la mère de Guillaume jusqu'à ce soir, le mari au travail ... À nous la liberté!
Sarah	Tu veux venir avec moi, je pensais faire une balade dans Paris?
Marie-Claire	Mais pourquoi pas? Ma main est encore douloureuse mais je ferais bien attention. Tu n'aurais pas envie d'aller au Louvre?
Sarah	Le Louvre ... non, ça ne me dit rien et puis nous n'aurions pas assez de temps, il y a toujours une telle queue!
Marie-Claire	Oui, je sais, si j'avais le temps ... et l'argent ... je sortirais beaucoup plus souvent.
Sarah	Écoute, si on allait au Musée d'Orsay on pourrait juste aller voir les Impressionnistes, non? Et après si on voulait, on aurait assez de temps pour faire les grands magasins: le Bazar de l'Hôtel de Ville ou je ne sais pas moi ...
Marie-Claire	Je suis d'accord pour le Musée d'Orsay mais au lieu du Bazar de l'Hôtel de Ville on pourrait aller à la Samaritaine.
Sarah	C'est d'accord et on ira prendre une tasse de thé tout en haut, à la terrasse du magasin.

être de bonne humeur   *to be in a good mood*
de meilleure humeur   *in a better mood*
se sentir mieux   *to feel better*
douloureux/se   *painful*
Cela ne me dit rien (colloquial).   *I don't fancy it.*
au lieu de   *instead of*
une telle queue   *such a queue*
les gosses   *kids* (similar to **les gamins** but slightly prejorative)

Link the following English phrases to the French.

1) It shows!
2) The kids are at Guillaume's mother's.
3) Do you fancy going to the Louvre?
4) We would not have enough time.
5) We would have time to go to the department stores.
6) We'll go for a cup of tea at the terrace at the top.

(a) Nous n'aurions pas assez de temps.
(b) Cela se voit.
(c) On ira prendre une tasse de thé tout en haut à la terrasse.
(d) Les gosses sont chez la mère de Guillaume.
(e) Tu as envie d'aller au Louvre?
(f) On aurait assez de temps pour faire les grands magasins.

Comment ça marche?

1 Faire

Faire can mean a lot more than *to make* or *to do*.

> faire les grands magasins *to go window-shopping,* Lit. *to do the shops*
> faire du lèche-vitrine *to go window-shopping*, Lit. *to do window licking*

Faire is also used to express that someone has done it all:

> Il a fait la Chine, l'Afrique, l'Amérique du Sud ... *He's done China, Africa, South America...*

2 The conditional and the imperfect

You have already met and used the conditional tense (see Unit 7, page 72). It conveys the notion that if conditions were fulfilled something would happen. It is used frequently in conversational French, especially with a few verbs which you are now familiar with:

Je voudrais faire une balade	*I would like to ...* (**vouloir**)
Je devrais rentrer chez moi	*I ought to...* (**devoir**)
On pourrait aller au cinéma	*We could ....* (**pouvoir**)
Il faudrait partir avant la nuit	*We should ...* (**falloir**)

Here are two verbs in the conditional and the conditional verb ending pattern:

Aller	Finir	Ending pattern for all verbs in the conditional		
j'irais	je finirais	je	_____	**rais**
tu irais	tu finirais	tu	_____	**rais**
elle irait	elle finirait	elle	_____	**rait**
nous irions	nous finirions	nous	_____	**rions**
vous iriez	vous finiriez	vous	_____	**riez**
ils iraient	ils finiraient	ils	_____	**raient**

You have noticed before that within one short conversation people use many different tenses. The imperfect tense and the conditional are often used together in the same sentence to convey the notion that if the condition was (imperfect) right something would (conditional) happen.

Look at the examples in the dialogue on page 227. First of all note that **si** *if*, together with a verb in the imperfect is often used with the conditional:

Si ça allait mieux on pourrait peut-être sortir.	*If you were better we could go out.*
Si j'avais le temps et l'argent je sortirais beaucoup plus souvent.	*If I had more time and money I would go out more often.*
Si on allait au Musée d'Orsay on pourrait aller voir ...*	*If we went to the Musée d'Orsay we could go and see ...*

The emerging pattern here is therefore:

■ **si** + verb in the imperfect + verb in the conditional

or

■ verb in the conditional + **si** + verb in the imperfect

It is also possible to have the conditional on its own with the condition unspoken but present in the mind of the speaker and understood by the listener:

Nous n'aurions pas assez de temps.   *We would not have enough time.*

Note that when the doubt is lifted or when the condition is fulfilled the future tense is used instead of the conditional:

On ira prendre une tasse de thé ...   *We'll go for a cup of tea ...*

It has been agreed by the sisters that this is exactly what they will do rather than what they would like to do.

Reminder: The ending pattern for the future tense is as follows:

je	—**rai**	nous	—**rons**
tu	—**ras**	vous	—**rons**
elle	—**ra**	ils	—**ront**

(Also see page 107)

☑ À vous maintenant!

1 Faites des phrases

Find the ending for each of the sentences in the left-hand column.

1) Si je savais son numéro de téléphone je...	(a) réussirait à ses examens.
2) Si j'étais riche je ...	(b) iraient à l'hôpital.
3) Si Corinne travaillait mieux elle ...	(c) n'aurait pas d'accidents.
4) Si vous aviez le temps qu'est-ce que vous ...	(d) ferais un voyage autour du Monde.
5) S'il conduisait moins vite il ...	(e) saurais ce qui se passe. (**savoir**, *to know*)
6) Si tu lisais le journal tu ...	(f) nous changerait les idées.
7) S'ils étaient malades ils ...	(g) lui téléphonerais.
8) Si on allait au cinéma, ça ...	(h) feriez?

Point info

Paris

The following Paris landmarks are mentioned in the dialogue:

Le Louvre is a vast art gallery and museum on the right bank of the Seine which used to be the residence of French kings before they moved to Versailles. In 1989 a large glass pyramid was added to it which in fact operates as a large dome for the underground reception area.

Le Musée d'Orsay is an old main line station which stopped being used for main-line purposes as long ago as 1939. Since 1986 it has been an art museum and a cultural centre which houses many works of the Impressionists.

Le Bazar de l'Hôtel de Ville and **la Samaritaine** are two large and very old department stores. The first is near l'Hôtel de Ville (**la Mairie de Paris**) and **la Samaritaine** is a tall building opposite **le Pont-Neuf** (the oldest bridge in Paris, despite its name). It has seven floors and a roof terrace from where you have a wonderful view over Paris. All these places are within close walking distance from the métro station **Châtelet**. From **le Châtelet** you can also walk to the **Forum des Halles**, where **le Centre Pompidou** was built in the 1970s on the site of **les Halles**, which used to be the vegetable market for the capital. Le Forum des Halles is a very lively part of Paris.

2 Qu'est-ce que tu ferais?

Sarah et Marie-Claire sont assises à la terrasse de la Samaritaine. Elles se relaxent un peu en jouant un jeu.

Listen to/Read the dialogue, and answer the questions.

(a) What game are they playing?
(b) What would she have if it happened and why?

Listen/Read again.

(c) Why would she live in Paris?
(d) Would she carry on working?

Listen/Read once more.

(e) When would she swim?
(f) What would she do in Paris? (try to list everything mentioned, but if not, find at least three)
(g) Who would be with her in her paradise?

(h) Write a caption for the picture, taking account of what Marie-Claire says she would do if she had time and money.

Sarah	Dis-moi Marie-Claire, honnêtement et sans tricher, ce que tu ferais vraiment si tu gagnais le gros lot au Loto?
Marie-Claire	Alors d'accord ... euh ... Eh bien j'aurais un grand appartement à Paris, parce que j'adore vivre à Paris, et une maison sur la Côte d'Azur parce que j'aime bien le soleil.
Sarah	Tu continuerais à travailler?
Marie-Claire	Euh, non! Comme cela j'aurais plus de temps pour moi.
Sarah	Et qu'est-ce que tu ferais avec tout ce temps?
Marie-Claire	J'irais à la piscine tous les jours, je lirais tous les livres que je voudrais, j'irais au cinéma, au théâtre, à l'Opéra, dans de très bons restaurants. Et puis de temps en temps je ferais des petits voyages quelque part, au sport d'hiver par exemple. C'est dingue tout ce qu'on pourrait faire!
Sarah	Tu serais toute seule dans ton paradis?
Marie-Claire	Non, je serais avec toute ma famille, toi y compris!
Sarah	Merci, ma chère, c'est très aimable à toi!

> **sans tricher**   *no cheating*
> **c'est dingue**   *it's crazy* (colloquial expression)
>   also **dingo**: **il est dingo** *he is mad*

À vous maintenant!

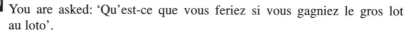 2 Qu'est-ce que vous feriez?

You are asked: 'Qu'est-ce que vous feriez si vous gagniez le gros lot au loto'.

(a) Work out how you would say that you would have a house in Brittany, that you would have a boat, that you would go fishing and watch TV in the evening.

(b) How would you say that you would take a trip round the world?

(c) Listen to the audio and check your answers.

3 Les jeux instantanés (*scratch cards*)

Vous avez acheté une carte jeu. Vous l'avez grattée (gratter *to scratch*). Est-ce que vous avez gagné?

Look at the scratch card and answer these two questions.

(a) What is the rule of the game?
(b) What is the cost of this scratch card?

Gagner, cela n'arrive pas qu' aux autres

(Lit. *Winning does not happen only to others.*
In other words: *It could be **you!***)

---

4 Avez-vous gagné au Loto?

Look at the following grid . There are two days of the week when the Loto is drawn and on each of these days there are two draws within a few minutes of one another.

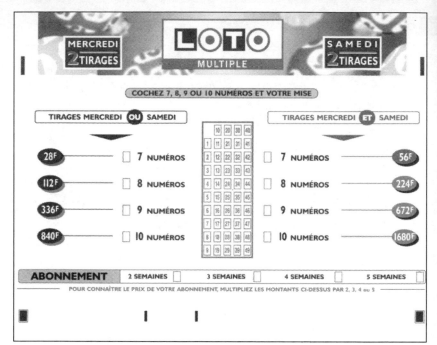

(a) On which days is the lottery drawn each week?
(b) How much would you pay if you opted for eight numbers on only one of the two days?
(c) How much would you pay if you opted for eight numbers on both days?
(d) How many numbers would you be able to tick for 1680F?
(e) Up to how many weeks could you have a subscription for?
(f) How much would you pay for four weeks, having ticked eight numbers for both days?

5 Vous avez coché?

Tick eight numbers on the loto card above. In order to win anything you need to get between three and six numbers correctly.

Écoutez et voyez si vous avez gagné! Ne trichez pas!

Pas de chance? Mais si vous aviez choisi les bon numéros, vous auriez gagné le gros lot …

3 Un peu de littérature

Here is an extract from *Dora Bruder*, a novel by the contemporary French writer Patrick Modiano.

> *Elle allait certainement le dimanche retrouver ses parents qui occupaient encore la chambre du 41 boulevard Ornano. Je regarde le plan du métro et j'essaye d'imaginer le trajet qu'elle suivait. Pour éviter de trop nombreux changements de lignes, le plus simple était de prendre le métro à Nation, qui était assez proche du pensionnat. Direction Pont de Sèvres. Changement à Strasbourg-St-Denis. Direction Porte de Clignancourt. Elle descendait à Simplon, juste en face du cinéma et de l'hôtel.*

(Editions Gallimard 1997, page 46)

And here's what the Larousse dictionary says about Patrick Modiano:

> **MODIANO** (Patrick), écrivain français né à Boulogne-Billancourt en 1945. Ses romans forment une quête de l'identité à travers un passé douloureux et énigmatique

Did you understand it all? Now answer these questions.

(a) What did Dora most certainly do on Sundays?
(b) Where did her parents live?
(c) What is the author imagining?
(d) At which station would she catch the métro? Where would she get out?
(e) How many changes did she have to make?
(f) What was there next to the hotel?
(g) What is Modiano's date of birth?
(h) What are his novels mainly about?

trajet *route*		**roman** *novel (book)*
éviter *avoid*		**quête** *enquiry*
pensionnat *boarding school*		**à travers** *through*
écrivain *writer*		**douloureux** *painful*

22 | **LES GRÈVES**
Strikes

In this unit you will learn about:

■ French television
■ possessive adjectives and pronouns
■ strikes and French trade unions

 ## 1 C'est le mien!

 C'est vendredi soir. Les enfants sont tous les deux dans la chambre d'Ariane. Soudain on entend des cris: ils se disputent. Leur père va voir ce qu'il se passe.

 Listen to/Read the dialogue, and answer the questions.

(a) Why are they fighting?
(b) Where is Pierre's game?
(c) Whose game has he got now?

Listen/Read again.

(d) Who shouted?
(e) What does Pierre claim he can prove?
(f) What does Guillaume tell them to do?

Listen/Read once more.

(g) Why does Pierre call Ariane a liar?
(h) How does she retaliate?
(i) What does Guillaume tell them to do?

Ariane donne un coup de pied à Pierre

Ariane	Donne-moi ça! C'est à moi!
Pierre	Non, c'est le mien!
Ariane	Mais non, tu as laissé le tien chez Bonne Maman et tu le sais bien!
Guillaume	Qu'est-ce que c'est que tout ce bruit? Qui a crié?
Ariane	C'est Pierre, il a pris mon jeu et il dit que c'est le sien!
Pierre	Mais elle est complètement dingue! C'est le mien, je peux te le prouver!
Ariane	Je te dis que ce n'est pas le tien!
Guillaume	Bon, ça suffit! Vous allez venir vous asseoir avec nous dans la salle de séjour et vous allez regarder la télé tranquillement. Il y a un programme très intéressant sur les animaux.
Ariane	J'aime pas les animaux!
Pierre	Menteuse! Aïe!! Elle m'a donné un coup de pied dans la jambe!
Guillaume	Bon, c'est terminé pour ce soir. Ni jeux, ni télé mais le lit! Immédiatement!

---

un cri   *a shout (cri is another*
    faux-ami, *to cry is* **pleurer**)
crier   *to shout*
un coup de pied   *a kick*

menteuse/menteur   *liar*
ni ... ni ...   *neither ... nor*
Ça suffit!   *That's enough!*

Link the following English phrases to the equivalent French expressions.

1) Give me that!
2) You left yours at Grandma's.
3) What's all this noise?
4) It's mine and I can prove it to you!
5) That's enough!
6) She kicked me in the leg.
7) You are going to come and sit with us.
8) No games, no TV but bed!

(a) Ça suffit!
(b) Elle m'a donné un coup de pied dans la jambe.
(c) Vous allez venir vous asseoir avec nous.
(d) Donne-moi ça!
(e) Ni jeux, ni télé mais le lit!
(f) Tu as laissé le tien chez Bonne Maman.
(g) Qu'est-ce que c'est que tout ce bruit?
(h) C'est le mien, je peux te le prouver!

⊡ Comment ça marche?

1 Possessive adjectives and pronouns

Possessive adjectives and pronouns are used to say that something belongs to someone. The following examples show three different ways of saying something belongs to 'me':

C'est **à moi**
C'est **mon jeu**/C'est **le mien**
C'est **ma chambre**/C'est **la mienne**
Ce sont **mes chaussures**/Ce sont **les miennes**
Ce sont **mes crayons**/Ce sont **les miens**

To express possession you can choose between:

1) an emphatic pronoun: **c'est à moi**, when you are talking about something you can point to;
2) a possessive adjective before a noun: **mon jeu**, **mes chaussures**. Remember, the adjective agrees with the gender and number of the noun it accompanies;
3) A possessive pronoun which replaces the noun altogether: **le mien**, **les miennes**. Here the form of the pronoun depends on the number and gender of the noun it replaces.

Study the following table which shows the whole range of possessive adjectives and pronouns and also the use of the emphatic pronoun, following a preposition (in this case **à**).

Emphatic pronouns	Possessive adjectives	Possessive pronouns
C'est **à moi**	C'est **mon/ma** ... Ce sont **mes** ...	C'est **le mien/la mienne** Ce sont **les miens/les miennes**
C'est **à toi**	C'est **ton/ta** ... Ce sont **tes** ...	C'est **le tien/la tienne** Ce sont **les tiens/les tiennes**
C'est **à lui/ à elle**	C'est **son/sa** ... Ce sont **ses** ...	C'est **le sien/la sienne** Ce sont **les siens/les siennes**
C'est **à nous**	C'est **notre** ... Ce sont **nos** ...	C'est **le nôtre/la nôtre** Ce sont **les nôtres**
C'est **à vous**	C'est **votre** ... Ce sont **vos**...	C'est **le vôtre/la vôtre** Ce sont **les vôtres**
C'est **à elles/ à eux**	C'est **leur** ... Ce sont **leurs** ...	C'est **le leur/la leur** Ce sont **les leurs**

À vous maintenant!

1 Au bureau des objets trouvés

Maintenant vous êtes au bureau des objets trouvés (*lost property office* but literally *found property*). You report that you have lost seven items in the following order: umbrella, roller skates, reading glasses, wallet, keys, bag and watch. Work through the grid below, item by item, and say if the object shown to you is yours or not. (The gender of the article is indicated).

Exemple:

Vous	J'ai perdu mes lunettes de soleil (*sunglasses*).
Employée	Ce sont les vôtres?
Vous	Non, ce ne sont pas les miennes.

Employée du bureau des objects trouvés		Vous
(a) C'est votre parapluie?	(masc.)	Non, ce n'est pas …
(b) Ce sont vos patins à roulettes?	(masc.)	Oui, ce sont …
(c) Ce sont vos lunettes?	(fem.)	Oui …
(d) C'est votre portefeuille?	(masc.)	Non …
(e) Ce sont vos clefs?	(fem.)	Oui …
(f) C'est votre sac?	(masc.)	Oui …
(g) C'est votre montre?	(fem.)	Non …

2 Oui c'est le mien

This time all the items are yours (the items are the same as above but not in the same order). Listen to the audio and claim your property.

Exemple:

Employée	Ce sont vos lunettes de soleil?
Vous	Oui, ce sont les miennes.

Bonne continuation!

2 On regarde la télé

Il est neuf heures. Les enfants sont couchés. Marie-Claire regarde le programme de télévision.

Look at the TV listings for this evening, listen to the audio, and answer the questions below.

LUNDI 27 OCTOBRE 1997

TELEVISION

TF1 F2 F3 C+ 5e M6 Câble
ARTE · et satellite

TF1	F2	F3	C+	5e/ARTE	M6
20.45	20.55	20.50	20.35	20.45	20.45

LA BELLE VIE
Téléfilm humoristique français de Gérard Marx (2/2) (1997). 120 min. VF. Avec : Jean Yanne (Julius), Danièle Evenou (Linda), Paulette Dubost (Mamé), Vanessa Devraine (Fanny), Christian Rauth (Gaspard). Une famille d'origine modeste devient milliardaire et rachète un château pour y habiter.

22.55
LE DROIT DE SAVOIR
Magazine présenté par Charles Villeneuve. «Un enfant à tout prix». Un reportage réalisé par Cathelyne Hemery, David Gosset et Philippe Véron en 1997. L'adoption d'enfants à l'étranger, en particulier au Viêt-nam et en Russie.

URGENCES
Série médicale américaine. Deux épisodes : Se voiler la face. - Boomerang. VF. 90 min.

22.40
MOTS CROISÉS
Magazine présenté par Arlette Chabot et Alain Duhamel. «Quelle école pour nos enfants?» Invités : Claude Allègre, Alain Madelin.
23.50 En fin de compte.
23.55 Journal.

MOTS CROISES
le magazine politique mensuel de la rédaction présenté par **Arlette CHABOT Alain DUHAMEL**
ce soir 22h35 **2** *France*

LES CONQUÉRANTS DE CARSON CITY
Film américain d'André De Toth (1952). Western. 84 min. VF. Avec : Randolph Scott (Jeff Kincaid), Lucille Norman (Susan Mitchell), Raymond Massey (Big Jack Davis). Un ingénieur se bat pour l'ouverture d'une ligne de chemin de fer.
22.20 La dernière séance. Au sommaire : Actualités. - Tex Avery.
22.50 Soir 3.

23.15
TERREUR À L'OUEST
Film américain d'André De Toth (1954). Western. 80 min. VO. Avec : Randolph Scott (Jim Kipp), Marie Windsor (Alice William), Dolorès Dorn (Julie). Un justicier solitaire poursuit trois criminels dont il ignore encore le signalement.
0.35 La dernière séance. Tex Avery.

RIDICULE
Film français de Patrice Leconte (1996). Comédie. 102 min. VF. En 16/9. Redif le 30. Avec : Charles Berling, Fanny Ardant. Un jeune noble naïf et passionné découvre les artifices et les dangers de la cour de Versailles.
22.15 Flash infos.

22.20
PARTY
Film franco-portugais de Manoel de Oliveira (1996). 90 min. VF. 1ère diff. Redif le 28. Avec : Michel Piccoli, Irène Papas. Un séducteur impénitent s'efforce de charmer sa jeune hôtesse, lors d'une garden-party.
23.55 Caméléone. Film de Benoît Cohen (1996). Policier. 92 min. VF. En 16/9. Dern. diff.

LA LEÇON DE PIANO
Film de Jane Campion (1992). 125 min. VO. En 16/9. Avec : Holly Hunter (Ada), Harvey Keitel (Baines). Une jeune pianiste muette entre deux hommes, en Nouvelle-Zélande.
22.40 Kinorama.

22.55
L'ARGENT
Film de Robert Bresson (1983). 85 min. VF. Avec : Christian Patey (Yvon), Sylvie van der Elsen.
0.15 Court circuit - Bon voyage. Court-métrage d'A. Hitchcock.
0.45 La rate. Téléfilm de Martin Buchhorn.
2.15 Tracks.

D.A.R.Y.L.
Film américain de Simon Wincer (1985). Science-fiction. 100 min. VF. Avec : Barret Oliver (Daryl), Mary Beth Hurt (Joyce Richardson), Kathryn Walker (Ellen Lamb). Un robot rêve de devenir un humain.

22.40
COUPS POUR COUPS
Film américain de Deran Sarafian (1990). Policier. 90 min. VF. Avec : Jean-Claude Van Damme (Louis Burke), Robert Guillaume (Naylor). Pour enquêter sur une série de meurtres inexpliqués dans un pénitencier, un inspecteur de police endosse l'identité d'un gangster.

Film français de Patrice Leconte (1989). Drame. 90'. En 16/9. **21.50** La main gauche du seigneur. Film américain d'Edward Dmytryk (1955). Aventures. VO. 85'. En 16/9. **23.20** La femme secrète. Film français de Sébastien Grall (1986). Comédie dramatique. 90'. En 16/9. **0.55** Secret mortel. Film américain de Michael Scott (1995). Policier. 88'.

CINÉ CINÉFIL
20.30 Arsène Lupin. Film américain de Jack Conway (1932). Policier. NB. VO. 86'. **22.00** Fanny Elssler. Film allemand de Paul Martin (1937). Romanesque. NB. VO. **23.25** Fabiola. Film italien d'Alessandro Blasetti (2/2) (1949). Aventures. NB. 90'. **0.45** L'empereur de Californie. Film allemand de Luis Trenker (1936). Western. NB. VO. 90'.

(a) Guillaume has heard on the news that lorry drivers might go on strike. When is the strike likely to start?
(b) Why is he telling Sarah?
(c) What is Sarah's first reaction?

Listen again.

(d) What has already started on Canal+?
(e) Which programme would Guillaume like to watch after the film?
(f) Why should it interest Sarah?

Now read the dialogue.

Guillaume   Sarah, je viens de voir la fin du journal, les routiers menacent de se mettre en grève à partir de dimanche, ça pourrait affecter ton voyage de retour!

Sarah   Super! Comme cela je resterais à Paris! Sérieusement parlant, je ne pense pas que l'Eurostar soit affecté par le blocage des routes mais on ne sait jamais. On verra bien!

Marie-Claire   Au fait il y a *Ridicule* qui passe à Canal+. Ça fait presque une demi-heure que cela a commencé.

Sarah   Parce que vous avez Canal+ maintenant?

Marie-Claire   Oui, c'est surtout pour les nouveaux films puisque nous ne sortons presque pas.

Sarah   Eh bien c'est bien! Alors on regarde le film?

Guillaume   Oui mais je voulais voir *Mots Croisés* après.

Marie-Claire   Ah oui, c'est vrai. Toi qui aimes la politique, Sarah, ça t'intéressera sûrement.

---

le journal (d'information)/les informations/les infos   *the news*
les routiers   (short for **chauffeurs routiers**)   *lorry drivers*
mots-croisés   *crosswords* Here, on France 2, it is the name of a televised political debate between politicians (the title plays on the expression **mots croisés**)

Link the following English phrases to the equivalent French expressions.

1) I have just seen the end of the news.
2) It could affect your return journey.
3) We'll see.
4) You can never tell.

(a) On ne sait jamais.
(b) Les routiers menacent de se mettre en grève.
(c) Puisque nous ne sortons presque jamais.

5) Lorry drivers are threatening
to go on strike.

6) Since we hardly ever go out.

(d) On verra.

(e) Ça pourrait affecter ton voyage de
retour.

(f) Je viens de voir la fin du journal.

À vous de choisir

Look at the TV listing opposite above and answer the questions overleaf
(there may be more than one answer for some of the questions).

| **VF: Version Française** *dubbed* **VO: Version Originale** *with subtitles* |

In response to each question indicate which channel you would watch and
at what time.

(a) If you wanted to watch a film in English?

(b) If you wanted to watch a medical comedy?

(c) If you wished to see the late night news?

(d) If you wanted to watch a political debate?

(e) If you wanted to watch a programme on the adoption of children from
other countries?

(f) If you fancied watching a science-fiction film?

(g) If you wanted to see *Monsieur Hire*, a film you have been meaning to
see for a long time?

(h) On which condition would you be able to watch it?

(i) Look at the small ad for *Mots Croisés*. Can you find the word which
indicates that it is a monthly programme?

(j) What is the theme of this month's debate?

Point info

Les grèves et les syndicats

Less than a quarter of French workers belong to a trade union but when
serious issues are raised there is usually a spontaneous response from the
vast majority of people within a profession or an industry. Workers join in
if a strike is called whether they are members of a trade union or not. All
categories of workers go on strike at one time or other and take to the
streets. Doctors, nurses, dentists, teachers and even lawyers (see headlines
at the end of this section) go on strike when they need to put pressure on
the government.

There are two main trade unions in France, both cover all trades and professions and have within them groupings for the various categories of workers. The difference between them is now a historical division which no longer applies but still marks each one's tendencies:

La CGT (**C**onfédération **G**énérale du **T**ravail) was traditionally affiliated to the French Communist Party. It has not significantly declined since the demise of communism.

La CFDT (**C**onfédération **F**rançaise **D**émocratique du **T**ravail) is more aligned with the French Socialist Party.

There are also two much smaller trade union organisations:

FO (**F**orce **O**uvrière – the name means *workers' power*) is of a moderate and reformist tendency.

La CFTC (**C**onfédération **F**rançaise des **T**ravailleurs **C**hrétiens) is a Christian trade unionists' organisation.

Quote from a lorry driver interviewed on France Inter: **'Ce que nous n'obtiendrons* pas par la négociation, nous l'obtiendrons par la rue.'** For this reason strikes by some categories of workers such as **les routiers** *lorry drivers* have a wide impact!

* future of **obtenir**, *to obtain*

Menace de grève des avocats
Les bâtonniers protestent contre le manque de moyens.

Les bâtonniers is a term sometimes used when referring to barristers. They are threatening to go on strike because of insufficient funding.

3 Que disent les journaux?

Read the following newspaper article and answer the questions overleaf.

Patrons routiers mettez-vous d'accord!
Les négociations continuent

«**P**atrons, mettez-vous d'accord, on se revoit mardi!» C'est ce
qu'ont déclaré les représentants des syndicats de chauffeurs
routiers en quittant la salle des negociations vendredi à minuit. Les
quatre principaux syndicats, CFDT, CGT, FO et CFTC ont déposé un
préavis de grève pour le dimanche 2 novembre au soir. Pour éviter un
blocage du territoire il faudrait que les patrons acceptent les
revendications des chauffeurs routiers: 10 000F par mois pour 200
heures de travail pour les routiers les plus qualifiés.

les patrons	*the bosses*	**aboutir**	*to reach a successful outcome*
des pourparlers	*talks*	**l'enjeu**	*the stake*
un préavis	*advance notice*	**réclamer**	*to claim*

(a) When will the trades unions be meeting the bosses?
(b) When did the last negotiating session take place?
(c) At what time did it end?
(d) When are they planning to go on strike?
(e) What do the lorry drivers wish to achieve?

 Qui dit quoi?

Now read this description of the negotiations, before answering the
questions opposite.

Les positions avant le blocus

Fédérations patronales (UFT, UNOSTRA)	Syndicats (CFDT, CGT, FO, CFTC)
◆ Calcul annuel des salaires ◆ 120 000F par ans pour 200 heures de travail par mois en l'an 2000 ◆ Hausse de salaires de 1,5 à 4% pour tous et de 3,5 a 5% pour les routiers les plus qualifiés	◆ 120 000F par an pour 200 heures de travail par mois immédiatement ◆ Paiement de la prime de 3000F ◆ Diminution du temps de travail ◆ Pas d'annualisation ◆ Salaire horaire autour de 50F

Say whether the following statements are made by the lorry drivers or by the bosses. Mark each sentence with **R** for **Routiers** or **P** for **Patrons**.

(a) 120 000F in the year 2000
(b) Bonus payment of 3000F
(c) Salary increase between 1.5% and 4%
(d) Around 50F per hour
(e) Reduction of working hours
(f) Pay worked out on an annual basis
(g) Up to 5% increase for top lorry drivers

Les mots cachés

Find ten words used in the newspaper article opposite meaning the following:

payment, increase, bonus, strike, decrease, salary, calendar, hourly, drivers, trades unions

C	A	L	E	N	D	R	I	E	R	A	S
H	A	U	S	S	E	R	G	R	E	V	E
A	S	D	F	G	G	H	J	U	N	T	H
U	S	A	S	A	E	R	T	Y	U	J	B
F	Y	E	R	T	H	P	R	I	M	E	G
F	N	Q	S	A	Z	X	C	V	E	G	H
E	D	E	A	H	O	R	A	I	R	E	U
U	I	E	L	R	N	M	L	U	A	R	Y
R	C	L	A	D	F	R	G	H	T	M	A
S	A	D	I	M	I	N	U	T	I	O	N
G	T	E	R	S	G	E	R	Y	O	G	K
B	S	I	E	T	R	E	D	Z	N	E	L

23 | LA VIE DE FAMILLE
Family life

In this unit you will learn about:

■ the cinema
■ sport in France
■ one more past tense: the pluperfect

1 Moi, j'en ai ras-le-bol!

C'est samedi matin et Marie-Claire est débordée!

Listen to/Read the dialogue. You need to concentrate on what the various people in the family are planning to do. Complete the empty boxes according to what each person is doing in the morning, afternoon and evening.

Saturday	**Marie-Claire**	**Guillaume**	**Sarah**	**Ariane**	**Pierre**
Morning	Housework Shopping				
Afternoon		Football match	Cinema		
Evening	Cinema	·		At home	

débordée	*snowed under*	**aider**	*to help*
le ménage	*housework*	**en avoir ras-le-bol**	*to be fed up*
la rentrée	*start of the new school year*	(lit. *up to the brim*)	
		ranger	*to tidy up*

Ariane	Maman, c'est aujourd'hui que tu nous emmènes au cinéma? Tu avais dit qu'on irait voir *Hercule* …
Marie-Claire	Oui ma chérie, mais nous n'avons pas encore décidé ce que nous allons faire aujourd'hui.
Pierre	Tu nous avais promis!
Marie-Claire	Oui je sais mais c'est un peu compliqué …
Guillaume	Marie-Claire, je t'avais prévenue qu'aujourd'hui c'est le sport toute la journée… Je pars dans cinq minutes, là …
Marie-Claire	Quoi? Mais où vas-tu?
Guillaume	Mais je te l'ai dit avant-hier! Ce matin je vais à Bercy faire une partie de tennis avec les copains du bureau et cet après-midi je vais au foot avec Lionel. On va voir Paris - Saint Germain. C'est le premier match de la saison, on ne peut pas rater ça!
Marie-Claire	Il est possible que tu me l'aies dit mais j'avais complètement oublié. Moi j'en ai ras-le-bol! Je comptais sur toi pour m'aider à faire le ménage et les courses pour la semaine prochaine. Tu as sans doute oublié que c'est mardi, la rentrée!
Sarah	Bien, moi je vous propose une solution: Guillaume tu vas à Bercy et à ton match de foot, les enfants, ce matin on va tous aider Marie-Claire avec le ménage et les courses et si vous avez bien travaillé, je vous emmènerai voir *Hercule* cet après midi. Maman profitera du calme pour se reposer.
Ariane	Super! Je vais ranger ma chambre. Tu viens Pierre?
Guillaume	Et moi, ce soir je garderai les enfants et vous deux vous pourrez aller au cinéma si vous en avez envie.

Link the following English phrases to the equivalent French expressions.

1) You had said we would go and see…	(a) On va tous aider.
2) I was counting on you to help with the shopping.	(b) On ne peut pas rater ça.
3) I told you the day before yesterday.	(c) Je garderai les enfants.
	(d) Tu avait dit qu'on irait voir.
4) I shall look after the children.	(e) Je te l'ai dit avant-hier.
5) We are all going to help.	(f) Je comptais sur toi pour les courses.
6) We can't miss that!	

🖥 Comment ça marche?

1 The pluperfect

This is another past tense, used for an action which took place prior to something else happening:

Tu avais dit qu'on irait
    voir Hercule.

*You had said that we would go
and see Hercules.*

Ariane is reminding her mother what had been said prior to today.

There is very little difference between the structures of the pluperfect and the perfect tense.

■ Perfect: **avoir** or **être** in the present tense + past participle

■ Pluperfect: **avoir** or **être** in the imperfect tense + past participle

J'**ai** dit	*I have said*	Elle **est** partie	*She has left*
J'**avais** dit	*I had said*	Elle **était** partie	*She had left*

Other examples in the dialogue:

Tu nous avais promis.	*You had promised.*
Je t'avais prévenue.	*I had warned you.*
J'avais oublié.	*I had forgotten.*

Note that in many cases the pluperfect and the perfect are used in the same sentence, for example when:

■ something was planned, said or done but more recent events altered the situation:

Schumacher **avait voulu** gagner mais à Jerez **il a tout perdu** dans un accrochage avec Jacques Villeneuve.
Schumacher had wanted to win but he lost everything in a collision with Jacques Villeneuve.

■ something is done as a consequence of a prior state of things:

Le garçon **a volé** des pommes parce qu'il **n'avait** pas **mangé** depuis deux jours.
The boy stole some apples because he hadn't eaten for two days.

Check that you know your past participles:

prendre	pris
pouvoir	pu
devoir	dû
boire	bu
pleuvoir	plu
perdre	perdu
avoir	eu

 # À vous maintenant!

1 Terminez les phrases

Find a suitable end for each of the sentences.

1) Sylvie avait beaucoup travaillé
2) Les Durand avaient gagné le gros lot
3) J'avais pris mon parapluie
4) Loïc avait dit qu'il viendrait à Paris
5) Les jeunes avaient trop bu
6) Laurent était allé en Angleterre pour les vacances
7) Il a appelé la police
8) Le voleur est entré sans effort

(a) mais malheureusement il n'a pas pu.
(b) pour déclarer qu'on lui avait volé sa voiture.
(c) on avait dû laisser la porte ouverte.
(d) et elle a réussi son examen.
(e) et il a décidé d'y rester.
(f) malheureusement ils ont tout perdu.
(g) alors il n'a pas plu.
(h) et ils ont eu un accident.

Point info

Les Français et le sport

Lots of people are keen to watch sports on TV but not so keen to participate. The attitude to sport has been changing slowly though. In the 80s and 90s most French towns started to build well-equipped sports centres. If you want one, look for a sign saying: **Salle omnisports**. The biggest sports centre in France is **Le Palais Omnisports de Paris-Bercy** – a vast centre built mainly for indoor games and also for international competitions, with a capacity for 17,000 spectators. French people are also getting away from lazy beach holidays and spending more time walking, cycling through the countryside on their **VTT** (**Vélos Tous**

Terrains, *mountain bikes*), surfing and wind surfing, skiing, swimming and sailing. And when you hear some French people say: **Je fais du footing**, what they mean is that they go jogging. **Jogging** is also used.

But spectator sports are as popular as ever with **Le Tour de France Cycliste** (watched by millions from the road sides) at the top of the list and **le foot** close second, and third, horse racing, **la course de chevaux/ hippique**. In the dialogue, Guillaume is going to **Le Parc des Princes** to see his team **Paris Saint Germain**. **Paris SG** or **le PSG** is the only first division club in Paris.

Les clubs français

All French football clubs have their own name:

Auxerre: **Association Jeunesse Auxerroise**
Bordeaux: **Les Girondins de Bordeaux**
Guingamp: **En avant Guingamp** (*Forward Guinguamp* – from a tiny Brittany town)
Marseille: **Olympique de Marseille**
Lens: **Racing Club de Lens**
Monaco: **Association Sportive de Monaco**
Nantes: **Football Club Nantes Atlantique**

Many sporting events take place or finish in Paris every year. Look at the table below:

Calendrier annuel des évènements sportifs à Paris

DATES ET ÉVÈNEMENTS SPORTIFS	LIEUX: OÙ DANS PARIS
Premier janvier Départ du Rallye de Paris-Dakar	Esplanade de Vincennes
Dernier dimanche de janvier Prix d'Amérique (*course de chevaux*)	Hippodrome de Vincennes
Février – mars Tournoi des Cinq Nations (rugby)	Parc des Princes
Avril Marathon de Paris Festival d'Arts Martiaux	À travers Paris Palais Omnisports de Bercy
Première quinzaine d'avril (un dimanche) Prix du Président de la République	Hippodrome d'Auteuil

Fin mai / début juin Internationaux de France de Tennis	Stade Roland-Garros
Juin Finale de la coupe de France de Football Course des serveuses et garçons de café	Parc des Princes Des Champs-Elysées à la Bastille
Troisième dimanche de juin Grand Steeple-Chase	Hippodrome d'Auteuil
Dernier dimanche de juin Grand Prix de Paris	Hippodrome de Longchamp
Mi-juillet Arrivée du Tour de France Cycliste	Champs-Elysées (départ et arrivée)
Mi-septembre (un samedi) Prix d'été	Hippodrome de Vincennes
Premier dimanche d'octobre Prix de L'Arc de Triomphe	Hippodrome de Longchamp
Octobre Les vingt Kilomètres de Paris (course à pied)	Tour Eiffel
Deuxième dimanche d'octobre Course de côte de voitures anciennes (*uphill race*)	Rue Lepic (Montmartre)
Fin octobre Tennis: Le Tournoi de Paris (*Paris Open*)	Paris-Bercy

À vous maintenant!

2 Les évènements sportifs

Listen again at the table of sporting events in Paris, and answer these questions.

(a) How many types of sporting events are listed?
(b) What are they?
(c) When is the barmen and women's race?
(d) Where does it take place?
(e) When is the Prix du Président de la République?
(f) What race starts and finishes at the Eiffel Tower?

3 Un peu de lecture

The old affininity between France and Canada – more specifically with Québec, means that Villeneuve, who is francophone, receives full media attention in France.

Read this newspaper extract and answer the questions:

TEL EST PRIS QUI CROYAIT PRENDRE

Eh oui! Michel Schumacher (Ferrari) fait la grimace : il a tout perdu dans un accrochage au quarante-huitième tour. Jacques Villeneuve (Williams Renault) par contre rit: il a gagné! Le Québécois est devenu dimanche à Jerez le champion du monde de Formule 1, à l'issue du Grand Prix d'Europe. C'est Mika Hakkinen (McLaren) qui a remporté cette dernière épreuve du Championnat du Monde de la saison. Epreuve que l'on pressentait explosive et qui a ravi les supporters de Villeneuve et déçu ceux de Schumaker.

(a) The headline is the French equivalent of a well-known English proverb. Can you tell which it is?

(b) Who won the last race of the season?

(c) At what point did Schumacher lose the championship?

(d) Villeneuve is laughing, is Schumacher laughing too?

(e) What were people expecting at this event?

2 Aller au cinéma

 Sarah et Marie-Claire ont finalement décidé d'aller au cinéma. Elles regardent la liste des films que l'on montre au cinéma du quartier. Il y a neuf films au choix. Elles en discutent.

Listen to the audio and look at the programme of films showing **Aux Arcades**. Then answer the questions.

You will need to stop the audio for each of the films mentioned.

(a) Why does Sarah say that she will let Marie-Claire choose the film?

(b) Can you tell what the two women say about each of the nine films?

(c) Which film do they choose in the end?

(d) Who did Guillaume Depardieu act with in *Tous les matins du monde*?

(e) How many of the films are forbidden to under-twelves?

Cinémas
Arcades

LE MONDE PERDU : « Jurassic Park suite », et probablement pas fin. Steven Spielberg procède à la résurrection de ces chers (ô combien) dinosaures. Les surprises sont rares, mais effets spéciaux et trouvailles visuelles fascinent une nouvelle fois. Terreur garantie. A 13 h 50, 16 h 20, 19 h 40 et 22 h 10.

LE MARIAGE DE MON MEILLEUR AMI : une jeune femme éconduite va tout faire pour détruire le mariage de son ex-amant. Une traditionnelle comédie américaine de P.-J. Hogan avec une amusante Julia Roberts et Dermot Mulroney. A 14 h, 16 h, 20 h et 22 h.

BREAK DOWN, POINT DE RUPTURE : (int. - 12 ans). Pour retrouver sa femme enlevé par un routier, un homme va devoir affronter les pillards de l'autoroute. Un « Road movie » haletant et nerveux, de Jonathan Mostow avec Kurt Russel et Kathleen Quinlan. A 14 h, 16 h et 20 h.

WESTERN : Il était une fois … Paco et Nino qui marchaient sur les routes de Bretagne, à la recherche de l'amour. Un road-movie de Manuel Poirier, véritable hymne à l'amitié récompensé par le prix du jury à Cannes. A 14 h, 16 h 30, 19 h 45 et 22 h 15.

BEAN : un « désastre ambulant », détruit tout ce qu'il touche … Une série culte ne suffit pas à faire un bon film et Rowan Atkinson est loin de Jerry Lewis ou Peter Sellers. A 14 h, 16 h 30, 20 h et 22 h 15.

THE FULL MONTY : des chômeurs décident de créer un groupe de strip-tease masculin … Ni trivial, encore moins graveleux, ce nouveau film anglais de Peter Cattaneo est aussi touchant que drôle. Une réussite … A 14 h, 16 h 30, 20 h et 22 h.

PORCO ROSSO : ancien combattant de 14-18, l'aviateur Marco doit à une mystérieuse malédiction le fait d'être affublé d'un visage de cochon. A 16 h 30.

RENCONTRE DU 3ᵉ TYPE : d'étranges événements se produisent en des points différents du globe. Ainsi une escadrille portée disparue pendant la guerre à la suite d'une rencontre avec une soucoupe volante, est retrouvée intacte dans le désert. A 16 h 30.

MARTHE : un film émouvant et juste de Jean-Louis Hubert, avec Guillaume Depardieu et Clothilde Courau, qui montre comment l'amour peut tenter de faire renaître à la vie un homme qui côtoie la mort … A 14 h, 16 h 30, 19 h 55, 22 h 15.

Sarah	Je te laisse choisir parce que je sors beaucoup plus souvent que toi à Londres. À moins que ce soit un navet, j'aimerais sûrement ton choix.
Marie-Claire	Regardons la liste ensemble alors, comme cela, nous pourront choisir toutes les deux. Alors … *Le Monde Perdu*, non, on reviendra voir ça avec les enfants. *Le Mariage de Mon Meilleur Ami …*
Sarah	Oui, j'aimerais bien voir celui-là, j'adore Julia Roberts, je la trouve drôle et tendre en même temps.
Marie-Claire	Moi aussi, j'aime beaucoup. C'est un choix possible. *Point de Rupture*, non, ça ne me dit rien. *Western*, ça a l'air bien mais un peu trop sérieux pour ce soir. *Bean*, encore un pour les enfants.
Sarah	*The Full Monty*, je l'ai vu à Londres. C'est superbe, comme film, drôle mais sérieux à la fois. Vous devriez aller le voir, toi et Guillaume!
Marie-Claire	Et oui! *Porco Rosso*, je ne sais pas ce que c'est … Oh la la … un homme avec un visage de cochon … non merci, très peu pour moi. *Rencontre du 3° type*, déjà vu … et *Marthe*, avec Guillaume Depardieu et Clotilde Courau. Apparemment c'est très bien fait.
Sarah	Ça j'aimerais bien le voir celui-là. J'irais voir *My Best Friend's Wedding* en version originale à Londres!
Marie-Claire	Alors c'est décidé, on y va. J'espère qu'il est aussi bon acteur que son père.
Sarah	Oui, il est chouette! Tu ne l'as pas vu dans *Tous les matins du Monde*? Il jouait avec Gérard Depardieu.

le cinéma de quartier	*local cinema*	**un visage de cochon**	*a pig's face*
un navet	*a flop* (lit. *a turnip*)	**drôle**	*funny*
		chouette	*great* (lit. *owl*)

 **J'aimerais voir…**

Now it's your turn to say (in French) which film you would like to see.

(a) Say you would like to see *Rencontre du 3ème Type* because you like science-fiction films.

(b) Say you have already seen *Le Monde Perdu*.

(c) Say you have seen *Bean* and that you laughed a lot.

(d) Say you will go and see *The Full Monty* in England.

(e) Say you don't fancy seeing *My Best Friend's Wedding*.

✔À vous maintenant!

4 Un peu de lecture

Read this short article from *Ouest-France* and answer the questions.

Cinéma: Spielberg tourne à Omaha

Avant la projection du «Monde perdu» au festival du film américain, Steven Spielberg était en Normandie, vendredi. A une centaine de kilomètres de Deauville, le réalisateur achevait le tournage de «Saving Private Ryan», au cimetière américain d'Omaha Beach.

Avec ce film, le créateur de « E.T. » délaisse le grand spectacle et les dinosaures. «Saving Private Ryan» est le récit héroïque d'un capitaine incarné par Tom Hanks. Ce dernier fait la promesse à une mère de protéger son fils, la veille du 6 juin 1944.

(a) Where was Spielberg at the time of this article?

(b) How far is it from Deauville?

(c) According to this article what has Spielberg given up?

(d) What is *Saving Private Ryan* about?

(e) What part does Tom Hanks play?

5 Abonnez-vous

Et si vous aimez vraiment le cinéma abonnez-vous!

The form on the next page is for a year's subscription to *Les Cahiers du Cinéma*, the oldest and most famous cinema magazine which, from its early days, has been influential on French cinema.

Fill in the form (but do not send it) and answer these questions.

(a) What was the special offer?

(b) How many magazines would you receive for that price?

(c) What is 120F?

(d) What does **CB** stand for on the form?

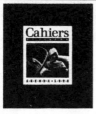

En vous abonnant aux CAHIERS DU CINEMA,
vivez tous les mois les grands moments
du cinéma, et recevez en cadeau
l'agenda 1998 des *Cahiers du cinéma.*

**OUI, JE M'ABONNE AUX
CAHIERS DU CINEMA**
pour un an (12 numéros)
pour 330 F au lieu de 450 F*.
J'économise 120 F
et je recevrai en cadeau
l'agenda 1998
des Cahiers du cinéma**.

Renvoyez-nous dès aujourd'hui cette carte dans
une enveloppe timbrée adressée aux Cahiers du
cinéma (9 passage de la Boule Blanche 75012
PARIS).
*Prix de vente chez votre marchand de journaux.
**Délais de réception : 3 semaines.
Offre réservée à la France métropolitaine.
Etranger : nous consulter au 33-01-43 43 92 20

NOM ⎿⏥⏥⏥⏥⏥⏥⏥⏥⏥⏥⏥⏥⏥⏥⏥⏥⏥⎿
Prénom ⎿⏥⏥⏥⏥⏥⏥⏥⏥⏥⏥⏥⏥⏥⏥⏥⏥⎿
Adresse ⎿⏥⏥⏥⏥⏥⏥⏥⏥⏥⏥⏥⏥⏥⏥⏥⏥⎿
⎿⏥⏥⏥⏥⏥⏥⏥⏥⏥⏥⏥⏥⏥⏥⏥⏥⏥⎿
Commune ⎿⏥⏥⏥⏥⏥⏥⏥⏥⏥⏥⏥⏥⏥⏥⏥⎿
Code postal ⎿⏥⏥⏥⏥⎿
Bureau distributeur ⎿⏥⏥⏥⏥⏥⏥⏥⏥⏥⏥⏥⏥⏥⎿

Règlement :
    ❏ Chèque bancaire   ❏ C C P
    ❏ CB ⎿⏥⏥⏥⏥⏥⏥⏥⏥⏥⏥⏥⏥⏥⏥⎿

Date d'expiration..............................

Signature : ....

CDC HS 07 10 - offre valable jusqu'au 31/03/98

 6 Test: les acteurs

How much do you know about film actors? Test your knowledge.

■ **Test : les acteurs**

1 Lequel de ces acteurs est un
authentique héros de la Seconde
Guerre mondiale (le plus médaillé)?
A Robert Taylor.
B Audie Murphy.
C Van Johnson.

2 Quel comique avait la réputation de
ne jamais rire?
A Harold Lloyd.
B Max Linder.
C Buster Keaton.

3 Lequel de ces comédiens joue dans
« Emmanuelle » au côté de Sylvia
Kristel ?
A Alain Cuny.
B Charles Denner.
C Michel Auclair.

4 Lequel de ces rôles a été interprété
par Sean Connery?
A Richard Cœur de Lion
B Lancelot
C Mazarin

5 Qui est le mari de la comédienne Annette Benning ?
A Jack Lemmon.
B Warren Beatty.
C Sam Elliot.

6 Dans quel film Alain Souchon incarne-t-il un pompier appellé « PinPon » ?
A Le vol du sphinx.
B Tout feu tout flamme.
C L'été meutrier.

7 Lequel de ces trois comédiens n'a jamais interprété un rôle de femme ?
A Robin Williams.
B Dustin Hoffman.
C Jack Nicholson.

8 Quel acteur américan a tourné un film en France avec Jean Gabin ?
A George Kennedy.
B Robert Stack.
C Lee Marvin.

9 Lequel de ces acteurs était chanteur avant de faire du cinéma ?
A Paul Meurisse.
B Pierre Brasseur.
C Bernard Blier.

10 Quel acteur jouait le rôle du commandant de bord du Boeing dans « Airport »?
A James Woods.
B Dean Martin.
C John Huston.

11 Quel acteur était à ses débuts le compagnon de Jean-Pierre Darras sur les scènes de cabarets ?
A Philippe Noiret.
B Pierre Arditi.
C Jean Rochefort.

12 Quel acteur a tourné son dernier film en compagnie de Marilyn Monroe ?
A Clark Gable.
B Montgomery Clift.
C John Cassavetes.

24 | UN REPAS FAMILIAL
A family meal

In this unit you will learn:

■ about French meals
■ recipe vocabulary
■ how to talk about the family
■ how to talk about travelling
■ **qui** and **que** (relative pronouns)

1 Mettre le couvert

 La famille se retrouve chez tante Eliane, Rue du Docteur Blanche, à Passy dans le seizième arrondissement de Paris. Bruno, un de ses fils, fait son service militaire* mais aujourd'hui il est en permission. Son autre fils, Daniel, travaille à l'étranger.

* Compulsory Military Service to be abolished with effect from 2000.

Listen to the audio and answer the questions.

(a) What does aunt Eliane ask the children to do?
(b) What does she ask them to be careful with?
(c) What does she give them to take to Bruno?
(d) What will they drink with the meal?

> *Menu de*
> *Tante Eliane*
> *Dimanche 31 août*

Listen again, several times if necessary.

(e) And now write down Tante Eliane's menu in French and say what it means.

Tante Eliane	Vous venez avec moi dans la salle à manger les petits, vous allez m'aider à mettre le couvert.
Ariane	Moi, je sais mettre le couvert.
Pierre	Et moi aussi je sais.
Tante	Alors faites bien attention à ma vaisselle, surtout les verres. Alors vous faites comme cela. La petite assiette sur la grande assiette, la fourchette à gauche, le couteau à droite et la cuillère à dessert devant le verre. Voilà, c'est bien!
Pierre	On a fini!
Tante	Bon, tu veux demander à Bruno de m'ouvrir la bouteille de vin blanc qui est au frigo? Tiens, donne-lui le tire-bouchon.
Ariane	Qu'est-ce qu'on mange? J'ai faim!
Tante	Ah! J'aime bien que les enfants aient de l'appétit! Je vous ai préparé un très bon menu. Alors comme entrée on a du bon melon et après je vais vous servir une truite au champagne et raisins avec des pommes de terre sautées.
Pierre	Et pour le dessert?
Tante	Ah mais avant le dessert il y a de la salade et du bon fromage et pour le dessert ... une tarte aux pommes!
Pierre et Ariane	Miam-miam!

Le couvert

In the dialogue can you find the French for the following items of crockery, cutlery, etc.?

(a) a glass
(b) a plate
(c) a knife
(d) a fork

(e) a spoon
(f) crockery/dishes
(g) a corkscrew

Link the following English phrases to the equivalent French expressions.

1) You are going to help to set the table.
2) Mind my dishes.
3) Do you mind asking Bruno to open the bottle of wine for me?

(a) Donne-lui le tire-bouchon.
(b) Et pour le dessert ... une tarte aux pommes.
(c) J'aime que les enfants aient de l'appétit.

4) Give him the corkscrew.
5) I like it when children have an appetite.
6) And for dessert ... an apple tart.

(d) Vous allez m'aider à mettre le couvert.
(e) Faites attention à ma vaisselle.
(f) Tu veux demander à Bruno de m'ouvrir la bouteille de vin?

Point info

La cuisine et la nourriture *Cooking and food*

French home cooking has been very traditional for a long time but now people are starting to experiment. There is also the influence of North-African cooking such as couscous-based dishes which are integrated into what people eat at home.

There is a slight attempt to eat things other than meat for the main course. However, the pattern of serving the lettuce after the main course, followed by the cheese followed by dessert is absolutely standard.

An important family meal on a special occasion such as a wedding, a communion or a christening (**un baptême**) would probably have either a sea food dish to start with or **un plateau de charcuterie** with various cooked meats. There would be a fish course followed by a meat dish. Traditionally only one vegetable is served, often a potato dish. Big family reunions often take place around the table and often last for hours. Lots of wine tends to be served.

Everyday cooking can be more sober but even when people are on their own they take pleasure in cooking something nice: **se mijoter un bon petit plat**. **Mijoter** means *to stew*, but in terms of French cooking, **mijoter** means cooking slowly, with care and attention, just the correct proportion of ingredients, making sure that the sauce is just right.

2 Une bonne recette: La grande truite au champagne et aux raisins frais.

Before you can read this recipe you need a few items of vocabulary which are new to you. Some can be guessed but others need to be learnt. The vocabulary can be divided into three categories: nouns of ingredients, adjectives describing the condition of the ingredients, and instructions (here verbs in the infinitive). Once you can read this recipe you can tackle others.

In each of the three boxes below match the equivalent French and English expressions. Some have already been done for you.

Qu'est-ce qu'il faut?

Les ingrédients
1) échalotes
2) beurre
3) champignons
4) jaunes d'œufs
5) feuilles d'aneth fraîches
6) sel et poivre

(a) mushrooms
(b) salt and pepper
(c) shallots
(d) fresh dill leaves
(e) butter
(f) egg yolks

Les procédés (*processes*) **et les ustensiles de cuisine**
7) le temps de cuisson
8) ébullition
9) la lèchefrite ⎯⎯⎯⎯⎯⎯→
10) le four ⎯⎯⎯⎯⎯⎯→

(g) boiling point
(h) cooking time
(i) cooking pan (in oven)
(j) the oven

Comment sont nos ingrédients?

11) épluché(e)(s) ⎯⎯⎯⎯⎯⎯→
12) lavé(e)(s)
13) vidé(e)(s) ⎯⎯⎯⎯⎯⎯→
14) hâché(e)(s) ⎯⎯⎯⎯⎯⎯→
15) chauffé(e)(s)

(k) peeled
(l) heated
(m) gutted (emptied)
(n) chopped
(o) washed

Maintenant que faut-il faire?

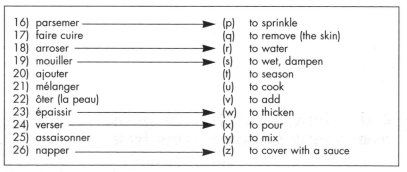

16) parsemer ⎯⎯⎯⎯⎯⎯→
17) faire cuire
18) arroser ⎯⎯⎯⎯⎯⎯→
19) mouiller ⎯⎯⎯⎯⎯⎯→
20) ajouter
21) mélanger
22) ôter (la peau)
23) épaissir ⎯⎯⎯⎯⎯⎯→
24) verser ⎯⎯⎯⎯⎯⎯→
25) assaisonner
26) napper ⎯⎯⎯⎯⎯⎯→

(p) to sprinkle
(q) to remove (the skin)
(r) to water
(s) to wet, dampen
(t) to season
(u) to cook
(v) to add
(w) to thicken
(x) to pour
(y) to mix
(z) to cover with a sauce

Et voilà! La cuisine de A à Z!
Vous pouvez maintenant suivre n'importe quelle recette française!

 Lisez la recette! Now read carefully the recipe for trout in champagne overleaf, and answer the questions which follow.

UNE ENVIE DE VRAI

à découvrir la truite de France et ses recettes mode et tradition

AU FOUR,
EN FETE, LA GRANDE TRUITE
AU CHAMPAGNE ET RAISINS FRAIS

Ingrédients

- 1 grande truite d'env. 2,5 kg
- 3 échalotes
- 100 g de beurre
- 125 g de champignons de Paris
- 1/2 bout. de champagne
- 10 grains de raisin noir frais épluchés
- 10 grains de raisin blanc frais épluchés
- Asperges
- 125 g de crème fraîche
- 2 ou 3 jaunes d'œufs
- Baies de poivre rose
- Feuilles d'aneth fraîches
- Sel et poivre

Temps de cuisson
Environ 45 minutes.

Préparation pour 6/8 personnes.

La truite étant vidée et lavée, saler et poivrer l'intérieur. Garnir le fond d'une léchefrite d'une feuille d'aluminium, la parsemer d'échalotes hâchées et de champignons, y déposer la truite, après avoir enveloppé la tête et la queue de papier d'aluminium. Saler, poivrer, mouiller avec la moitié du champagne, couvrir le plat d'aluminium.

Faire cuire à 200°C (thermostat 6) pendant 45 minutes environ. Une ou deux fois en cours de cuisson, arroser la truite de champagne chauffé en soulevant la feuille d'aluminium.

Sortir la truite et ôter la peau des deux côtés. Dresser sur un plat de service. Pour la sauce, à ébullition, verser le jus de cuisson dans une casserole, ajouter la crème mélangée aux jaunes d'œufs. Assaisonner, faire épaissir, ajouter grains de raisins et baies de poivre rose et napper la truite.

(a) This recipe is for how many persons?
(b) How long will it take to cook?
(c) How much champagne is used?
(d) What must be done to the champagne before pouring it on the trout?
(e) When do you need to add the champagne?
(f) What needs to be done to the trout's tail and head?

À vous maintenant!

1 Un peu de diététique

Avez-vous un bon équilibre alimentaire? Pour le savoir, testez-vous.

Cochez les cases qui correspondent à vos habitudes alimentaires.

VOS HABITUDES ALIMENTAIRES	Toujours	Parfois	Jamais
1) Vous buvez de l'eau tout au long de la journée?			
2) Vous optez pour les fruits et légumes?			
3) Vous restez raisonnable avec le gras et le sucre?			
4) Vous consommez des fibres?			
5) Vous préférez le poisson et les volailles?			
6) Vous consommez des céréales?			
7) Vous utilisez des huiles végétales?			
8) Vous déjeunez copieusement et dînez légèrement?			
9) Vous limitez votre consommation d'alcool?			
10) Vous mangez avec plaisir et en bonne compagnie?			
Mots-clefs: le gras (fat), la volaille (poultry), parfois (sometimes)			

La solution:

Pour chaque question où vous avez coché la première colonne: accordez-vous 1 point; la deuxième colonne: 2 points; et la troisième: 3 points.

Et le verdict:

De 1 à 12 points: C'est bien! Vous avez un régime équilibré.

De 13 à 23 points: Encore un petit effort! Vous pouvez mieux faire et vous faire du bien.

De 24 à 30 points: C'est le désastre! Vous allez à la catastrophe à moins de faire quelque chose immédiatement.

3 Des nouvelles de la famille

Tout le monde est encore à table, la truite au champagne est délicieuse, le vin est bon et on échange des nouvelles de la famille.

Listen to the audio and answer the questions.

(a) Where is Daniel now?
(b) When is he coming back to France?
(c) Does he like it?
(d) Is he married?

Listen again.

(e) Who is Tante Eliane going to Canada with?
(f) Why is she going with her?

Listen once more.

(g) When are they leaving? From where?
(h) When are they returning?

un ordinateur	*a computer*	**ma belle-sœur**	*my sister-in-law*
célibataire	*single* (applies to men	**à cause de**	*because of*
	or women)		

Sarah	Au fait, comment va Daniel?
Tante Eliane	Il va bien, il voyage beaucoup … Euh … en ce moment il est au Japon mais il rentrera en France à Noël.
Sarah	Ah bon! Ça fait combien de temps qu'il est là-bas?
Tante	Oh, à peu près trois mois. Il travaille pour une firme qui fabrique des ordinateurs et en ce moment il passe trois mois en France et trois mois au Japon.
Sarah	Ça lui plaît?

Tante	Ah oui, énormément. Et puis tant qu'il est célibataire il n'y a pas de problèmes. Oh mais je ne vous ai pas dit? Cette fois-ci c'est moi qui pars en voyage!
Marie-Claire	Ah bon! Et où vas-tu?
Tante	Au Canada! J'y vais avec ma belle-sœur qui habite à Nantes. C'est un voyage organisé. Ils avaient acheté les billets et maintenant son mari ne peut pas y aller à cause de son travail alors j'y vais à sa place.
Guillaume	Et quand est-ce que tu pars?
Tante	Eh bien le départ de Nantes est le 12 octobre et nous rentrons le 21.
Marie-Claire	Bon, alors on te souhaite un bon voyage et n'oublie pas de nous envoyer une carte postale, hein!

Link the following English phrases to the equivalent French expressions.

1) How long has he been there?
2) He works for a firm which manufactures computers.
3) as long as he is single …
4) I am going with my sister-in-law.
5) Don't forget to send a post card.
6) It's a package tour.

(a) C'est un voyage organisé.
(b) tant qu'il est célibataire …
(c) N'oublie pas de nous envoyer une carte postale.
(d) Ça fait combien de temps qu'il est là-bas?
(e) J'y vais avec ma belle-sœur.
(f) Il travaille pour une firme qui fabrique des ordinateurs.

Comment ça marche?

1 Qui or que?

These are relative pronouns. Although similar, they have two different functions:

■ **Qui** *who, which, that* represents people or objects. It acts as the subject of the verb:

une firme qui fabrique des ordinateurs
c'est **moi qui** pars

In the two examples above **qui** represents tthe noun which precedes it and which is the subject of the sentence. **Que** links two sentences, making one longer and more elegant sentence:

C'est ma belle sœur. Elle habite à Nantes. Becomes **C'est ma belle sœur qui habite à Nantes**.

■ **Que/qu'** *which, that, whom* also links two sentences, but it represents the direct object of the sentence. It represents people or objects.

Le voyage que je vais faire est un voyage organisé.

In this type of sentence **que** is placed immediately before the subject. This should be more obvious in the next two examples:

Regarde, c'est **le type que** j'ai   *Look, it's the guy I saw yesterday.*
vu hier.

Here **que** represents **le type** (the object). **Que** precedes **j'** (the subject) who did the action of seeing the man (the object).

Regarde, c'est **le type qui** a vu   *Look, it's the guy who saw the*
l'accident.   *accident.*

In this sentence **qui** represents **le type** (here the subject) who saw the accident (the object).

Qui is always followed by a verb, sometimes preceded by an indirect pronoun:

C'est toi qui lui as donné les clefs!   *It's you who gave her the keys!*

In the above example, **qui** represents the subject **toi**. In the following sentence **que** represents the object **les clefs** and precedes the subject **tu**. Note that as the object **les clefs** precedes the verb, the past participle agrees with the number and gender of the object (donn**ées**):

Voici les clefs que tu lui as données. *Here are the keys you gave him.*

☑ À vous maintenant!

2 Remplissez les blancs

In each of the sentences fill the gap(s) with **qui, que** or **qu'**.

(a) Ce _____ j'aime ce sont les enfants _____ sont polis!
(b) La recette _____ je préfère c'est celle de la truite aux amandes.
(c) Le film _____ je voulais voir passe à la télé ce soir.
(d) Ce sont les années _____ j'ai passées en Angleterre à apprendre l'anglais _____ me seront les plus utiles.
(e) C'est toi _____ as les clefs?
(f) Pourquoi est-ce _____ ce sont toujours les mêmes _____ décident?

3 Un peu de lecture

Tante Eliane shows her family what she is going to see in Canada.

Look at the schedule for days 5, 6 and 7.

8 930 F

Départ de Nantes

PROGRAMME

JOUR 5
MONTRÉAL-QUÉBEC
Petit déjeuner à l'hôtel. Départ pour la visite guidée, métropole cosmopolite, Montréal présente mille et un visages, mille et un éclats. Vous découvrirez le centre-ville et ses gratte-ciel, le Vieux Montréal et ses rues recouvertes de gros pavés, le Vieux Port qui offre une fenêtre sur St-Laurent, l'Eglise Notre-Dame, le Mont-Royal, l'Ile Ste-Hélène, le Jardin Botanique et le Stade Olympique. Départ pour Québec. Déjeuner à la Cabane à Sucre Chez Pierre. Dîner de homard au restaurant le Monte Carlo. 5e nuit hôtel LE COTTAGE ou similaire.

JOUR 6
QUÉBEC
Petit déjeuner à l'hôtel. Départ de l'hôtel pour la visite guidée de la ville Québec, berceau de la civilisation française en Amérique du Nord. La seule ville fortifiée au Nord du Mexique. Vous verrez le Vieux-Québec, le Château Frontenac, la Place Royale, la Colline Parlementaire et la Citadelle. Déjeuner et temps "libre" dans le Vieux Québec pour découvrir ses boutiques et musées à pied. Dîner au restaurant La Cage aux Sports. 6e nuit Hôtel LE COTTAGE ou similaire.

JOUR 7
QUÉBEC-CHARLEVOIX
Petit déjeuner à l'hôtel. Départ pour la région de Charlevoix, nous ferons quelques arrêts, premier arrêt aux Chutes Montmorency (1 fois et-demi la hauteur des Chutes du Niagara). Déjeuner à Tadoussac, suivi de temps libre pour visiter ce très beau petit village ou faire l'excursion des baleines (en option) pour les autres nous ferons la viste du Manoir Richelieu. Dîner à votre hôtel. 8e nuit au MANOIR CHARLEVOIX.

| **les gratte-ciel** *skyscrapers* | **un homard** *a lobster* |
| **des pavés** *cobblestones* | **des baleines** *whales* |

Vrai ou faux?

Say whether the following statements based on the schedule are true or false.

(a) They will see skyscrapers in Tadoussac.

(b) Québec is one of two fortified towns north of Mexico.

(c) There is a lobster dinner at the end of day 7.

(d) The excursion to see the whales is optional.

(e) There will be some free time to see old Quebec.

(f) Mont-Royal offers a window on the St Laurent.

(g) Montmorency Falls are one and a half times higher than Niagara Falls.

(h) There is a guided tour of Tadoussac.

(i) Québec is the cradle of French civilisation in North America.

(j) L'Ile Ste Hélène is a church.

Cherchez l'erreur

Attention, dans le texte pour Jour 7 il y a **une petite erreur d'imprimerie** (*a small printing error*). L'avez-vous découverte?

25 SI ON ACHETAIT UNE MAISON?
What if we bought a house?

In this unit you will learn:

■ how to express sadness and feeling depressed
■ the order of pronouns
■ about planning to buy a house in France
■ some legal requirements when buying a property

1 Avant le départ

Toute la famille accompagne Sarah à la gare du Nord d'où elle doit repartir pour Londres.

Listen to the audio once, and answer these questions.

(a) Why is Sarah feeling a bit low?
(b) How does Ariane feel about Sarah's departure?
(c) Is Sarah looking forward to going back to work?

Listen again.

(d) Who is Marie-Claire going to 'phone tonight?
(e) Why tonight?

Listen once more.

(f) What is Mrs Burgess planning to do? (two things)
(g) What does Guillaume suggest?
(h) Does Marie-Claire think it is a good idea?

J'ai le cafard.

Feeling depressed:
Il a le cafard
Il est déprimé
Il n'a pas la pêche (colloquial)
Il n'a pas le moral

Now read the dialogue.

Sarah	Ah la la, je n'ai pas envie de rentrer!
Guillaume	Eh bien reste!
Sarah	Non … je ne peux pas, seulement j'ai toujours un peu le cafard quand je quitte la France.
Ariane	Moi non plus je ne veux pas que tu partes. On est triste quand tu t'en vas!
Marie-Claire	Tu regrettes de ne pas avoir accepté l'offre d'emploi chez Gallimard?
Sarah	Non, pas du tout, je n'y pensais même plus. Non, ce n'est pas grave, je suis un peu déprimée mais ce n'est tout de même pas de la grosse dépression! C'est tout simplement que je n'ai pas la pêche quand il s'agit de reprendre le travail!
Marie-Claire	En fait de déprime il ne faut pas que j'oublie de téléphoner à Maman ce soir. C'est la rentrée pour elle aussi demain et, en général, elle non plus elle n'a pas le moral avant de reprendre les cours.
Sarah	Alors fais bien attention. Elle va sûrement te faire part de ses projets: elle voudrait prendre sa retraite à cinquante-cinq ans et s'acheter une petite maison dans le Midi.
Marie-Claire	Oui je sais, elle m'en a déjà parlé. Elle dit que cette idée, c'est toi qui la lui as donnée!
Guillaume	Et si on achetait une maison entre nous tous! On pourrait peut-être trouver quelque chose de pas trop cher à rénover …
Marie-Claire	Ah oui! Dis Guillaume et qui est-ce qui les ferait, ces rénovations?

triste *sad*	**Gallimard** *one of the most*
faire part de *to inform about*	*important French publishing*
un faire-part de naissance/	*companies*
mariage/décès *announcement*	
of birth/wedding/death	

 Link the following English phrases to the equivalent French expressions.

1) Do you regret turning down Gallimard's job offer?	(a) Elle m'en a déjà parlé.
2) I was no longer thinking about it.	(b) Elle voudrait prendre sa retraite à 55.
3) before going back to school.	(c) Je n'y pensais même plus.
4) She has already spoken to me about it.	(d) avant de reprendre les cours.
5) She would like to retire at 55.	(e) Tu regrettes de ne pas avoir accepté l'offre d'emploi chez Gallimard?

Comment ça marche?

1 Order of pronouns: le, la, les and lui

In the following sequence, the nouns in the sentence are replaced by pronouns:

> Tu as donné **cette idée à Maman.**
> Tu **lui** as donné cette idée. (**lui** represents **à Maman**)
> Tu **l'**as donnée à Maman. (**la / l'** represents **cette idée**)
> Tu **la lui** as donnée.

Word order, especially the order of pronouns may appear difficult but there is a simple principle which can help: **le, la** and **les** are weaker pronouns, in terms of sound, than **lui** and **leur**. They are always placed before **lui** or **leur**:

> J'ai donné **mon billet au contrôleur**: Je **le lui** ai donné.

> J'ai donné **mon permis de conduire aux gendarmes**: Je **le leur** ai donné.

In a negative sentence there are even more words to line up. The same principle applies:

> Je ne le lui ai pas donné.
> Je ne le leur ai pas donné.

In more slovenly speech there is a tendency to rush all the pronouns together and to drop **ne** (which is weaker than **pas**) and also **le**:

> J'lui ai pas donné.

and in the affirmative too there is a tendency to drop **le**:

> J'lui ai donné.

The two examples above are not what you are advised to say but you will hear them frequently.

2 Moi aussi *me too* / moi non plus *me neither*

These two expressions are frequently used. They are strictly direct responses, agreeing with something someone else has said:

Je n'aime pas les départs!   Response: **Non, moi non plus.**
Elle adore les voyages!   Response: **Oui, moi aussi.**

À vous maintenant!

1 Vous êtes d'accord

Listen to the audio and react to what is being said. You agree with everything said:

Exemples:

Statements	Responses
Je n'ai jamais aimé le football.	Non, moi non plus!
Nous avons souvent visité la Bretagne.	Oui, moi aussi! /nous aussi!

2 Chez le notaire

Depuis plusieurs mois déjà, Dominique et son copain Gildas ont décidé d'acheter une petite maison dans le Finistère. Ils en ont trouvé une qu'ils aiment beaucoup mais avant de faire les démarches nécessaires ils ont décidé de s'adresser à Maître Le Corre leur notaire.

À VENDRE
S'ADRESSER À
Me le Corre Notaire à Lanvec Tel: 02 98 7154

Read the dialogue below and answer these questions.

(a) Why are Gildas and Dominique consulting a lawyer?
(b) What would they like to find out?

Read the dialogue again.

(c) How did they find the house?
(d) Have they contacted the owner?
(e) Have they seen the house?
(f) What would they like the lawyer to do?

Read once more.

(g) Who would check the present owner's civic status?
(h) What are Gildas and Dominique going to do?

un notaire *notary, a lawyer who deals specifically with property and family transactions such as wills, donations, etc.* **Maître** *(abbreviation **Me**) a notaire's title* **l'état civil** *civic status*	**l'urbanisme** *town planning department* **recueillir des renseignements** *to gather information/to do a search* **le compromis de vente: l'avant-contrat** *the pre-contract*

Gildas	Nous avons trouvé une petite maison que nous aimerions acheter. Nous avons pensé qu'il serait peut-être préférable de nous adresser à vous d'abord.
Me Le Corre	Vous avez eu tout à fait raison. Il vaut toujours mieux s'adresser à un notaire puisque c'est obligatoirement le notaire qui se chargera de rédiger l'acte de vente.
Dominique	Comment pouvons-nous être certains qu'il n'y a aucun problème avec la propriété et les propriétaires actuels?
Me Le Corre	C'est le rôle du notaire de le découvrir. Mais comment avez-vous trouvé la maison en question?
Dominique	Nous avons vu une petite annonce dans le journal, tout simplement.
Gildas	Oui, nous sommes allés voir la maison et nous pensons que c'est exactement ce que nous cherchions. Jusqu'ici c'est tout.
Me Le Corre	Et vous n'avez pas pris contact avec les propriétaires?

Gildas	Non, pas encore. Nous avons préféré venir en discuter avec vous d'abord.
Dominique	Vous pourriez organiser une visite de la maison parce que pour le moment nous ne l'avons vue que de l'extérieur?
Me Le Corre	Oui bien sûr mais la mission du notaire va beaucoup plus loin que cela: si vous me chargez de l'affaire, je vous informe, je vous conseille, je vérifie l'état civil du vendeur, je peux aussi recueillir des renseignements d'urbanisme ...
Gildas	Pour vérifier s'il n'y a pas d'autoroute ou autres constructions en projet?
Me Le Corre	Exactement. Je vous préparerais le compromis de vente, c'est-à-dire un avant-contrat, et ensuite le contrat si tout va bien.
Gildas	Eh bien nous allons réfléchir mais de toute façon nous reviendrons vous voir.

Link the following English phrases to the equivalent French expressions.

1) It would be preferable to consult you first.

2) You were absolutely right.

3) The lawyer will take care of drawing up the deeds of sale.

4) We've only seen it from the outside.

5) if you ask me to take care of the business

6) We are going to think about it.

(a) Vous avez eu tout à fait raison.

(b) si vous me chargez de l'affaire

(c) Nous ne l'avons vue que de l'extérieur.

(d) Nous allons réfléchir.

(e) Il serait peut-être préférable de nous adresser à vous d'abord.

(f) Le notaire se chargera de rédiger l'acte de vente.

Vrai ou faux?

Say which of the following statements are true or false.

(a) Dominique and Gildas have visited the house and they like it.

(b) They saw the advert in a newspaper.

(c) They have been in contact with the vendor.

(d) They have found exactly what they were looking for.
(e) They have asked the lawyer to start the search as soon as possible.
(f) He can get information from the planning department.
(g) By law the deed of sale has to be prepared by a lawyer.
(h) The notaire's mission is to inform and to advise.

Point info

Acheter une maison

If you decide to buy a house in France it is wise to go through a **notaire**. If you don't know a **notaire** you may know someone who does or you can find one by looking out for a prominent oval brass sign with the symbol of justice embossed on it. You may find that you need a **notaire** who speaks English so that he can explain the details of the transaction to you. You might like to find a helpful **notaire** before you have a property in mind.

If you have found a house you would like to buy, you have to be absolutely sure that you want it and that you won't change your mind, because, once you have signed a pre-contract, **compromis de vente** or **avant-contrat**, there is no going back unless the search has revealed elements which would render the pre-contract nul and void, such as the fact that the property is threatened by some planning development or that the vendor is not solvent.

On signing **le compromis de vente** you engage yourself to buy the property by paying a deposit, **le dépôt de garantie,** a sum of money between 5% and 10% of the value of the property.

Following the signing of **le compromis de vente** there is a mandatory delay for the lawyer to carry out the necessary checks and to prepare the deed of sale. Your financial position and the availability of a mortgage will also be checked. If the search reveals something untoward, the sale will be stopped and you will receive your deposit back. If all the conditions are fulfilled then the sale must go ahead. If for some external reasons you then breach the pre-contract, you lose your deposit to the vendor. On the other hand, if the vendor is no longer willing to sign the contract, **signer le contrat**, then the sale is dealt with by a tribunal. This means that **le compromis de vente** is a solid guarantee both for vendor and buyer. There is no gazumping in France.

À vous maintenant!

 2 Acheter ou vendre dans les meilleures conditions

In the leaflet opposite read carefully the desirable and necessary stages which apply if you sell or buy a property. Some are the same for both parties.

conseil/avis *advice*	**le bien** *the property*
conseils patrimoniaux *advice*	**l'achat/l'acquisition** *the*
on the property	*purchase*
mise au point *preparation*	**la vente** *the sale*
les frais *expenses*	

On the leaflet the first nine points can be referred to as **A** (**acquisition**) and the next nine **V** (**vente**).

Indicate which stage of the proceedings the following statements refer to.

Exemple:

Advice on opportunity to buy: **1A**

Advice on sale opportunity: **1V**

(a) Advice on the price of the property
(b) Cost evaluation (including legal cost)
(c) Advertising the offer
(d) Property evaluation
(e) Organisation of the visit of the property
(f) Preparation of the pre-contract
(g) Preparation of the deed of sale
(h) Search for suitable property in the area

 3 La maison de votre choix

You too have decided to buy a small house in Brittany, so you have been looking at the small ads. Today's newspaper offers 13 properties for sale: Look at the adverts, reproduced on page 278.

à aménager/aménageable *to*	**un grenier** *an attic/loft*
modernise/convertion	**de la pierre** *stone*
agrandissement *extension*	**jardin clos** *enclosed*
une grange *a barn*	*garden/secluded*
démolir *to pull down*	

ACHETER OU VENDRE DANS LES MEILLEURES CONDITIONS

La transaction immobilière notariale s'adresse à tous les particuliers, acquéreur ou vendeur d'un bien immobilier. En neuf étapes, le notaire vous assure un service rigoureux et professionnel, dans les meilleures conditions financières et de délai.

L'acquisition en 9 étapes

1. Conseils sur l'opportunité de l'achat.
2. Recherche des biens à vendre dans la région.
3. Organisation de la visite du bien.
4. Avis sur le prix et conseil personnalisé.
5. Evaluation des frais.
6. Information sur les meilleures conditions de crédit.
7. Mise au point de l'avant-contrat.
8. Elaboration et signature de l'acte authentique de vente.
9. Conseils patrimoniaux.

La vente en 9 étapes

1. Conseils sur l'opportunité de la vente.
2. Evaluation proposée du bien.
3. Examen des conditions de la vente.
4. Signature d'un mandat avec ou sans exclusivité.
5. Publicité de l'offre.
6. Accueil des acquéreurs potentiels et organisation de la visite du bien.
7. Mise au point de l'avant-contrat.
8. Elaboration et signature de l'acte authentique de vente.
9. Conseils patrimoniaux.

Say which property would suit you if you were looking for the following:

(More than one advert may apply)

(a) a small house by the sea
(b) a four-bedroom house
(c) ruins to renovate
(d) a secluded garden
(e) preferably a stone house in the centre of a small town or a village
(f) a house with potential for extension
(g) vacant property
(h) reduced legal cost

VENTES MAISONS

1) Vends **GRANGE à démolir**, petite et grande portes + escalier en pierre de taille. Tél. 02.98.66.39.41

2) **PONT-DE-BUIS**, maison pierres, **2 niveaux**, terrain permis agrandissement, **meublée**. 160.000 F. Libre. Tél. 02.98.77.31.66.

3) Particulier vend **GUISCRIFF**, maison, cuisine, chambre, sanitaires, grenier aménageable, terrain, dépendances. 120.000 F. à débattre. Bon état. Tél. 02.97.44.61.37

4) **PONT-CROIX** place de l'Eglise, maison pierre **4 chambres**, grenier aménageable, jardinet, dépendances à rénover, possibilité commerce. 560.000 F à débattre. Tél. 02.98.71.39.81

5)
Vends maison **SAINT-MARTIN-DES-CHAMPS**, quartier calme, jardin clos, cave, garage extérieur, **6 CHAMBRES**, chauffage gaz. 750.000 F. Tél. 01.60.66.31.71.

6) Idéal pour loisirs et retraite, **MOËLAN-SUR-MER**, aur cœur d'un village proche plage, commerce et port, maison traditionnelle, jardin et parking privés, **3 chambres**, séjour, kitchenette équipée, belles prestations, frais notaires réduit. 380.000 F. Tél. 02.98.37.69.75

7) A saisir entre mer et campagne, dans un cadre exceptionnel, 200 m plage, entre **CONCARNEAU ET LA POINTE DE TRÉVIGNON**, maison plus terrain, chambres, séjour, cuisine, belle prestation, frais de notaire réduit, 465.000 F. Tél. 02.98.27.69.39.

8) **FOREST-LANDERNEAU**, maison **T5**, 5 chambres, salon, séjour, cuisine, chaminée, grand sous-sol, jardin 1.300 m², chauffage électrique. Tél. 02.98.77.66.33.

9) Vends maison **CHATEAULIN**, **4 chambres**, salon, séjour, cuisine, cheminée, grand sous-sol, 1er étage à aménager, terrain arboré. 685.000 F. Tél. 02.98.96.66.71

10) **LESCONIL**, sur plage, grande maison, standing, confortable, toute l'année, jardin clos, dépendances, 1.550.000. Particulier. Tél. 02.98.44.65.66.

11) Vends maison **CHATEAULIN**, **3 CHAMBRES**, salon-séjour, cuisine, grand sous-sol, 1er étage à aménager, terrain arboré, 675.000 F. Tél. 02.98.74.75.45

12) Vends région **PRIZIAC, 2 maisons ruines superbes**, encadrements fenêtres, portes, terrain à proximité. Tél. 02.98.75.63.20.

13) **PONT-L'ABBÉ centre-ville**, vends maison pierre, jardin clos, calme, 625.000 F accès direct jardin public. Tél. 02.98.78.91.49 (heures repas).

4 Le notaire vous pose des questions

You are four different customers. Using the ads opposite for guidance, answer Me Le Corre's question (he asks everyone the same thing):

Me Le Corre: **Qu'est-ce que vous recherchez exactement?**

Client(e) 1 *You are looking for a small stone house close to the coast.*
Client(e) 2 *You are looking for a five-bedroom house with a cellar.*
Client(e) 3 *You are looking for a small house with a secluded garden.*
Client(e) 4 *You are looking for a small house with a convertible loft.*

5 Trouvez les intrus *Find the odd ones out*

(a) In the ads above there is one property for sale which is never going to be liveable in. Which one is it?
(b) Which is the only one mentioning a fireplace?
(c) Which property has direct access to the park?
(d) Which property could be developed for commercial purposes?
(e) Which is the only one which already has building permission for an extension?

BONNE CHANCE!

R5 | CINQUIÈME UNITÉ DE RÉVISION

☑ 1 Les loisirs et vous: sondage d'opinion

 This is a real French opinion poll. For part A pretend you are Stéphane Jacquelin:

■ You like science-fiction films and psychological drama
■ You enjoy TV programmes on classical music, religion and philosophy. You also like TV games shows
■ You regularly read history magazines

Put a circle around **1 (oui)** for all the activities mentioned above and circle **2 (non)** for all the others.

A. Aimez-vous?
(Une réponse par ligne. Entourez le 1 ou le 2.)

	oui	non
(a) Les films d'arts martiaux (karaté, kung fu …). C.32	1	2
(b) Les films de science-fiction. C.33	1	2
(c) Les films musicaux, disco, rock… C.34	1	2
(e) La musique pop, le rock. C.36	1	2
	1	2

(f) Les variétés, les chansons. C.37	1	2
(g) Les livres érotiques ou suggestifs. C.38	1	2
(h) Je suis intéressé(e) par les émissions TV et les magazines sur la musique classique. C.39	1	2
(i) Je suis intéressé(e) par les émissions TV sur la religion, la philosophie. C.40	1	2
(j) J'aime les journaux sur la santé, les informations médicales. C.41	1	2
(k) J'aime les émissions de jeux à la télévision. C.42	1	2
(l) Je lis régulièrement un ou des magazines (revues) d'histoire. C.43	1	2

B Les sports

For part B circle as many answers as you like to find our if you are sporty, or a TV sports fan.

B. Parmi les sports suivants, lesquels pratiquez-vous et lesquels aimez-vous regarder? (Répondez à chaque colonne. Autant de réponses que vous voulez.)

	Je pratique	Je regarde
Tennis, autres sports à raquettes.	1	2
Cyclisme.	1	2
Courses de voiture et de motos.	1	2
Jogging ou athlétisme.	1	2

■ Vous totalisez entre 7 et 8 points vous êtes un fanatique du sport!

 2 Encore une bonne recette, simple et rapide à réaliser

en dés *diced*	**un brin de menthe** *a leaf of mint*
des pignons de pin *pine*	**un four à micro-ondes**
kernels	*Microwave oven*

Read the recipe and answer the questions.

COUSCOUS PILAF

PRÉPARATION: 20 minutes
CUISSON: 5 minutes
POUR 2 PERSONNES
○ 1 petite pomme évidée, épluchée et coupée en dés
○ 50 g de céleri blanc en petits morceaux
○ 50 g de jeunes oignons en fines rondelles
○ 1 cuillère à soupe de raisins secs blancs
○ 2 moitiés d'abricot sec en petits morceaux
○ 30 g de pignons de pin grillés
○ 2 cuillères à café de margarine, 175 ml d'eau
○ 75 ml de nectar d'abricots ou de poires
○ ¹/2 cuillère à café de curry en poudre
○ 40 g de couscous
Pour la garniture: un brin de menthe

RÉALISATION
Mettez la pomme, le céleri, les oignons, les raisins, les abricots, les pignons de pin et la margarine dans le plat et mélangez. Placez le plat à couvert au four à micro-ondes pendant 2 minutes. Ajoutez l'eau, le nectar et le curry au mélange et remettez le plat, à couvert, 3 minutes au four. Incorporez le couscous au mélange aux fruits, couvrez le plat et laissez gonfler le couscous pendant 5 minutes. Disposez le couscous pilaf sur un plat et garnissez avec la menthe.

(a) How long does it take to prepare from beginning to end?
(b) How much liquid is required in all?
(c) How do you prepare the onions?
(d) How much curry powder is needed?
(e) What can you use if you don't have apricot juice?
(f) How many raisins do you need?
(g) What is the mint for?
(h) What do you add the water and juice to?
(i) At what stage do you add the couscous?
(j) How long does the dish need to rest before serving?

KEY TO THE EXERCISES

Unit 1

À vous 1 (a) Bonjour Madame Corre! (b) Au revoir Marie-Claire. (c) Bonne nuit Paul! (d) Bon après-midi Mademoiselle! (e) Salut Marcel! (f) À tout à l'heure/à bientôt Monsieur Jarre.
Comment ça va? Monsieur Blanchard is feeling fine; Madame Lebrun is feeling so so. À **vous 2** 1(c) 2(a) 3(e) 4(f) 5(d) 6(b) À **vous 3 Dialogue 1:** (c) New Year **Dialogue 2:** (b) Françoise's birthday **Dialogue 3:** (a) Estelle and Paul's wedding À **vous 4 D1**(c) **D2**(b) **D3**(c) **5** (a) un kilo de pommes (b) trente-deux francs (c) un sandwich au fromage (d) une bière (e) la gare **5 Dans la rue** (a) the post office (b) the tourist office (c) the supermarket (d) the Citroën garage

Unit 2

1 (a) Alain (b) Claire (c) Paris (d) Marseille **Enchanté de faire votre connaissance** (d) Je suis de Paris. (e) Enchanté de faire votre connaissance. À **vous 1** (a) Je m'appelle François(e). (b) Je suis de Boulogne. À **vous 2** (a) Between 2 and 10 (b) Twenty numbers for each draw (c) 20F for two draws and 10F for one (d) The winning numbers are: 21, **45**, 53, 65, **9**, 50, **11**, 13, 24, 37. (Winning numbers in our grid are in bold type) **2 Je suis la mère d'Isabelle** (a) Isabelle's mother (b) David's (c) no – she's French (d) Mark Thompson (e) in England (f) J'habite en Angleterre. (g) La tante de David. (h) Je vous présente Madame ... (i) Mon fils. (j) Ma fille. **3 Tu as quel âge?** (a) J'ai douze ans. (b) Mon frère, il a quatorze ans. (c) Je n'ai pas de frère. (d) Moi aussi! (e) Tu as quel âge? À **vous 3** (a) J'ai vingt et un ans. (b) Il a trente-huit ans. (c) Elle a soixante-neuf ans. (d) Il a quarante ans. **4 Vous parlez français?** (a) French and English (b) Both (c) French (d) Il est professeur de français. (e) Cela dépend. (f) Je parle français ou anglais. (g) Je parle français à la maison. (h) Les enfants parlent couramment les deux langues. (i) Il parle bien le français. À **vous 4** 1(c), 2(e), 3(d), 4(a), 5(b) À **vous 5** (a) Grand-mother (b) Father (c) Aunt (d) Cousin (e) Brother

Unit 3

1 En stage (Natalie) (a) 36 (b) yes (c) two (d) Yes (e) Cinema, travelling, reading, photography (f) Je suis professeur d'histoire. (g) J'aime voyager.

(h) J'habite à Vannes en Bretagne. (i) J'aime aller au cinéma. (j) Je n'aime pas faire le ménage. **2 Antoine** (a) 29 (b) Paris (c) German (d) Watching films and sports on TV, photography and travelling (e) Je demeure à Paris. (f) J'aime bien regarder des films à la télé. (g) J'ai horreur des voitures. (h) Je vais au travail à vélo. **Comment ça marche? Alors** moi: *so*; **Alors** je vais au travail à vélo: *therefore* **3 Monique** (a) 45 (b) Her husband (c) At the post office (d) A little (e) She hates it (f) Je travaille à la poste. (g) Je parle un peu l'anglais. (h) Je n'ai pas d'enfants. (i) J'apprends le vietnamien. **4 Pierre** (a) 52 (b) Monique (c) At Renault (d) In Dijon (e) Ma mère est veuve. (f) Je travaille chez Renault. (g) Elle habite chez nous. (h) J'adore les voyages et la lecture. (i) Je n'aime pas la télé sauf les documentaires. (j) Je comprends un peu l'anglais. **À vous 1** Je m'appelle Anne-Marie Pélerin. J'ai quarante-cinq ans. J'habite à Boulogne. Je suis dentiste. Je parle français, anglais et allemand. J'adore le football et la photographie. **À vous 2**:

NAMES	QUESTIONS	ANSWERS
Natalie		Je m'appelle Natalie
Antoine		J'ai vingt-neuf ans
Natalie	Quelle est votre profession?	
Monique		Je travaille à la poste
Pierre	Où habitez-vous?	
Antoine	Quelles langues parlez-vous?	
Monique	Vous aimez le sport?	
Pierre		Oui, je suis marié avec Monique

À vous 3 (a) Faux (b) Faux (c) Vrai (d) Vrai (e) Vrai (f) Faux

Unit 4

1 Au pont cinq (a) five (b) eight (c) Information desk. Deck 7 (d) It's in the evening (they say **bonsoir**) (e) 017 **Linked phrases:** 1 (d) 2 (e) 3 (a) 4 (b) 5 (c) **À vous 1** 1 (d) 2 (f) 4 (g) 6 (b) 7 (c) 11 (a) 12 (h) 13 (j) 15 (e) 17 (i) **À vous 2** (a) C'est au pont sept. (b) C'est au pont neuf. (c) C'est au pont sept. (d) C'est au pont neuf. (e) C'est au pont sept. **2 Est-ce qu'il y a un cinéma?** (a) Yes, there are two (they are large video screens) (b) No (c) *Star Wars* (d) 23.00 (e) 45F **Linked phrases:** 1 (c) 2(d) 3 (a) 4 (b) **À vous 3** (a) 140F (b) 99F (c) 75F for 10 packets (d) 85F

Unit 5

1 Pour aller à … (a) 2) (b) 2) (c) 3) **Linked phrases:** 1 (e), 2 (c), 3 (a), 4 (f), 5 (d), 6 (b) **2 Vous tournez à gauche** (a) Dominique (b) A passer-by (c) 500 metres (d) Not at all **Linked phrases:** 1 (f) 2 (g) 3(a) 4 (b) 5 (c) 6 (d) 7 (e) **À vous 1** (a) Et toi **tu** connais? (b) Vous allez/vous tournez **À vous 2** 1 (c) 2 (a) 3 (c) **À vous 3** Q1: Le petit aquarium SVP? Q2: La cathédrale SVP? Q3: Le Musée SVP? **À vous 4** (a) C'est à droite. (b) C'est à 200 m. (c) Non, c'est tout près. (d) C'est tout droit. (e) C'est à gauche.

R1 **(1) Profiles A** Nom: Burgess; Prénom: Sarah; Âge: 28 ans; Adresse: 12
Stella Avenue, Londres SW2; Numéro de téléphone: 0181 476 5656; Nationalité:
britannique; Nationalité du père: britannique; Nationalité de la mère: française;
Profession: éditeur, Lieu de travail: Hodder & Stoughton, Londres, Aime: les
voyages, le cinéma, la lecture; N'aime pas: le sport à la télévision **B** Nom:
Périer; Prénom: Dominique; Âge: 36 ans; Adresse: 5 Avenue de la Vieille Ville;
St Nazaire; France; Numéro de téléphone: 02 40 45 1811; Nationalité: française,
Nationalité du père: française; Nationalité de la mère: française; Profession:
professeur de philosophie; Lieu de travail: lycée de St Nazaire; Aime: les chats,
l'opéra, les musées d'art; N'aime pas: la télévision, les voitures **(2) Une**
promenade à St Malo (1) from (c) to the station, (2) from (e) to the swimming
pool, (3) from (d) to the cathedral, (4) from (a) to the castle (3) **Orthographe**
des nombres vingt and **cent** only have **s** in the plural if they come at the end of
the number e.g. deux cents, quatre vingts, but deux cent trois, quatre-vingt-cinq

Unit 6

1 Où stationner? (1) 2h30 (2) ay /bz (3) a) 2h30 b) 24 hours (4) 15F (5) Several
hundreds (6) A maximum of 2 hours (the cost 8F is the cost of 2 hours in the
short stay car park) **2 Tu as de la monnaie?** (1) (a) (2) 3 to 4 hours (3) 15 F (4)
With the following coins: (a) 50c x2, (c) 2F x 2 and (d) 5F x 2 **Linked phrases:**
1 (e), 2 (d), 3 (f), 4 (a), 5 (c), 6 (b) **À vous 1** (a) monnaie (b) me repose (c) reste
(d) argent (e) argent **3 À l'heure française** (a) **votre** déjeuner, **ton** déjeuner

(b)	Q1	Q2	Q3
Femme		12.30	11.00
Homme	7.00		about midnight
Fille	7.15		10.00
Garçon		12.30	9.00

(c) The woman (d) Midnight **À vous 2** 1 (e), 2 (h), 3 (a), 4 (b), 5 (c), 6 (g), 7 (f),
8 (d) **À vous 3** (a) 4 am (b) 2pm **À vous 4** (a) 5th channel (b) Saturday 9 August
at 2.30pm and Wednesday 13 August at 12.30pm (c) At what altitude do giant
pandas live? **À vous 5** (a) 1 July to 31 August (b) No the Manor is closed at the
weekend between 1 September and 30 June (c) 10 am to 11.30 and 2.30 to 6 pm
(d) From 10 am to 3 pm (e) School parties and groups of 10+ (f) It's free (g)
Musée ouvert **toute** l'année, **Tous** les jours du 1er juillet au 31 août (h) In
French, unless names for the days of the week and the months of the year are at
the beginning of a sentence they are spelt without capital letters.

Unit 7

1 Choisir un hôtel 1 (c), 2 (e), 3 (f), 4 (b), 5 (a), 6 (d) **Symbols** 1 (h), 2 (j), 3
(k), 4 (m), 5 (b), 6 (c), 7 (n), 8 (a), 9 (i), 10 (d), 11 (e), 12 (g), 13 (f), 14 (l) **2**
Quelques renseignements (1) One room for two people for one night, in a

3 star hotel with sea view (2) A hotel where he/she can take a small dog (3) One room for one person in a not too expensive hotel with restaurant and swimming pool (4) A large room for three people in a hotel with a lift (disabled daughter in wheelchair) **À vous 1** (a) Je voudrais une chambre pour une personne avec vue sur la mer. (b) Je voudrais une chambre double dans un hôtel. (c) Nous cherchons un hôtel avec piscine. (d) On voudrait une chambre d'hôtel pour le week-end **3 Chambre d'hôtes** (a) Chez des agriculteurs (b) Pour une ou plusieurs nuits (c) Un petit déjeuner campagnard (d) Vos hôtes vous serviront **Services "plus"** (a) dentifrice (b) chauffe biberon (c) sèche-cheveux (d) brosse à dents (e) crème à raser (f) télécopie **4 Un petit hotel** (a) Yes (b) No, there are plenty of restaurants in St Malo. (c) Yes (d) No but they can phone to check availability. (e) Cela devrait être possible. (f) Pouvez-vous nous renseigner? (g) Vous vous chargez des réservations? (h) Non, je suis désolé Madame! (i) Nous passons quelques jours dans la région. **À vous 2** (a) (inside the old town) (b) 18 (c) Yes, they have English TV channels (d) A lift (e) Between 220F and 330F

Unit 8

1 Quel hôtel choisir? (a) Station Hotel (b) It's convenient, easy with luggage and it's the cheapest. (c) Near the station (d) Madame Olivier (e) More comfortable **Linked phrases:** 1 (c), 2 (a), 3 (f), 4 (e), 5 (b), 6 (h), 7 (d) **À vous 1** (a) Faux (b) Vrai (c) Faux **À vous 2** (a) Café des Amis (b) Café du Port (c) Café de la Vieille Ville (d) Café de l'Europe

À vous 3

```
C Q A D H B G T I C R V
H A P D E O U Y T N H I
S Q R X G L T WT T Y E
H O T E L D U P O R T I
R E G T D F M E D A W L
T G H W A B F P F M F I
A N G L A I S V I L L E
A M G L B I S Q C R U P
B C V N F T H W A Q S F
```

À vous 4 The SEAT Ibiza is one of the least expensive and one of the richest cars. **2 À l'hôtel de la Plage** (a) yes (b) two nights (c) third floor (d) 25 (e) from 8 to 10 am (f) at 11 pm **Linked phrases:** 1 (e), 2 (d), 3 (a), 4 (f), 5 (g), 6 (c), 7 (b) **À vous 5** (1) Lécaille (2) Gaétan (3) Yannick Tanguy **À vous 6** (a) Je prends/peux, Tu peux/prends, Il /elle/on prend/peut, Nous prenons, Vous prenez, Ils/elles peuvent/prennent (b) Vous **prendrez** ... Oui nous le **prendrons** (c) Where there is a will there is is a way.

Unit 9

1 C'est à côté du... (a) Try to find a post office (b) Yes (PTT) (c) A tour of the

ramparts (d) 2 An hour's time **Linked phrases:** 1 (e), 2 (a), 3 (f), 4 (h), 5 (g), 6
(c), 7 (d), 8 (b) **Vrai ou faux?** (a) Faux (b) Vrai (c) Faux (d) Faux (e) Faux

À vous 1

A	B	C	D
1. M & Mme Olivier	vont	choisir	des cartes postales
2. Tu	vas	faire	une promenade
3. Sarah Burgess	va	prendre	le petit déjeuner au lit
4. Vous	allez	visiter	la vieille ville
5. Je	vais	rester	à St Malo
6. On	va	chercher	du travail
7. Les enfants	vont	téléphoner	à ton frère
8. Nous	allons	voir	le dernier film de Spielberg

2 Une si jolie petite ville! 4 (f), 7 (a), 8 (d), 10 (c), 15 (b), 16 (e), 17 (h)
Directions from Pl. de la République Passant: camping municipal **Vous:**
camping ... charcuterie **Passant:** mairie **Vous:** bibliothèque **3 Qu'est-ce qu'on
va faire?** (a) Mum (b) The girl (c) Take the little train to St Malo (d) Dad (e)
What they will do tomorrow **Linked phrases** 1 (d), 2 (e), 3 (a), 4 (b), 5 (f), 6 (c)
À vous 2 (a) The intra-muros (the old town) and places around St Malo (b) It is
the starting place and the end of the train ride (c) No, only in July and August

R2 (1) A trip to England for two (2) 14 September (3) The town and the tourist office.

Unit 10

1 Où est-ce qu'on mange? (a) A picnic (b) The other side of the street (c) 50F
all included **Linked phrases:** 1 (g), 2 (e), 3 (a), 4 (f), 5 (b), 6 (h), 7 (d), 8 (c) **À
vous 1** (a) Chauvinism (b) When it is a question of cuisine/cookery (c) two (d)
The chefs and French restaurants (e) China and Italy (f) one **2 Les repas...** (a)
Fine food and good meals (b) Christening, communion or confirmation, a
wedding, an exam result, a birthday, Christmas and the New Year. (c) 7 to 8pm
(d) Children (e) **Souper** is later than **dîner** and it is also a lighter meal. (f) At the
canteen, cafeteria, restaurant or at home if they are close to their work place. **3
Où est-ce qu'on mange ce soir?** (a) 4 and 7, (b) 1 and 5, (c) 4, (d) 2 and 3, (e)
6, (f) 4, (g) 6, (h) 3, (i) 5, (j) 7 **4 Le goûter à la ferme** (a) Orchards and cider
making (b) Apple juice or cider (c) jams (d) Every afternoon from 1 May to 15
September (e) You need to book **À vous 2** (a) Le 15 août (b) A partir de 19h30
(c) Soupe de poissons, moules et frites et dessert (d) Cinquante-cinq francs

Unit 11

1 Il va faire de l'orage (a) This afternoon (b) To listen to the weather forecast
(c) The Pyrenees, the Alps and Corsica (d) 3, (e) 4, (f) 2, (g) 2, (h) 2 and 3 **Point
info** (1) Bretagne, Caen (2) Lille (3) Strasbourg, Nord-est (4) Poitou-Charentes,
Limousin (5) Bordeaux (6) Auvergne, Lyon (7) Marseille et Nice, Corse **À vous
1** (a) Poitou-Charentes and Limousin, Aquitaine, Midi-Pyrénées, Auvergne,
Rhône-Alpes, Languedoc-Roussillon (b) Bretagne and Normandie, Nord-

Picardie, Ile-de-France, Nord-Est, Bourgogne, Franche-Comté (c) The same as the areas with thunderstorms (d) & (e) Nord-Picardie, Ile de France (f) Pourtour méditerranéen, Corse (g) Nord-Est, Bourgogne, Franche-Comté (h) Pays de Loire **À vous 2** (a) 1) à Dublin 2) à Athènes 3) à Moscou 4) à Oslo (b) 1) A Varsovie le temps est ensoleillé 2) Il fait de l'orage

Unit 12

1 Un peu de lecture 1 (b), 2 (c), 3 (a), 4 (c), 5 (b) **À vous 1** (1) Je viens d'arriver à Paris. (2) Tu viens de finir tes examens. (3) Jean-Paul vient de gagner le gros lot au loto. (4) Nous venons de visiter St Malo. (5) Vous venez de choisir un menu. (6) Elles viennent de voir un bon film. **À vous 2** (1) J'ai écouté les infos à la radio. (2) Tu as fini ton travail. (3) On a mangé des moules-frites. (4) Nous avons choisi un hôtel pas trop cher. (5) Vous avez posté vos cartes postales. (6) S & D ont réservé une cabine. **2 Au café de la Baie** (a) No Sarah orders a draft beer and Dominique a shandy (b) Ice cream (c) No, she is on a diet (d) Sarah (e) Dominique. Sarah paid last time (f) 56F (g) Yes 4F (g) Je vous apporte la carte (h) Prends un sorbet il y a moins de calories (i) Une glace à la fraise et un sorbet au citron (j) Tu as payé la dernière fois (k) Quelques minutes plus tard (l) Un peu plus tard **Perfect tense:** Vous avez choisi, tu as payé; **Present tense:** je vous sers, je conduis, je vous apporte, tu prends, je suis, prends, il y a, paie; **Immediate future:** je vais prendre, nous allons prendre. **3 Au restaurant** (a) A table by the window (b) No, they ask for the menu (c) A children's menu (d) Yes (e) It's only available at lunch time (f) Two menus at 127F, two children's menus and a bottle of Muscadet
À vous 3

	Menus (prix)	First course	Second course	Cheese	Dessert
Luc	127F	Scallops	Monkfish	No	Icecream
Florence	285F	Sea food platter	Lobster	Cheese	Choice of dessert
Vous	170F	6 oysters served hot with seaweed	Grilled scallop kebab	Cheese	Strawberry ice cream

Unit 13

1 Il y a une déviation (a) There is a diversion in 500m (b) 50km/hour (c) Service station (d) On the right **Linked phrases:** 1 (e), 2 (h), 3 (g), 4 (b), 5 (f), 6 (a), 7 (c), 8 (d) **À vous 1** 1 (a) or (c), 2 (e), 3 (d), 4 (b), 5 (f), 6 (a) or (c) **À vous 2** (3) Vérifier la pression des pneus **À vous 3** 1) C, 2) A, 3) B, 4) a full tank of diesel, 20 litres of leaded 4 star petrol, 30 litres of unleaded petrol

À **vous 4** (a) A16 (b) N43 (c) D940 **2 Les panneaux** (a) The end of the area where
the signs apply (b) Blue (c) Red (d) A blue square **Checklist** 1) 3) 4) 6) 7) 9) 10)
3 Les informations...

Accidents	Type of vehicle involved in the accident	Place where accident occurred	No. of people killed	No. of people injured
1	Portuguese coach and lorry	RN10	8	24
2	Bicycle and a car	St Nazaire	1	–
3	Four cars	D940 Calais–Boulogne	1	8

À **vous 5** 1 (f), 2 (g), 3 (a), 4 (d), 5 (e), 6 (c), 7 b

Unit 14

1 L'appart de Dominique (a) Fourth floor (b) No (c) Yes, the view is great, it's
cheap and the neighbours are quiet (d) There is no lift (e) Going up and down
stairs (f) Dominique and her boyfriend (g) The sea **Linked phrases:** 1
(h), 2 (e), 3 (g), 4 (k), 5 (b), 6 (c), 7 (d), 8 (f), 9 (j), 10 (a), 11 (i) **Comment ça
marche** 1) je le loue; si, les voilà; l'à décoré; tu la vois? 2) appartement; clefs;
appartement; mer. À **vous 1** 2, 3, 5, 6, 7, 9, 10, 14, 16, 17, 20 **2 Où loger?**
(a) Her mother (b) A room in the university campus (c) Rent a studio flat or
share a flat with one or two girl friends. (d) She is going to find a holiday job.
Linked phrases: 1 (d), 2 (f), 3 (a), 4 (e), 5 (c), 6 (b) **3 Corinne cherche...**
1) 4 (a, b, d and j) 2) b 3) k and g (although g is too expensive for her) 4) 2500F
5) a À **vous 2** 1 (e), 2 (g), 3 (a), 4 (f), 5 (d), 6 (c), 7 (b)

Unit 15

1 Rien dans le frigo (a) Milk, cheese, yogurts, butter, bread, fish, fruit and
vegetables, washing up liquid and tins of cat food (b) Her cat (c) Her neighbour
(d) Film for her camera, batteries for her torch, white wine and a cake (e) For
Sarah and Dominique's evening meal (f) A pair of shoes and a pullover (g) No
(h) Green (i) Fish counter **Linked phrases:** 1 (e), 2 (f), 3 (h), 4 (b), 5 (c), 6 (a),
7 (d), 8 (g) **Dom. plaisante** Sarah has just told Dominique that red does not suit
her. In reply Dominique suggests that they move on to the fish counter, saying
that she hopes they don't sell goldfish. The French word for goldfish is **poisson
rouge** (lit. *red fish*). **On va a quel rayon?** 3, 12, 13, 21, 22, 23, 24, 25, 26, 28,
33, 36 and 40 À **vous 1** 1 (e), 2 (f), 3 (a), 4 (b), 5 (d), 6 (c) À **vous 2** (a) White
nectarines (b) 1 to 3 August (c) A Sunday (d) In the town centre on Tuesday 12
and Wednesday 13 August (e) Bedding (f) 32,000F (g) Wednesday 6 August (h)
Furniture **2.1** Bayonne ham: six slices; garlic sausage: 12 slices; farmhouse pâté:
250g; Greek mushrooms: 200g; scallops: 4

2.2

P	A	C	C	D	M	N	G	H	I	L	P	K
A	D	S	E	A	P	O	M	M	E	S	O	D
M	S	Q	R	D	S	A	T	E	E	G	M	H
P	E	T	I	T	S	P	O	I	S	K	M	K
L	R	G	S	F	T	Y	M	S	E	L	E	H
E	A	R	E	B	A	N	A	N	E	S	S	A
M	I	O	S	D	C	E	T	A	P	A	D	R
O	S	I	Z	A	H	R	E	T	O	U	E	I
U	I	R	C	V	O	B	S	M	I	A	T	C
S	N	E	R	H	U	S	G	D	R	D	E	O
S	C	A	R	O	T	T	E	S	E	E	R	T
E	T	U	Y	U	H	N	F	D	S	V	R	S
S	F	X	J	V	B	C	A	S	W	R	E	M

À **vous 3** 1) True 2) False: it takes 2.5 kg of fresh peas to get 1 kg when frozen 3) False: there are over 100 4) True 5) True 6) False: only 4 star freezers are adequate 7) False: vitamins are kept intact 8) True

Unit 16

1 Je suis animateur 1 (b) 2 (c) 3 Sports, photography, music and travel 4 Morocco 5 three weeks 6 18 young people and 3 adults 7 With their families 8 Young Moroccans **Linked phrases** 1 (h), 2 (f), 3 (e), 4 (g), 5 (a), 6 (b), 7 (d), 8 (c) À **vous 1** 1 (c) Djamel is the youth worker who organised the journey. 2 (e) Sarah and Dominique arrived at Gildas's. 3 (f) I went up the Eiffel Tower. 4 (a) The young people went to Morocco. 5 (b) You went away with a group of young people? 6 (d) The group stayed three weeks in Morocco. À **vous 2** (a) Vous aussi vous êtes allée au Maroc avec le groupe? (b) Combien de jeunes y sont allés/sont allés au Maroc? (c) Vous êtes restés combien de temps? (d) Vous avez rencontré des jeunes marocains? **2 Je suis né en France** (a) If it was the first time he had been to Morocco (b) In France (c) His parents and sisters (d) About ten times (e) Arabic (f) Three: Arabic, French and English À **vous 3** 1 (c), 2 (e), 3 (a), 4 (b), 5 (d) À **vous 4** (a) 50%: cinquante pour cent (b) 48%: quarante-huit pour cent (c) 65%: soixante-cinq pour cent (d) 32%: trente-deux pour cent À **vous 5** (a) Not much (b) Acting (c) Also a footballer (d) They exchanged their skin colour (presumably they used make-up) (e) Part of the fight against racism (f) At the Real Madrid stadium (g) A friendly match, as part of the Year against Racism (h) Maradona and Weah (i) 1) leurs couleurs de peau 2) une équipe 3) les feux de l'actualité 4) les plus grands joueurs du monde 5) l'aspirant-acteur 6) le signe de l'amitié et de la solidarité

(j)

K	N	A	U	B	M	J	A	K	L	Y	P
C	N	T	R	E	T	M	O	N	D	E	E
S	U	O	R	E	D	F	I	G	H	H	A
O	V	S	E	E	L	U	T	T	E	G	U
L	E	Q	U	B	F	M	I	Y	M	F	V
I	A	S	A	Z	A	C	E	B	M	U	E
D	U	A	D	G	B	L	W	A	E	I	O
A	N	N	E	E	W	S	L	A	E	D	G
R	S	T	U	V	J	O	U	L	U	R	S
I	T	D	E	F	E	N	S	E	U	R	J
T	A	E	Y	Q	U	I	O	P	N	R	M
E	Q	U	I	P	E	X	A	Z	F	R	S

R3 1) 6-d-m/o 2) 8-f-n 3) 1-b-q 4) 5-a-j 5) 9-g-l 6) 7-h-r 7) 2-c-m/o 8) 3-i-p 9) 4-e-k

Unit 17

1 Mon père était professeur (a) It's very good (b) Sarah is bilingual (c) Her mother and her father (d) He died (e) Five years ago (f) Fine (g) Because he is tiring Sarah out with his questions (h) Her room (i) Two years ago
1.2

Noms	profession/métier	*profession/job*
Dominique	Prof de Philo	*Philosophy teacher*
Sarah	Editrice	*Editor*
Mme Périer	Pharmacienne	*Pharmacist*
M. Périer	Viticulteur	*Wine grower*
Mr. Burgess	Professeur d'allemand	*German teacher*
Mrs. Burgess	Professeur de français	*French teacher*

À vous 1 (a) Je dansais (b) Je skiais/je faisais du ski (c) Je faisais du basket (d) J'allais à la pêche (e) Je faisais de la planche à roulettes (f) Je jouais du piano
2 À l'ANPE (a) He does not know (b) He was a baker's apprentice (c) He works full-time as a baker (d) Go out to clubs in the evening (e) 5am (f) In a pharmacy **Linked phrases:** 1 (d), 2 (f), 3 (a), 4 (c), 5 (b), 6 (e) **3 Le contrat** 1) Between 16 and 26 2) two years 3) It can be extended to three and reduced to one 4) Two months 5) The contract can be broken 6) Five weeks 7) Six weeks before the date of birth and ten afterwards 8) (a) four days (b) three days 9) General and technical 10) Between one and two weeks per month
À vous 2 (a) Je m'intéresse aux métiers de la restauration. (b) Je m'intéresse à la photographie. (c) Je m'intéresse aux métiers de la bouche. (d) Je m'intéresse aux métiers de la santé. (e) Je m'intéresse aux métiers de l'habillement. **À vous 3** (a) 3,48F (b) Look at 36.17 on your Minitel (c) Job offers (d) You can look up all

adverts for the last fortnight (e) You can send your CV immediately via the Internet (f) Sales assistants, doorman, confectioner, waitresses, apprentice (in a delicatessen), home helps (g) Secretarial jobs or accountancy, sales, electrician (h) At least 26 (i) You must be dynamic, motivated and interested in information technology (j) Maths, physics, chemistry, economics or management

Unit 18

1 Vous prenez le TGV? (a) She has to go back to work (b) Bordeaux, les Landes and the local wine (c) She likes it a lot (d) To Paris (e) By train (TGV) (f) 3 hours (g) 12 hours (h) To make her train reservation (i) Between 3 and 4pm (j) Her sister **Linked phrases:** 1 (d), 2 (f), 3 (a), 4 (g), 5 (b), 6 (c), 7 (h), 8 (e) **À vous 1** 1 (b), 2 (c), 3 (d), 4 (a), 5 (f), 6 (e) **À vous 2** (a) Ça prend deux heures (b) Ça prend cinq heures (c) Ça prend deux heures cinquante (d) Ça prend une heure cinq **2 Au guichet de la gare** (a) 1h45 (b) return tickets (c) on Thursday (d) 10.09 (e) 10.37 (f) It arrives at Poitiers just in time for lunch (g) No (h) Book her ticket at the ticket machine **Linked phrases:** 1 (d), 2 (e), 3 (b), 4 (h), 5 (a), 6 (c), 7 (f), 8 (g) **À vous 3** (a) Je voudrais réserver un billet pour Paris SVP. (b) Non, je voyage demain. (c) Je prends le train de sept heures cinq. (d) Non, je prends un billet simple. C'est combien? **À vous 4** (a) une soirée (b) ans (c) jours (d) ans **3 Les points de vente...** (a) Vrai (b) Faux (c) Vrai (d) Vrai (e) Faux (f) Faux (g) Vrai **3.2**

A	R	R	I	V	E	E	S	A	R	T	Y	U	C	V	B	M	B	T	A
Z	E	F	G	H	N	M	K	L	O	S	E	R	A	T	A	Z	C	V	L
D	S	I	M	P	L	E	F	S	D	F	G	H	O	R	A	I	R	E	L
R	E	W	A	S	V	B	G	N	M	J	D	E	P	A	R	T	S	V	E
G	R	A	N	D	E	S	L	I	G	N	E	S	D	I	A	S	W	B	R
T	V	S	A	F	T	F	E	D	D	T	Y	U	I	N	G	S	A	N	I
F	A	A	W	E	G	A	H	F	E	S	V	O	Y	A	G	E	G	D	R
V	T	S	S	D	G	U	J	I	U	Y	T	R	D	G	F	A	O	F	E
B	I	L	L	E	T	T	E	R	I	E	F	F	R	D	X	N	G	T
C	O	F	F	G	I	O	K	L	Y	F	D	F	G	A	S	C	R	T	O
V	N	D	U	W	R	M	D	G	T	R	R	M	I	N	I	T	E	L	U
N	E	E	J	E	G	A	R	E	S	F	F	F	U	D	B	F	S	Y	R
G	U	I	C	H	E	T	F	Z	A	G	F	G	K	E	J	G	T	U	A
M	F	D	H	A	B	I	L	L	E	T	D	U	Y	V	K	H	A	E	E
O	G	F	N	S	S	Q	H	G	L	N	S	I	T	I	U	J	U	A	I
P	B	H	F	S	A	U	K	E	R	K	G	K	F	T	T	H	R	D	O
V	A	L	A	B	L	E	L	K	L	H	U	U	D	E	R	T	A	F	U
N	P	O	I	N	T	S	D	E	V	E	N	T	E	S	D	S	N	C	F
F	H	W	E	T	G	G	U	I	T	H	U	T	D	S	E	F	T	G	Y
G	S	D	M	O	N	T	P	A	R	N	A	S	S	E	S	R	S	E	A

Unit 19

1 Sarah téléphone à sa sœur (a) 19.15 (b) 19.05 She will not get compensation (her train was less than 30 minutes late) (c) No (d) To telephone her sister (e) A telephone card **2 Allô!** (a) 15 (b) 01– 48 05 39 16 (c) At the hospital (d) Opening a tin of cat food (e) Not really (f) Marie-Claire's children (g) Get a taxi (h) No she knows her way very well **Linked phrases:** 1 (d), 2 (g), 3 (e), 4 (h), 5 (b), 6 (c), 7 (a), 8 (f)

À vous 1

Names	Questions on the cassette	Your answer
Nadine	A quelle heure avez-vous téléphoné à Nadine?	Je lui ai téléphoné à onze heures trente
Mathieu	à Mathieu?	Je lui ai téléphoné à midi
Chantal et Marc	à Chantal et Marc?	Je leur ai téléphoné à dix-sept heures quinze
Votre sœur	... à votre sœur?	Je leur ai téléphoné à dix-huit heures quarante cinq
Vos parents	... à vos parents?	Je leur ai téléphoné à vingt heures dix
Votre fiancé/e	à votre fiancée?	Je lui ai téléphoné à vingt-deux heures vingt-cinq

À vous 2 (a) A (b) Summer (c) 10 (d) 04 (e) 01 (f) It cannot be sold **À vous 3** 1 G), 2 J), 3 I), 4 H), 5 F), 6 A), 7 B), 8 D), 9 C), 10 E) **3 À l'hôpital: maux et blessures** 1 (g) mal au dos 2 (e) blessé aux genoux en tombant de vélo 3 (d) mal à la tête 4 (b) mal aux dents 5 (f) bras cassé 6 (c) main brûlée avec un fer 7 (h) coupé le pied 8 (a) piqûres de moustiques infectées **J'ai mal au ventre** (a) No (b) Stomach (c) 38.2 degrees (it's slightly high) (d) appendicitis (e) Nothing at all (f) Breakfast (g) 10 am (h) She should be kept at the hospital for observation **Linked phrases:** 1 (c), 2 (a), 3 (d), 4 (e), 5 (f), 6 (b) **À vous 4** (a) Wednesday 19 March 1997 at 8.30pm (b) Dr Friat (c) Backache (d) Salle polyvalente (*village hall*) (e) C.H.U. of Brest

Unit 20

1 Je te prie… Calendar of events (a) Chatting to her sister (b) Will take the children out to the Bois de Boulogne zoo and go for a walk (c) All go to the cinema (d) Lunch at Tante Eliane (e) Gare du Nord: register train ticket (f) Takes Eurostar back to London (g) Starts work in London **Linked phrases:** 1 (c) 2 (e) 3 (g) 4 (h) 5 (b) 6 (a) 7 (d) 8 (f) **À vous 1** (a) Il n'y a pas de mal (b) Ce n'est pas

grave (c) Ne vous inquiétez pas (d) Cela ne fait rien **2 Acheter des tickets** (a)
No they have got some (b) Half-fare (c) Children (d) She needs to think which
kind of ticket she needs to buy (e) A carnet of tickets (f) Direction Porte de
Vincennes (g) Because they may be able to have a ride on the little train at the
Bois de Boulogne **À vous 2** 1 (c), 2 (e), 3 (f), 4 (b), 5 (a), 6 (d) **Linked phrases**
(a) Card A (b) B is for museums and monuments, C is for Disneyland and D is a
telephone card (c) In all RER and RATP stations (d) Marne la Vallée/Chessy
(Disneyland station) (e) Card A (f) For 1, 3 or 5 days (g) All metro and RER
stations, bus terminals, shops and tobacconists with the RATP sign, ticket
machines (h) 45F

R4

1 (a) Work experience (b) Administration and management (c) No (d) It was
eight weeks of their holidays (e) It gave them their first contact with the world
of work **2** 1) Fast food and cafeteria: (c) (b) (d) 2) Telephone marketing and
opinion polls: (g) (a) (i) 3) Leaflets distribution: (h) (f) (e)

Unit 21

On pourrait sortir (b), (c), (e), (f) (g) Marie-Claire is feeling much better and
she will be careful (b) More time and money **Linked phrases:** 1 (b), 2 (d), 3 (e),
4 (a), 5 (f), 6 (c) **À vous 1** 1 (g), 2 (d), 3 (a), 4 (h), 5 (c), 6 (e), 7 (b), 8 (f) **2
Qu'est-ce que tu ferais?** (a) Marie-Claire is imagining what she would do if she
won the jackpot. (b) A large appartment in Paris and a house on the
Mediterranean. (c) Because she loves Paris. (d) No, she would have all the time
to herself. (e) Every morning. (f) She would go to the cinema, theatre, opera,
fine restaurants. (g) All her family including Sarah **À vous 2** 1) J'aurais une
petite maison en Bretagne, j'aurais un bateau, j'irais à la pêche et le soir je
regarderais la télé. 2) Je ferais un voyage autour du monde. **À vous 3** (a) Three
identical sums of money on the card and you win that amount (b) 10F **À vous 4**
(a) Wednesdays and Saturdays (b) 112F (c) 224F (d) 10 (e) 5 (f) 896F **À vous 5**
Winning numbers: 35, 8, 15, 28, 13, 45, 11, 25; bonus number is 12 **3 Un peu
de littérature** (a) She would go and meet her parents (b) In a hotel room at 41
Boulevard Ornano (c) Her journey (d) Nation. Simplon (e) One (f) A cinema (g)
1945 (h) A quest for the identity of people and their painful and enigmatic past

Unit 22

1 **C'est le mien** (a) Over a game (b) He left it at his grandmother's (c) Ariane's
(d) Pierre (e) That it is his game (f) To go and sit down in the living-room and
watch TV (g) Because she says she does not like animals (h) She kicks Pierre (i)
Go to bed **Linked phrases:** 1 (d), 2 (f), 3 (g), 4 (h), 5 (a), 6 (b), 7 (c), 8 (e) **À
vous 1** (a) Non ce n'est pas le mien. (b) Oui ce sont les miens. (c) Oui ce sont
les miennes. (d) Non ce n'est pas le mien. (e) Oui ce sont les miennes. (f) Oui
c'est le mien. (g) Non ce n'est pas la mienne. **À vous 2** Q1: Ce sac est à vous?
R1: Oui c'est le mien. Q2: Ce sont vos clefs? R2: Oui ce sont les miennes. Q3:
C'est votre montre? R3: Oui c'est la mienne. Q4: Ce sont vos patins à roulettes?

R4: Oui ce sont les miens. **2 On regarde la télé** (a) From Sunday (b) It might affect her return journey (c) Good she can stay in Paris! (d) A film called *Ridicule* (e) **Mots-Croisés** (f) Because she is interested in politics **Linked phrases:** 1 (f), 2 (e), 3 (d), 4 (a), 5 (b), 6 (c) **À vous de choisir** (a) Channel 5 (ARTE) at 20.45 (b) F2 at 20.55 (c) TF1: 0.45/F2: 23.55/F3: 22.50/C+: 22.15 (d) F2: 22.40 (e) TF1: 22.45 (f) M6: 20.45 (g) Cable TV: 20.30 (h) If you had cable TV (i) *Mensuel* (j) 'Which school for our children?' **3 Que disent les journaux?** (a) On Tuesday (b) Friday (c) Around midnight (d) 2 November in the evening (e) 10.000F (£1000 approx.) per month for 200 hours' work **Qui dit quoi?** (a) P, (b) R, (c) P, (d) R, (e) R, (f) P, (g) P

Les mots cachés

C	A	L	E	N	D	R	I	E	R	A	S
H	A	U	S	S	E	R	O	R	E	V	E
A	S	D	F	G	G	H	J	U	N	T	H
U	$	A	S	A	E	R	T	Y	U	J	B
R	Y	E	R	T	H	P	R	I	M	E	G
F	N	Q	$	A	Z	X	C	V	E	G	H
E	D	E	A	H	O	R	A	I	R	E	U
U	I	E	L	R	N	M	L	U	A	R	Y
R	C	L	A	D	F	R	G	H	T	M	A
$	A	D	I	M	I	N	U	T	I	O	N
G	T	E	R	S	G	E	R	Y	O	G	K
B	$	I	E	T	R	E	D	Z	N	E	L

Unit 23
1 Moi, j'en ai ras-le-bol!

Saturday	Marie-Claire	Guillaume	Sarah	Ariane	Pierre
Morning	Housework Shopping	**Bercy Sports centre, playing tennis with his office friends**	**Housework and shopping**	**Housework and shopping**	**Housework and shopping**
Afternoon	**Having a rest at home**	Football match	Cinema	Cinema	Cinema
Evening	Cinema	**At home looking after the children**	Cinema	At home	At home

Linked phrases: 1 (d), 2 (f), 3 (e), 4 (c), 5 (a), 6 (b) **À vous 1** 1 (d), 2(f), 3 (g), 4 (a), 5 (h), 6 (e), 7 (b), 8 (c) **À vous 2** (a) Around 10 (b) Car rally, horse racing, rugby, running (marathon and 20k), martial arts, tennis, football, waiters' races, cycling: Tour de France, vintage cars race (c) In June (d) From the Champs-Elysées to Bastille (e) On a Sunday during first two weeks of April (f) A 20 km

run **À vous 3** (a) The tables are turned (b) Mika Hakkinen (c) 48th lap (d) No, he is grimacing (e) It would be explosive **2 Aller au cinéma** (a) Because she gets more opportunities to go out and see films in London (b) *Lost World:* a film to see with the children, *My Best Friend's Wedding:* would like to see it, *Point de Rupture:* don't fancy it, *Western:* too serious for tonight, *Bean:* to see with the children, *The Full Monty:* great, funny and serious at the same time, *Porco Rosso:* don't want to see it, *Close Encounters of the Third Kind:* have seen it, *Marthe:* apparently very well made, would like to see it (c) *Marthe* (d) His father Gérard (e) One: *Point de Rupture* (**int.** = **interdit**: *forbidden*)
2 J'aimerais voir 2 (a) J'aimerais voir *Rencontre du 3ème Type* parce que j'aime les films de science-fiction. (b) J'ai déjà vu *le Monde Perdu.* (c) J'ai vu *Bean* et j'ai beaucoup ri. (d) J'irai voir *le Full Monty* en Angleterre. (e) *Le Mariage de Mon Meilleur Ami,* ça ne me dit rien. **À vous 4** (a) In Normandy (b) Around 100 km (c) Large-scale films and dinosaurs (d) An American Captain who promises to protect someone's son on the eve of 6 June 1944 (e) The captain **À vous 5** (a) Annual subscription of 330F instead of 450F (b) 12 (c) The savings (d) Carte bancaire **À vous 6** 1B, 2C, 3A, 4A, 5B, 6C, 7C, 8B, 9A, 10B, 11A, 12A

Unit 24

1 Mettre le couvert (a) To help her lay the table (b) Her crockery and her glasses (c) The corkscrew (d) White wine (e) **Menu de Tante Eliane:** Melon, *Melon*, Truite au champagne et raisins, *Trout in Champagne with grapes*, Pommes de terre sautés, *Sauté potatoes*, Salade, *Salad*, Fromage, *Cheese*, Tarte aux pommes, *Apple Tart* **Le couvert** (a) un verre (b) une assiette (c) un couteau (d) une fourchette (e) une cuillère (f) la vaisselle (g) une tire-bouchon **Linked phrases:** 1 (d), 2 (e), 3 (f), 4 (a), 5 (c), 6 (b) **2 Une bonne recette** Ingredients: 1 (c), 2 (e), 3 (a), 4 (f), 5 (d), 6 (b) Utensils: 7 (h), 8 (g), 9 (i), 10 (j) Preparation of ingredients: 11 (k), 12 (o), 13 (m), 14 (n), 15 (l) What to do: 16 (p), 17 (u), 18 (r), 19 (s), 20 (v), 21 (y), 22 (q), 23 (w), 24 (x), 25 (t), 26 (z) **Lisez la recette!** (a) 6 to 8 (b) 45 minutes (c) Half a bottle (d) Heated (e) Once or twice during the cooking time (f) They need to be wrapped in aluminium paper **3 Des nouvelles de la famille**(a) In Japan (b) For Xmas (c) Yes (d) No, he is single (e) Her sister-in-law (f) Because her brother-in-law cannot go (g) 12 October (h) 21 October **Linked phrases:** 1 (d), 2 (f), 3 (b), 4 (e), 5 (c), 6 (a) **À vous 2** (a) que, qui (b) que (c) que (d) que, qui (e) qui (f) que, qui **À vous 3** (a) Faux (b) Faux (c) Faux (d) Vrai (e) Vrai (f) Faux (g) Vrai (h) Faux (i) Vrai (j) Faux **Printing error:** In the last sentence for Day 7 of the visit it refers to la **8e nuit** instead of **7e.**

Unit 25

1 Avant le départ (a) Because she is leaving (b) sad (c) No (d) Their mother (e) Because she too is going back to work tomorrow (f) Retire at 55 and buy a small house in the South of France (g) All buy a house together and renovate it (h) Not really **Linked phrases:** 1 (e) 2 (c) 3 (d) 4 (a) 5 (b) **À vous 1** 1) S: J'adore la cuisine française R: Moi aussi 2) S: Je n'aime pas les voyages organisés R: Moi non plus 3) S: Nous aimons beaucoup la Bretagne R: Nous/moi aussi 4) S: Je n'aime pas la rentrée R: Moi non plus 5) S: Je déteste prendre l'avion R: Moi aussi 6) S: Je préfère rester chez moi R: Moi aussi **2 Chez le notaire** (a) Because they intend to buy a house (b) Whether there are any problems (c) An advert in a newspaper (d) No, not yet (e) Yes (f) Arrange a visit (g) The lawyer (h) Think about it **Linked phrases:** 1 (e), 2 (a), 3 (f), 4 (c), 5 (b), 6 (d) **Vrai ou faux?** (a) Faux (b) Vrai (c) Faux (d) Vrai (e) Faux (f) Vrai (g) Vrai (h) Vrai **À vous 2** (a) 4A, (b) 5A, (c) 5V, (d) 2V, (e) 3A, (f) 7A (g) 8A and 8V (h) 2A **À vous 3** (a) 6 and 7, (b) 8, (c) 12, (d) 5, 10, 13, (e) 2, 4, 13, (f) 2 (also 3, 9), (g) 2, (h) 6 **À vous 4** C1: Je cherche une petite maison de pierres près de la côte. C2: Je cherche une maison de cinq chambres avec cave. C3: Je cherche une petite maison avec jardin clos. C4: Je cherche une petite maison avec grenier aménageable **À vous 5** (a) 1 (b) 8 (c) 13 (d) 4 (e) 2

R5 1A Oui: b, d, h, i, k, l **Non:** a, c, e, f, g, j **2** (a) 25 minutes (b) 175 cl of water + 75 cl of juice (c) Thin slices (d) Half a teaspoon (e) Pear juice (f) One soup spoon (g) Garnish (h) The mixture (i) After the fruit mixture is cooked (j) Five minutes

TRANSCRIPT OF
LISTENING EXERCISES

Only the scripts of listening comprehensions or other listening exercises which are not already printed in the units are to be found in this section.

Unit 2

À vous maintenant! 1

Lucien Bonjour, je m'appelle Lucien. Et vous comment vous appelez-vous?
Vous Je m'appelle François.
Lucien Enchanté de faire votre connaissance. D'où êtes-vous?
Vous Je suis de Boulogne. Et vous?
Lucien Je suis de Bruxelles

À vous maintenant! 2

Et maintenant voici le tirage du loto. Les numéros gagants sont le 21, le 45, le 53, le 65, le 9, le 50, le 11, le 24 et le trente-sept.

À vous maintenant! 3

1) J'ai 21 ans. 2) Il a 38 ans. 3) Elle a 69 ans. 4) Il a 40 ans.

Unit 4

À vous maintenant! 3: C'est combien?

Dominique C'est combien les cigarettes?
Sarah Euh… c'est 75F les dix paquets.
Dominique Et le whisky?
Sarah C'est 99F.
Dominique Et le gin?
Sarah C'est 85F.
Dominique Et le Cognac?
Sarah C'est 140F.

Unit 5

À vous maintenant! 4

(a) Pour aller à la piscine s'il vous plaît? C'est à droite.
(b) Le musée SVP? C'est à 200 m.
(c) La cathédrale, c'est loin? Non, c'est tout près.
(d) Pour aller à l'office de tourisme SVP? C'est tout droit.
(e) Pour aller au château? C'est à gauche.

R1
Profil 1

Je m'appelle Sarah Burgess. J'ai 28 ans. J'habite 12 Stella Avenue, Londres SW2. Mon numéro de téléphone est 0181 476 5656. Je suis de nationalité britannique, mon père est de nationalité britannique, ma mère est de nationalité française. Je suis éditeur chez Hodder & Stoughton. J'aime les voyages, le cinéma, la lecture. Je n'aime pas le sport à la télévision.

Profil 2

Je m'appelle Dominique Périer. J'ai 36 ans. J'habite 5 Avenue de la Vieille Ville à St Nazaire en France. Mon numéro de téléphone est le 02 40 45 18 11. Je suis de nationalité française, mon père et ma mère sont de nationalité française. Je suis professeur de philosophie au lycée de St Nazaire. J'aime beaucoup les chats, l'opéra et les musées d'art. Je n'aime pas la télévision. Je n'aime pas les voitures.

Unit 6
À vous maintenant! 2: Quelle heure est-il?

(a) Il est dix-sept heures cinq. (b) Il est midi et demi. (c) Il est huit heures cinquante-six. (d) Il est sept heures moins le quart. (e) Il est une heure vingt. (f) Il est trois heures. (g) Il est onze heures quinze. (h) Il est minuit moins le quart.

3 À l'heure française

Femme	En général je me lève à sept heures et demie. Je déjeune à midi et demi et je me couche à onze heures. Le dimanche je me lève entre dix heures et dix heures et demie.
Homme	Je me lève à sept heures. Je prends mon déjeuner entre une heure et une heure et demie. Je me couche vers minuit.
Fille	Alors je me lève à sept heures et quart. Je déjeune à midi et je me couche à vingt-deux heures.
Garçon	Je me lève à six heures quarante-cinq. Je prends mon déjeuner à midi et demi et je me couche à neuf heures. Quelquefois le week-end je me couche à minuit.

À vous maintenant! 3

Jean-Pierre	Allô oui?
Martine	Salut Jean-Pierre, c'est Martine.
Jean-Pierre	Martine! Tu sais quelle heure il est? Il est quatre heures du matin ici!
Martine	Oh pardon! Il est deux heures de l'après-midi ici en Australie!

Unit 8
À vous maintenant! 6

1) **Sylvie Lécaille** Je m'appelle Mademoiselle Sylvie Lécaille. Lécaille ça s'épelle L-é-c-a-i-l-l-e.

2) **Gaétan Leberre** Alors mon nom c'est Gaétan Leberre. Gaétan ça s'épelle G-a-é-t-a-n et Leberre L-e-b-e-r-r-e.

3) **Yannick Tanguy** Je m'appelle Yannick Tanguy. Yannick ça s'épelle Y-a-n-n-i-c-k et Tanguy T-a-n-g-u-y.

Unit 10

À vous maintenant! 1

Pierre   Je crois que la cuisine française est la meilleure du monde.

Pascale Oui, moi je suis tout à fait d'accord avec vous. Nous avons les meilleurs chefs et les meilleurs restaurants.

Pierre   Vous avez raison et la preuve c'est que nos chefs sont demandés partout dans le monde.

Lionel   Eh bien moi je ne suis pas d'accord avec vous. Je crois qu'il y a de la bonne cuisine partout dans le monde. Qu'est-ce que vous pensez de la cuisine chinoise ou de la cuisine italienne par example? Moi je pense que c'est une question de goût, c'est tout!

À vous maintenant! 2

Michel C'est quel jour le souper marin?

Vous   Le 15 août.

Michel C'est à quelle heure?

Vous   C'est à partir de 19h30.

Michel Qu'est-ce qu'il y a au menu?

Vous   Soupe de poissons, moules, frites et dessert.

Michel C'est combien?

Vous   55F.

Unit 11

À vous maintenant! 2: Où sont-ils en vacances?

1) Bonjour, je m'appelle Fabienne. Dans la ville où je suis le temps est couvert et les températures sont entre 15 et 21 degrés.

2) Bonjour, je m'appelle Jérôme. Dans la ville où je suis il fait de l'orage et les températures sont entre 21 et 29 degrés.

3) Bonjour, je m'appelle Stéphanie. Dans la ville où je suis il fait de l'orage et les températures sont entre 7 et 12 degrés.

4) Bonjour, je m'appelle Alexandre. Dans la ville où je suis il fait de l'orage et les températures sont entre 12 et 23 degrés.

Unit 12

À vous maintenant! 3: Bon appétit!

Serveur   Monsieur-dame, qu'est-ce que vous avez choisi?

Florence Moi j'adore les fruits de mer. Je prends le menu à 285F.

Serveur   Excellent! Et pour Monsieur?

Luc   Alors moi je vais prendre le menu à 127F.

Serveur	Oui… et qu'est-ce que vous prendrez comme entrées?
Luc	Alors, comme entrée je prends la Coquille St Jacques à la Bretonne et puis comme plat principal je prends la Brochette de joues de Lotte à la Diable avec salade de saison.
Serveur	Très bien. Vous prendrez le plateau de fromage ou un dessert?
Luc	Je vais prendre un dessert… une glace si vous en avez.
Serveur	Certainement Monsieur.

*Une autre table … **vous**, un autre client*

Serveur	Vous avez choisi? Qu'est-ce que vous allez prendre?
Vous	Je vais prendre le menu à 170F.
Serveur	Et qu'allez-vous prendre comme entrée?
Vous	Je vais prendre les six huîtres chaudes avec cocktail d'algues.
Serveur	Oui, et comme plat principal?
Vous	Je vais prendre la Brochette de St Jacques au beurre blanc.
Serveur	Et après le plateau de fromage vous prendrez un dessert?
Vous	Oui, une glace à la fraise SVP.

Unit 13

À vous maintenant! 3

Marc	Je fais le plein de gazole.
Sandrine	Vingt litres de super SVP.
Bertrand	Trente litres d'essence sans plomb SVP.

3 Les informations: un weekend meurtrier sur les routes françaises

"Le weekend du quinze août a été marqué par de nombreux accidents de la route. L'accident le plus grave s'est produit sur la route nationale dix lorsqu'un car portugais a percuté un camion débouchant d'une route privée. Sur les 42 passagers huit ont été tués et 24 autres ont été blessés.

À St Nazaire un cycliste a été tué dans une collision avec une voiture et sur la D 940 entre Calais et Boulogne huit personnes ont été blessées dans un accident impliquant quatre voitures."

Unit 14

À vous maintenant! 2

Propriétaire	Allô, j'écoute!
1) Vous	J'ai vu une annonce pour un studio dans *Libé*. C'est bien ici?
Propriétaire	Oui, c'est bien cela.
2) Vous	C'est à quel étage?
Propriétaire	C'est au sixième.
3) Vous	Il y a un ascenseur?
Propriétaire	Euh, non mais monter et descendre les escaliers est excellent pour la santé!
4) Vous	Il y a le chauffage central?

Propriétaire	Non, le chauffage est électrique.
5) Vous	Il y a une cuisine?
Propriétaire	Oui il y a une cuisine moderne toute équipée.
6) Vous	C'est bien 2600F toutes charges comprises?
Propriétaire	C'est bien cela. Vous pouvez visiter aujourd'hui?
7) Vous	Je viendrais cet après-midi si vous êtes disponible.

Unit 16

À vous maintenant! 2: A votre tour de poser des questions

1) Vous	Vous aussi, vous êtes allée au Maroc avec le groupe?
Adidja	Oui, j'y suis allée.
2) Vous	Combien de jeunes sont allés au Maroc?
Adidja	Dix-huit. Huit filles et dix garçons.
3) Vous	Vous êtes restés combien de temps?
Adidja	Nous sommes restés trois semaines.
4) Vous	Vous avez rencontré des jeunes marocains?
Adidja	Oui, beaucoup. C'était formidable.

Unit 17

À vous maintenant! 1: À L'A.N.P.E. (II)

(a) Employé	Quel genre de métiers vous intéresse?
Vous	Je m'intéresse aux métiers de l'hôtellerie et de la restauration.
(b) Employé	Qu'est-ce qui vous intéresse?
Vous	Les métiers de la photographie.
(c) Employé	Qu'est-ce qui vous intéresse?
Vous	Les métiers de la bouche.
(d) Employé	Quel genre de métiers vous intéresse?
Vous	Les métiers de la santé.
(e) Employé	A quoi vous vous intéressez?
Vous	Aux métiers de l'habillement.

Unit 18

À vous maintenant! 2

Exemple:

Question	Ça prend combien de temps pour aller de Paris à Marseille par le TGV?
Vous	Ça prend quatre heures dix.

(a) Ça prend combien de temps pour aller à Nantes?
Ça prend deux heures.

(b) Ça prend combien de temps pour aller à Toulouse?
Ça prend cinq heures.

(c) Ça prend combien de temps pour aller à St Etienne?
Ça prend deux heures cinquante.

(d) Ça prend combien de temos pour aller à Lens?
Ça prend une heure cinq.

À vous maintenant! 3: À vous de réserver un billet

Vous	Je voudrais réserver un billet pour Paris SVP.
Employée	Vous voyagez aujourd'hui?
Vous	Non, je voyage demain.
Employée	Vous prenez le train de quelle heure?
Vous	Je prends le train de 7h 05.
Employée	Vous prenez un billet aller-retour?
Vous	Non, je prends un billet simple. C'est combien?

Unit 19

À vous maintenant! 1

(a) À quelle heure avez-vous téléphoné à Nadine?
Je lui ai téléphoné à onze heures trente.
(b) À quelle heure avez-vous téléphoné à Mathieu?
Je lui ai téléphoné à midi.
(c) À quelle heure avez-vous téléphoné à Chantal et à Marc?
Je leur ai téléphoné à 17h15.
(d) À quelle heure avez-vous téléphoné à votre sœur?
Je lui ai téléphoné à 18h45.
(e) À quelle heure avez-vous téléphoné à vos parents?
Je leur ai téléphoné à 20h10.
(f) À quelle heure avez-vous téléphoné à votre fiancé(e)?
Je lui ai téléphoné à 22h45.

Les maux et les blessures

Marie-José	J'ai mal au dos.
Alain	Je suis blessé aux genoux.
Adrienne	J'ai mal à la tête.
Benoît	J'ai mal aux dents.
Elise	Je crois que je me suis cassé le bras.
Julien	Je me suis brûlé la main avec le fer à repasser.
Cécile	Je me suis coupé le pied en marchant sur une bouteille cassée.
Didier	J'ai des piqûres de moustiques infectées.

Unit 21

À vous maintenant! 2

(a) Qu'est-ce que vous feriez si vous gagniez le gros lot au loto?
J'aurais une maison en Bretagne, j'aurais un bateau, j'irais à la pêche et je regarderais la télé.
(b) Est-ce que vous feriez des voyages?
Oui, je ferais un voyage autour du monde.

À vous maintenant! 5

Et voici les numéros gagnants pour le deuxiéme tirage du loto: le 35, le 8, le 15, le 28, le 13, le 45, le 11, le 25 et le 12 est le numéro supplémentaire.

Unit 22

À vous maintenant! 2

1) Ce sac est à vous?
   Oui, c'est le mien.
2) Ce sont vos clefs?
   Oui, ce sont les miennes.
3) C'est votre montre?
   Oui, c'est la mienne.
4) Ce sont vos patins à roulettes?
   Oui, ce sont les miens.

Unit 25

À vous maintenant! 1

1) J'adore la cuisine française.
   Moi aussi.
2) Je n'aime pas les voyages organisés.
   Moi non plus.
3) Nous aimons beaucoup la Bretagne.
   Moi aussi.
4) Je n'aime pas la rentrée.
   Moi non plus.
5) Je déteste prendre l'avion.
   Moi aussi.
6) Je préfère rester chez moi.
   Moi aussi.

À vous maintenant! 4

Mme Le Corre Qu'est-ce que vous cherchez exactement?
1)   Je cherche une petite maison de pierre près de la côte.
Mme Le Corre Qu'est-ce que vous cherchez exactement?
2)   Je cherche une maison de cinq chambres avec cave.
Mme Le Corre Qu'est-ce que vous cherchez exactement?
3)   Je cherche une petite maison avec un jardin clos.
Mme Le Corre Qu'est-ce que vous cherchez exactement?
4)   Je cherche une petite maison avec un grenier aménageable.

GRAMMAR SUMMARY

Adjectives

Adjectives are used to provide more information about nouns. In English they can appear in front of a noun or they can stand on their own after a verb such as *to be/to look/to seem*:

The *new* school opens today.   It looks *good*.

In French, adjectives have the same function but their spelling is affected by the noun they are linked with. Also they stand either before or after the nouns and in some cases the meaning of the adjective changes slightly according to where it is placed. The two factors which affect the spelling of adjectives are the gender and number of the noun:

un **joli petit** village	*a **pretty little** village*
une **jolie petite** ville	*a **pretty little** town*

In French, *village* is masculine and *town* feminine. -**e** indicates the feminine form except if the adjective finishes with an -**e** in its generic form:

un quartier **tranquille**	*a **quiet** district*
une région **tranquille**	*a **quiet** area*

Adjectives linked to plural nouns tend to take an -**s** but in some cases (as for the feminine) there are more drastic changes. If there is already an -**s** at the end of the adjective, it does not change in the plural form:

J'aime un **bon** verre de cidre **frais** avec des moules bien **fraîches**.	*I like a **good** glass of fresh cider with very **fresh** mussels.*
J'aime une **bonne** bière bien **fraîche** avec des fruits de mer bien **frais**.	*I like a **good cool** beer with very **fresh** seafood.*

Examples of a few adjectives which change more drastically:

Quel beau château!	*What a **beautiful** castle!*
Quelle belle journée!	*What a **beautiful** day!*
Quels beaux enfants!	*What **beautiful** children!*
C'est le tarif **normal**.	*It's the **normal** price.*
Ce sont des gens **normaux**.	*They are **normal** people.*
Ils mènent une vie **normale**.	*They lead a **normal** life.*

Ce sont des attitudes tout à fait **normales**.	*These are perfectly **normal** attitudes*.

Possessive adjectives: For the full list of words such as **mon, ma, mes** *my*, **son, sa, ses**, *her/his*, **votre** *your*, see page 238.

Adverbs

Just as adjectives provide more information about nouns, so adverbs tend to provide more information about verbs or adjectives:

Il marche **vite**.	*He walks **fast***.
Le voyage s'est **bien** passé.	*The journey went **well***.
Ils ne sont **nullement** fatigués.	*They are **not at all** tired*.

For easy recognition of a large number of French adverbs you need to note the following pattern: adjective in feminine form + -**ment** (equivalent of -**ly** in English):

Heureusement qu'il fait beau.	***Luckily** the weather is good*.
Les gendarmes sont arrivés **rapidement**.	*The policemen arrived **rapidly***.

An adverb can also provide information about another adverb:

Ils conduisent **trop vite**.	*They drive **too fast***.

Articles
The definite article

This term is given to *the* in English and to **la, le, l'** and **les** in French. **Le** is used in front of masculine nouns, **la** with feminine nouns, **l'** if a noun starts with a vowel or a mute **h**; **les** is used in front of nouns in the plural form:

À la naissance d'un enfant il faut déclarer **la** date, **le** lieu de naissance, **le** nom et **les** prénoms de **l'**enfant et **les** noms des parents.
*When a child is born you have to declare **the** date, **the** place of birth, **the** surname and first names of **the** child and **the** names of **the** parents*.

Auxiliary verbs

Auxiliary verbs are used as a support to the main verb, for example, I *am* working, you *are* working. Here *am* and *are* are used to support the verb *work*. By its very nature an auxiliary verb does not normally stand on its own, because it is the main verb which carries the meaning. *Working* gives us the information as to what activity is going on. **Avoir** *to have* and **être** *to be* are the main auxiliary verbs in the two languages and are mainly used to form past tenses. Others are **pouvoir** *can*, **venir de ...** *to have just ...*, also *to do* in English.

Est-ce que vous travaillez le samedi?	*Do you work on Saturdays?*
Je **viens de** voir un très bon film.	*I have just seen a very good film.*
J'ai perdu ma montre.	*I have lost my watch.*
Pourriez-vous m'indiquer la bonne route?	*Could you show me the right way?*
Ils **sont** partis de bonne heure.	*They left early/They have left early.*

The indefinite article

This is the term given to the words *a* and *an* in English and to **un, une, des** in French:

Il y a **des** jours où **un** rien me donne **un** mal de tête ou **une** migraine.

*There are **some** days when nothing much can give me **a** headache or **a** migraine.*

Comparatives

When we make comparisons, we need the comparative form of the adjective. In English this usually means adding *-er* to the adjective or putting *more*, *less* or *as* in front of it. In French you add **plus**, **moins** or **aussi** in front of adjectives:

Tu es **plus** fort que moi.   *You are stronger than me.*

Il est **plus** intelligent que son frère et beaucoup **moins** beau. Mais ils ont tout **aussi** mauvais caractère.

*He is **more** intelligent than his brother and **less** good-looking but they are just **as** bad tempered.*

Conjunctions

Conjunctions are words such as *and* and *although*. They link words, or clauses or sentences:

Nous sommes allés à Paris **mais** nous n'avons pas vu la tour Eiffel.

*We went to Paris **but** we did not see the Eiffel Tower.*

Nous avons fait une promenade **bien qu'il** pleuve.

*We went for a walk **although** it was raining.*

Je vous téléphonerai plus tard **si** vous voulez.

*I'll call you later **if** you want.*

Gender

In English, grammatical gender is only used for male and female persons or animals, so for example we refer to a man as *he* and a woman as *she*. Objects of indeterminate sex are referred to as having *neuter* gender. So a table is referred to as *it*. In French all nouns have a gender which is either masculine or feminine and although the gender of the word is linked to the sex of the person or the animal in most cases, there are very few guide lines to help you guess whether other nouns are feminine or masculine.

Le vélo de Paul et **la bicyclette** de Pierre: both words mean *bike* although one is masculine and the other feminine. In this case it is likely that **bicyclette** is feminine because it ends with **-ette** and words ending with **-ette** are usually feminine words e.g **une fillette** *a little girl*. It is not normally so easy to rationalise the reason for the gender of words. It is important to remember that it is the word which is feminine or masculine, not the object it refers to.

Imperative

The imperative is the form of the verb used to give orders, commands or advice:

Viens ici!	*Come here!* (order)
Roulez à droite.	*Drive on the right.* (command)
Faites attention en traversant la rue.	*Be careful when you cross the road.* (advice)
Écoutons les informations.	*Let's listen to the news.*
Regarde la télé.	*Watch TV.*
N'attrape pas froid!	*Don't catch a cold!*

The imperative is used for notices everywhere to direct or guide our actions:

Poussez! *Push!*	**Tirez!** *Pull!*
Cochez les cases. *Tick the boxes.*	**Ralentissez!** *Slow down!*

Infinitive

The infinitive is the basic form of the verb. This is the form that you will find in the dictionary. In English the infinitive is usually accompanied by the word *to*, e.g. *to go*, *to play*.

In French the infinitive form of a verb is noticeable by its ending. There are three major groups of verbs: **-er** verbs (ending in **-er**: **chercher**, **regarder**, **manger**), **-ir** verbs (ending in **-ir**: **choisir**, **finir**) and **-re** and **-oir** verbs (ending in **-re**: **prendre**, **attendre** or **-oir**: **vouloir**, **pouvoir**).

Verbs are used in the infinitive in two particular types of circumstances:

Je vais **acheter** du fromage.	*I am going to buy some cheese.*

A second verb is always in the infinitive, except when the first verb is **avoir** or **être**. A verb following a preposition such as **à**, **de**, **sans**, etc is always in the infinitive form.

J'ai passé toute la journée à **ranger** mes placards	*I spent the whole day **tidying up** my cupboards.*

Nouns

Nouns are words like **maison** *house*, **pain** *bread*, **beauté** *beauty*. A useful test of a noun is whether you can put **le, la** or **les** *the* in front of it.

Object

The term object expresses the 'receiving end' relationship of a noun and a verb. So, for instance **le facteur** *the postman* is said to be the object at the receiving end of the biting in the sentence:

Le chien a mordu **le facteur**.	*The dog bit **the postman**.*
J'ai donné **des fleurs** à **ma mère**.	*I gave **flowers** to **my mother**.*

In this particular example **des fleurs** is referred to as the direct object because there is nothing between it and the verb, and **ma mère** is referred to as the indirect object because it is linked to the verb with a preposition (**à, de**, etc).

It is important to know whether a noun is a direct or indirect object when it comes to using a pronoun to replace the noun.

Some verbs don't need an object:

Le chien a aboyé.	*The dog barked.*

Past participle

This is the name for the part of the verb which follows the auxiliary verbs **avoir** and **être** in the perfect and pluperfect tenses. Verbs ending with **-er** in the infinitive tend to have a past participle ending with **-é**. Other endings for past participles are **-i** for most **-ir** verbs, **-u** for most **-oir** verbs and **-is** for most **-re** verbs:

J'ai **regardé** la télé. (**regarder**, *to watch*)
Yannick a **fini** son travail. (**finir**, *to finish*)
Les garçons ont **voulu** partir en Angleterre. (**vouloir**, *to want*)
Ariane a **mis** le couvert. (**mettre**, *to put / to set the table*)

Prepositions

Words like **à** *at*, **avec** *with*, **de** *of the*, **dans** *in*, **chez** *at* someone's house, **pour** *for*, **sans** *without*, **sous** *under*, **sur** *on* are called prepositions. Prepositions often tell us about positions or relationships. They are normally followed by a noun or pronoun:

Ton livre est **sur** la table.	*Your book is **on** the table.*
Il a laissé son parapluie **dans** le train.	*He left his umbrella **in** the train.*
Voici un cadeau **pour** toi.	*This present is **for** you.*
Elle est sortie **avec** son copain.	*She went out **with** her boyfriend.*

Present participle

The part of a French verb which is often equivalent to -*ing* in English:

Ils sifflent en **travaillant**.	*They whistle while **working**.*
En **réfléchissant** bien ...	***Thinking** about it ...*
La chance **aidant** il a réussi son examen.	*With **the help of** luck he has passed his exam.*

Pronouns

Pronouns fulfil a similar function to nouns and often stand in the place of nouns which have already been mentioned:

La **maison** a plus de 200 ans.	*The **house** is over 200 years old.*
Elle est très belle.	***It** is very beautiful.*

(*House* is the noun and *it* is the pronoun.)

TABLE OF PRONOUNS

Subject pronouns	Reflexive pronouns	Direct object pronouns	Indirect object pronouns	Emphatic pronouns
je	me/m'	me/m'	me/m'	moi
tu	te/t'	te/t'	te/t'	toi
il	se/s'	le/l'	lui	lui
elle	se/s'	la/l'	lui	elle
on	se/s'			soi
nous	nous	nous	nous	nous
vous	vous	vous	vous	vous
ils	se/s'	les	leur	eux
elles	se/s'	les	leur	elles

For more explanations of pronouns, please refer to the following sections of the book: Unit 12 page 119 (emphatic pronouns), Unit 14 page 141 and Unit 19 page 203 (indirect object pronouns), Unit 22 page 238 (possessive pronouns) and Unit 25 page 271 (order of pronouns). For relative pronouns see relative clauses.

Reflexive verbs

When the subject and the object of a verb are one and the same, the verb is said to be reflexive:

Jean **se lève** à 6 heures.	*John **gets (himself) up** at 6 am.*
Je **me lave** bien.	*I wash **myself** thoroughly.*
Florence **s'est blessée**.	*Florence **hurt herself**.*

In French nearly all verbs can be reflexive if they are preceded by a reflexive pronoun:

Il a lavé sa chemise.	*He has washed his shirt.*
Il **s'est lavé** les mains.	*He **has washed his (own)** hands.*
Je regarde la télé.	*I watch TV.*
Je **me regarde** dans le mirroir.	*I **look at myself** in the mirror.*

When reflexive verbs are used in the perfect tense, they are always used with **être**. But when the same verb is not in its reflexive form, it takes **avoir** in the perfect tense.

Hélène **a coupé** du bois.	*Helen cut some wood.*
Hélène **s'est coupé** la main avec la scie.	*Helen cut her hand with the saw.*
J'**ai vu** la télé.	*I saw the TV.*
Je **me suis vue** à la télé.	*I saw myself on TV.*

Relative clauses and relative pronouns

A relative pronoun such as **que** *which/that*, or **qui** *who* can be used to provide more information about a noun which has just been mentioned. The resulting clause is called a relative clause:

Je connais la personne **qui habite à côté de chez toi**.
*I know the person **who lives next door to you**.*
La voiture **que je conduis** a presque dix ans.
*The car **(which) I drive** is nearly ten years old.*

(In French it is not possible to omit the relative pronoun **que**.) See page 265 for more about relative pronouns

Subject

The term 'subject' expresses a relationship between a noun and a verb. The subject is the person or thing doing the action, as here for instance:

Le chien a mordu le facteur.   ***The dog** bit the postman.*

Because it is the dog that does the biting, the dog is said to be the subject of the verb **mordre** *to bite*.

Superlatives

The superlative is used for the most extreme version of a comparison:

Ce magasin est **le moins cher** de tous.
*This shop is **the cheapest** of all.*
C'est **la plus belle** femme du monde.
*She is **the most beautiful** woman in the world.*

Le champion du monde de Formule Un, c'est **le meilleur** pilote du monde.
*The Formula One champion is **the best** driver in the world.*

See also page 154.

Tense

Most languages use changes in the verb form to indicate an aspect of time. These changes in the verb are referred to as 'tense', and the tense may be present, past or future. Tenses are often reinforced with expressions of time:

Past: Hier je suis allé à Londres. *Yesterday I went to London.*
Present Aujourd'hui je reste à la maison. *Today I am staying at home.*
Future: Demain je prendrai l'avion pour Berlin. *Tomorrow I'll be flying to Berlin.*

The course introduces verbs in the present tense. This includes the subjunctive (see pages 188 and 204) – a verbal form referred to as a 'mood', mostly used in the present to express regrets, doubts and uncertainties. Several past tenses are used throughout the course: the perfect tense (pages 115, 164 and 215), the imperfect (page 175) and the pluperfect (page 248). The future tense also features in the course (pages 107).

The conditional tense (pages 72 and 228) is used to indicate that if certain conditions were fulfilled something else would happen.

Verbs

Verbs often communicate actions, states and sensations. So, for instance, the verb **jouer** *to play* expresses an action, the verb **exister** *to exist* expresses a state and the verb **voir** *to see* expresses a sensation. A verb may also be defined by its role in the sentence or clause. It usually has a subject:

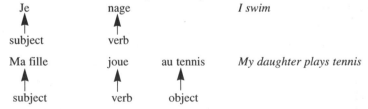

Irregular verbs

Life would be easier if all verbs behaved in a regular fashion. Unfortunately, all European languages have verbs which do not follow a set pattern and which are therefore commonly referred to as irregular verbs

There are 30 useful verbs in the verb table which follows. Most are irregular but, all the same, most can be used as a pattern for a few other verbs.

VERB TABLES

Trente verbes utiles (*Thirty useful verbs*)

1) Four regular verbs (with subject pronouns: **je, tu, il, elle, on, nous vous, ils, elles**)

Parler *to speak, to talk* Past participle: **parlé** Present participle: **parlant**

Present indicative *Présent de l'indicatif*	Perfect *Passé composé*	Imperfect *Imparfait*	Conditional *Conditionnel*	Future *Futur*	Present subjunctive *Présent du subjonctif*	Imperative *Impératif*
je parle	j'ai parlé	je parlais	je parlerais	je parlerai	(que) je parle	
tu parles	tu as parlé	tu parlais	tu parlerais	tu parleras	tu parles	parle
il/elle parle	il a parlé	il parlait	il parlerait	il parlera	il parle	
nous parlons	nous avons parlé	nous parlions	nous parlerions	nous parlerons	nous parlions	parlons
vous parlez	vous avez parlé	vous parliez	vous parleriez	vous parlerez	vous parliez	parlez
ils/elles parlent	ils ont parlé	ils parlaient	ils parleraient	ils parleront	ils parlent	

Remplir *to fill* Past participle: **rempli** Present participle: **remplissant**

Present indicative *Présent de l'indicatif*	Perfect *Passé composé*	Imperfect *Imparfait*	Conditional *Conditionnel*	Future *Futur*	Present subjunctive *Présent du subjonctif*	Imperative *Impératif*
je remplis	j'ai rempli	je remplissais	je remplirais	je remplirai	(que) je remplisse	
tu remplis	tu as rempli	tu remplissais	tu remplirais	tu rempliras	tu remplisses	remplis
il/elle remplit	il a rempli	il remplissait	il remplirait	il remplira	il remplisse	
nous remplissons	nous avons rempli	nous remplissions	nous remplirions	nous remplirons	nous remplissions	remplissons
vous remplissez	vous avez rempli	vous remplissiez	vous rempliriez	vous remplirez	vous remplissiez	remplissez
ils/elles remplissent	ils ont rempli	ils remplissaient	ils rempliraient	ils rempliront	ils remplissent	

Vendre *to sell* Past participle: **vendu** Present participle: **vendant**

Present indicative	Perfect	Imperfect	Conditional	Future	Present subjunctive	Imperative
je vends	j'ai vendu	je vendais	je vendrais	je vendrai	(que) je vende	
tu vends	tu as vendu	tu vendais	tu vendrais	tu vendras	tu vendes	vends
il/elle vend	il a vendu	il vendait	il vendrait	il vendra	il vende	
nous vendons	nous avons vendu	nous vendions	nous vendrions	nous vendrons	nous vendions	vendons
vous vendez	vous avez vendu	vous vendiez	vous vendriez	vous vendrez	vous vendiez	vendez
ils/elles vendent	ils ont vendu	ils vendaient	ils vendraient	ils vendront	ils vendent	

Se lever *to get up* Past participle: **levé** Present participle: **levant**. Note that there is an accent on the first **e** of **lever** when the following syllable has a neutral sound, e.g. **je me lève, je me lèverai**

Present indicative	Perfect	Imperfect	Conditional	Future	Present subjunctive	Imperative
je me lève	je me suis levé(e)	je me levais	je me lèverais	je me lèverai	(que) je me lève	
tu te lèves	tu t'es levé(e)	tu te levais	tu te lèverais	tu te lèveras	tu te lèves	lève-toi
il/elle se lève	il(elle) s'est levé(e)	il se levait	il se lèverait	il se lèvera	il se lève	
nous nous levons	nous nous sommes levés(es)	nous nous levions	nous nous lèverions	nous nous lèverons	nous nous levions	levons-nous
vous vous levez	vous vous êtes levé(s)(es)(e)	vous vous leviez	vous vous lèveriez	vous vous lèverez	vous vous leviez	levez-vous
ils/elles se lèvent	ils se sont levés	ils se levaient	ils se lèveraient	ils se lèveront	ils se lèvent	
		elles se sont levées				

2) Twenty-six irregular verbs

Aller *to go* Past participle: **allé** Present participle: **allant**

Present indicative	Perfect	Imperfect	Conditional	Future	Present subjunctive	Imperative
je vais	suis allé(e)	allais	irais	irai	aille	
tu vas	es allé(e)	allais	irais	iras	ailles	va
il/elle va	est allé(e)	allait	irait	ira	aille	
nous allons	sommes allés(e)	allions	irions	irons	allions	allons
vous allez	êtes allé(e)(s) (es)	alliez	iriez	irez	alliez	allez
ils/elles vont	sont allés(es)	allaient	iraient	iront	aillent	

S'asseoir *to sit* **assis** – **asseyant**

Present indicative	Perfect	Imperfect	Conditional	Future	Present subjunctive	Imperative
je m'assieds	me suis assis(e)	m'asseyais	m'assiérais	m'assiérai	m'asseye	
tu t'assieds	t'es assis(e)	t'asseyais	t'assiérais	t'assiéras	t'asseyes	assieds-toi
il/elle s'assied	s'est assis(e)	s'asseyait	s'assiérait	s'assiéra	s'asseye	
nous nous asseyons	nous sommes assis(es)	nous asseyions	nous assiérions	nous assiérons	nous asseyions	asseyons-nous
vous vous asseyez	vous êtes assis (e)(es)	vous asseyiez	vous assiériez	vous assiérez	vous asseyiez	asseyez-vous
ils/elles s'asseyent	se sont assis(es)	s'asseyaient	s'assiéraient	s'assiéront	s'asseyent	

Avoir *to have*: eu – ayant

Present indicative	Perfect	Imperfect	Conditional	Future	Present subjunctive	Imperative
j'ai	ai eu	avais	aurais	aurai	aie	
tu as	as eu	avais	aurais	auras	aies	aie
il/elle a	a eu	avait	aurait	aura	ait	
nous avons	avons eu	avions	aurions	aurons	ayons	ayons
vous avez	avez eu	aviez	auriez	aurez	ayez	ayez
ils/elles ont	ont eu	avaient	auraient	auront	aient	

Boire *to drink*: bu – buvant

Present indicative	Perfect	Imperfect	Conditional	Future	Present subjunctive	Imperative
je bois	ai bu	buvais	boirais	boirai	boive	
tu bois	as bu	buvais	boirais	boiras	boives	bois
il/elle boit	a bu	buvait	boirait	boira	boive	
nous buvons	avons bu	buvions	boirions	boirons	buvions	buvons
vous buvez	avez bu	buviez	boiriez	boirez	buviez	buvez
ils/elles boivent	ont bu	buvaient	boiraient	boiront	boivent	

Commencer *to begin*: commencé – commençant (ç is necessary to keep the sound /s/ before a, o or u)

Present indicative	Perfect	Imperfect	Conditional	Future	Present subjunctive	Imperative
je commence	ai commencé	commençais	commencerais	commencerai	commence	
tu commences	as commencé	commençais	commencerais	commenceras	commences	commence
il/elle commence	a commencé	commençait	commencerait	commencera	commence	
nous commençons	avons commencé	commencions	commencerions	commencerons	commencions	commençons
vous commencez	avez commencé	commenciez	commenceriez	commencerez	commenciez	commencez
ils/elles commencent	ont commencé	commençaient	commenceraient	commenceront	commencent	

Conduire *to drive*: conduit – conduisant

Present indicative	Perfect	Imperfect	Conditional	Future	Present subjunctive	Imperative
je conduis	ai conduit	conduisais	conduirais	conduirai	conduise	
tu conduis	as conduit	conduisais	conduirais	conduiras	conduises	conduis
il/elle conduit	a conduit	conduisait	conduirait	conduira	conduise	
nous conduisons	avons conduit	conduisions	conduirions	conduirons	conduisions	conduisons
vous conduisez	avez conduit	conduisiez	conduiriez	conduirez	conduisiez	conduisez
ils/elles conduisent	ont conduit	conduisaient	conduiraient	conduiront	conduisent	

Connaître *to know:* **connu – connaissant**

je connais	ai connu	connaissais	connaîtrais	connaîtrai	connaisse	connais
tu connais	as connu	connaissais	connaîtrais	connaîtras	connaisses	
il/elle connaît	a connu	connaissait	connaîtrait	connaîtra	connaisse	
nous connaissons	avons connu	connaissions	connaîtrions	connaîtrons	connaissions	connaissons
vous connaissez	avez connu	connaissiez	connaîtriez	connaîtrez	connaissiez	connaissez
ils/elles connaissent	ont connu	connaissaient	connaîtraient	connaîtront	connaissent	

Croire *to believe:* **cru – croyant**

je crois	ai cru	croyais	croirais	croirai	croie	crois
tu crois	as cru	croyais	croirais	croiras	croies	
il/elle croit	a cru	croyait	croirait	croira	croie	
nous croyons	avons cru	croyions	croirions	croirons	croyions	croyons
vous croyez	avez cru	croyiez	croiriez	croirez	croyiez	croyez
ils/elles croient	ont cru	croyaient	croiraient	croiront	croient	

Devoir *to have to (I must):* **dû – devant**

je dois	ai dû	devais	devrais	devrai	doive	dois
tu dois	as dû	devais	devrais	devras	doives	
il/elle doit	a dû	devait	devrait	devra	doive	
nous devons	avons dû	devions	devrions	devrons	devions	devons
vous devez	avez dû	deviez	devriez	devrez	deviez	devez
ils/elles doivent	ont dû	devaient	devraient	devront	doivent	

Dire *to say:* **dit – disant**

je dis	ai dit	disais	dirais	dirai	dise	dis
tu dis	as dit	disais	dirais	diras	dises	
il/elle dit	a dit	disait	dirait	dira	dise	
nous disons	avons dit	disions	dirions	dirons	disions	disons
vous dites	avez dit	disiez	diriez	direz	disiez	dites
ils/elles disent	ont dit	disaient	diraient	diront	disent	

Entendre *to hear*: entendu – entendant

Present indicative	Perfect	Imperfect	Conditional	Future	Present subjunctive	Imperative
j'entends	ai entendu	entendais	entendrais	entendrai	entende	
tu entends	as entendu	entendais	entendrais	entendras	entendes	entends
il/elle entend	a entendu	entendait	entendrait	entendra	entende	
nous entendons	avons entendu	entendions	entendrions	entendrons	entendions	entendons
vous entendez	avez entendu	entendiez	entendriez	entendrez	entendiez	entendez
ils/elles entendent	ont entendu	entendaient	entendraient	entendront	entendent	

Envoyer *to send*: envoyé – envoyant

Present indicative	Perfect	Imperfect	Conditional	Future	Present subjunctive	Imperative
j'envoie	ai envoyé	envoyais	enverrais	enverrai	envoie	
tu envoies	as envoyé	envoyais	enverrais	enverras	envoies	envoie
il/elle envoie	a envoyé	envoyait	enverrait	enverra	envoie	
nous envoyons	avons envoyé	envoyions	enverrions	enverrons	envoyions	envoyons
vous envoyez	avez envoyé	envoyiez	enverriez	enverrez	envoyiez	envoyez
ils/elles envoient	ont envoyé	envoyaient	enverraient	enverront	envoient	

Être *to be*: été – étant

Present indicative	Perfect	Imperfect	Conditional	Future	Present subjunctive	Imperative
je suis	ai été	étais	serais	serai	sois	
tu es	as été	étais	serais	seras	sois	sois
il/elle est	a été	était	serait	sera	soit	
nous sommes	avons été	étions	serions	serons	soyons	soyons
vous êtes	avez été	étiez	seriez	serez	soyez	soyez
ils/elles sont	ont été	étaient	seraient	seront	soient	

Faire *to do, to make*: fait – faisant

Present indicative	Perfect	Imperfect	Conditional	Future	Present subjunctive	Imperative
je fais	ai fait	faisais	ferais	ferai	fasse	
tu fais	as fait	faisais	ferais	feras	fasses	fais
il/elle fait	a fait	faisait	ferait	fera	fasse	
nous faisons	avons fait	faisions	ferions	ferons	fassions	faisons
vous faites	avez fait	faisiez	feriez	ferez	fassiez	faites
ils/elles font	ont fait	faisaient	feraient	feront	fassent	

Falloir *to be necessary (impersonal only):* Past participle: **fallu** No present participle

il faut	il a fallu	il fallait	il faudrait	il faudra	(qu')il faille	

Manger *to eat:* **mangé – mangeant** (**e** is added after the **g** in order to keep the soft sound before **a**, **o** and **u**)

je mange	ai mangé	mangeais	mangerais	mangerai	mange	
tu manges	as mangé	mangeais	mangerais	mangeras	manges	mange
il/elle mange	a mangé	mangeait	mangerait	mangera	mange	
nous mangeons	avons mangé	mangions	mangerions	mangerons	mangions	mangeons
vous mangez	avez mangé	mangiez	mangeriez	mangerez	mangiez	mangez
ils/elles mangent	ont mangé	mangeaient	mangeraient	mangeront	mangent	

Mettre *to put:* **mis – mettant**

je mets	ai mis	mettais	mettrais	mettrai	mette	
tu mets	as mis	mettais	mettrais	mettras	mettes	mets
il/elle met	a mis	mettait	mettrait	mettra	mette	
nous mettons	avons mis	mettions	mettrions	mettrons	mettions	mettons
vous mettez	avez mis	mettiez	mettriez	mettrez	mettiez	mettez
ils/elles mettent	ont mis	mettaient	mettraient	mettront	mettent	

Ouvrir *to open:* **ouvert – ouvrant**

j'ouvre	ai ouvert	ouvrais	ouvrirais	ouvrirai	ouvre	
tu ouvres	as ouvert	ouvrais	ouvrirais	ouvriras	ouvres	ouvre
il/elle ouvre	a ouvert	ouvrait	ouvrirait	ouvrira	ouvre	
nous ouvrons	avons ouvert	ouvrions	ouvririons	ouvrirons	ouvrions	ouvrons
vous ouvrez	avez ouvert	ouvriez	ouvririez	ouvrirez	ouvriez	ouvrez
ils/elles ouvrent	ont ouvert	ouvraient	ouvriraient	ouvriront	ouvrent	

Present indicative	Perfect	Imperfect	Conditional	Future	Present subjunctive	Imperative

Pleuvoir *to rain (impersonal only):* **plu – pleuvant**

Present indicative	Perfect	Imperfect	Conditional	Future	Present subjunctive	Imperative
il pleut	il a plu	il pleuvait	il pleuvrait	il pleuvra	(qu'il pleuve)	

Pouvoir *to be able to (I can):* **pu – pouvant**

Present indicative	Perfect	Imperfect	Conditional	Future	Present subjunctive	Imperative
je peux	ai pu	pouvais	pourrais	pourrai	puisse	
tu peux	as pu	pouvais	pourrais	pourras	puisses	
il/elle peut	a pu	pouvait	pourrait	pourra	puisse	
nous pouvons	avons pu	pouvions	pourrions	pourrons	puissions	
vous pouvez	avez pu	pouviez	pourriez	pourrez	puissiez	
ils/elles peuvent	ont pu	pouvaient	pourraient	pourront	puissent	

Prendre *to take:* **pris – prenant**

Present indicative	Perfect	Imperfect	Conditional	Future	Present subjunctive	Imperative
je prends	ai pris	prenais	prendrais	prendrai	prenne	
tu prends	as pris	prenais	prendrais	prendras	prennes	prends
il/elle prend	a pris	prenait	prendrait	prendra	prenne	
nous prenons	avons pris	prenions	prendrions	prendrons	prenions	prenons
vous prenez	avez pris	preniez	prendriez	prendrez	preniez	prenez
ils/elles prennent	ont pris	prenaient	prendraient	prendront	prennent	

Savoir *to know:* **su – sachant**

Present indicative	Perfect	Imperfect	Conditional	Future	Present subjunctive	Imperative
je sais	ai su	savais	saurais	saurai	sache	
tu sais	as su	savais	saurais	sauras	saches	sache
il/elle sait	a su	savait	saurait	saura	sache	
nous savons	avons su	savions	saurions	saurons	sachions	sachons
vous savez	avez su	saviez	sauriez	saurez	sachiez	sachez
ils/elles savent	ont su	savaient	sauraient	sauront	sachent	

Sortir *to go out*: **sorti – sortant**

je sors	suis sorti(e)	sortais	sortirais	sortirai	sorte	sors
tu sors	es sorti(e)	sortais	sortirais	sortiras	sortes	
il/elle sort	est sorti(e)	sortait	sortirait	sortira	sorte	
nous sortons	sommes sorti(e)s	sortions	sortirions	sortirons	sortions	sortons
vous sortez	êtes sorti(e)(s)	sortiez	sortiriez	sortirez	sortiez	sortez
ils/elles sortent	sont sorti(e)s	sortaient	sortiraient	sortiront	sortent	

Venir *to come*: **venu – venant**

je viens	suis venu(e)	venais	viendrais	viendrai	vienne	viens
tu viens	es venu(e)	venais	viendrais	viendras	viennes	
il/elle vient	est venu(e)	venait	viendrait	viendra	vienne	
nous venons	sommes venus(es)	venions	viendrions	viendrons	venions	venons
vous venez	êtes venu(e)(s)	veniez	viendriez	viendrez	veniez	venez
ils/elles viennent	sont venus(es)	venaient	viendraient	viendront	viennent	

Voir *to see*: **vu – voyant**

je vois	ai vu	voyais	verrais	verrai	voie	voie
tu vois	as vu	voyais	verrais	verras	voies	
il/elle voit	a vu	voyait	verrait	verra	voie	
nous voyons	avons vu	voyions	verrions	verrons	voyions	voyons
vous voyez	avez vu	voyiez	verriez	verrez	voyiez	voyez
ils/elles voient	ont vu	voyaient	verraient	verront	voient	

Vouloir *to want*: **voulu – voulant**

je veux	ai voulu	voulais	voudrais	voudrai	veuille	veuille
tu veux	as voulu	voulais	voudrais	voudras	veuilles	
il/elle veut	a voulu	voulait	voudrait	voudra	veuille	
nous voulons	avons voulu	voulions	voudrions	voudrons	voulions	veuillons
vous voulez	avez voulu	vouliez	voudriez	voudrez	vouliez	veuillez
ils/elles veulent	ont voulu	voulaient	voudraient	voudront	veuillent	

FRENCH–ENGLISH VOCABULARY

adj *adjective*
adv *adverb*
aux *auxiliary*
conj *conjunction*
dem pron *demonstrative pronoun*
f *feminine*
gen *generally*
impers *impersonal*
inv *invariable*
m *masculine*
n *noun*
nf *feminine noun*

nm *masculine noun*
nmf *masculine and feminine noun*
phr *phrase*
pl *plural*
pp *past participle*
prep *preposition*
qch *quelque chose* (something)
qn *quelqu'un* (somebody)
vi *intransitive verb*
vtr *transitive verb*
v refl *reflexive verb*
(v être) *takes être in perfect tense*

à prep *to; at; with*
abonné *nmf subscriber; season ticket holder*
abonnement *nm subscription; season ticket*
d'abord *phr first*
absolument *adv absolutely*
accident *nm accident; hitch; mishap*
accompagner *vtr to accompany, to go with*
accord *nm agreement;* **je suis d'~** *I agree*
accueil *nm welcome, reception; reception desk*
accueillant, -e *adj hospitable, welcoming*
accueillir *vtr to welcome; to receive; to greet*
acheter *vtr to buy*
acheteur, -euse *nmf buyer, purchaser*
acquéreur *nm buyer, purchaser*
acquérir *vtr to acquire; to purchase*
acquisition *nf purchase*
acteur, -trice *nmf actor/actress*
actif, -ive *adj active;* **la vie active** *working life*
activité *nf activity*
actuel, -elle *adj present, current*
addition *nf bill*
adieu *goodbye, farewell*
adorer *vtr to adore*
adresse *nf address*
  s'adresser a qn *v refl (+ v être) to speak to sb*
aéroport *nm airport*
affiche *nf poster*
agaçant, -e *adj annoying, irritating*
âge *nm age*
agence *nf agency;* **~ immobilière** *estate agents*
agglomération *nf town; (smaller) village*
agir *to act;* **s'agir de** *v impers* **de quoi s'agit-il?** *what is it about?; what's the matter?*
agréable *adj nice, pleasant*
aider *vtr to help*

ail, *pl* **~s** *or* **aulx** *nm garlic*
ailleurs *adv elsewhere* **d'ailleurs** *phr besides*
aimable *adj pleasant; kind; polite*
aimer *vtr to love; to like, to be fond of*
ainsi *adv thus*
ajouter *vtr to add (à to)*
alcool *nm alcohol*
alentour *adv* **la ville et la région ~** *the town and surrounding area*
alimentation *food;* **magasin d' ~** *food shop, grocery store*
Allemagne *nf Germany*
allemand, ~e *adj German; nm (lang) German*
aller *v aux* **je vais apprendre l'italien** *I'm going to learn Italian vi*
  comment ça va? *how are you?* *to go;* **s'en aller** *v refl (+ v être) to go, to leave*
allumer *vtr to light*
alors *adv then*
améliorer *vtr* **s'améliorer** *refl (+ v être) to improve*
aménagement *nm development*
aménager *vtr to convert; to do up [house, attic]*
amener *vtr to accompany to bring sb*
américain *adj American*
ami, -e *nmf friend*
amitié *nf friendship*
amusant, ~ e *adj entertaining; funny*
amuser *vtr to entertain;* **s'amuser** *v refl (+ v être) to have fun, to play;* **pour s'~** *for fun*
an *nm year*
ancien, -ienne *adj old*
anglais, ~e *adj English*
Anglais, ~e *nmf Englishman/Englishwoman*
Angleterre *nf England*

animal, ~e, *mpl* **-aux** *animal*
animateur, -trice *coordinator*
animer *vtr to lead*
année *nf year*
anniversaire *nm birthday*
ANPE *nf (abbr =* **Agence nationale pour l'emploi)** *French national employment agency*
août *nm August*
apercevoir *vtr to make out; to catch sight of*
apéritif *nm drink*
à-peu-près *nm inv approximation*
appareil *nm appliance; telephone;* **~ photo** *camera*
appartement *nm flat*
appeler *vtr to call*
s'appeler *v refl (+ v être)* **comment t'appelles-tu?** *what's your name?*
appétit *appetite*
apprendre *vtr to learn*
apprenti ~e *nmf apprentice*
apprentissage *nm apprenticeship*
après *adv afterward(s), after; later*
après-midi *nm/nf inv afternoon*
argent *nm money; silver*
arrêter *vtr to stop*
arrière *adj inv back*
arriver *(+ v être) vi to arrive*
arrondissement *nm administrative division*
s'asseoir *v refl (+ v être) to sit down*
assez *adv enough*
attendre *vtr to wait for*
au *prep (=* **à le)** *see* **à**
auberge *nf inn;* **~ de jeunesse** *youth hostel*
aujourd'hui *adv today*
aussi *adv too, as well, also*
aussitôt *adv immediately*
auteur *nm author*
autocar *nm coach*
automne *nm autumn*
autoroute *nf motorway*
autour de *phr around*
autre *other*
avant *adv before*
avant-hier *adv the day before yesterday*
avec *prep with*
avenir *nm future*
averse *nf shower (rain)*
avion *nm plane*
avis *nm inv opinion*
avocat *nm lawyer*
avoir *vtr to have*
avril *nm April*

bagage *nm piece of luggage*
baguette *nf French stick*
bain *nm bath*
balcon *nm balcony*
banlieue *nf suburbs*
bar-tabac *nm café (selling stamps and cigarettes)*
bas, basse *adj low*
bateau *nm boat, ship*
bâtonnier *nm president of the Bar*
bavarder *vi to talk to, to chatter*
beau, belle *adj beautiful; handsome; good; fine*
beaucoup *adv a lot*
beau-frère *nm brother-in-law*
Belgique *nf Belgium*
belle-mère *nf mother-in-law*
belle-soeur *nf sister-in-law*
besoin *nm need* **avoir ~ de** *to need*
bête *adj stupid, silly*
beur *nmf second-generation North African (living in France) (slang)*
beurre *nm butter*
bibliothèque *nf library*
bicyclette *nf bicycle*
bien *adj inv good; adv well*
bien que *phr although*
bière *nf beer*
bijou *nm piece of jewellery*
bilan *nm outcome, result*
bilingue *adj bilingual*
blanc, blanchè *adj white*
blessé, ~e *nmf injured or wounded man/woman*
blessure *nf injury*
bleu ~e *adj blue*
bois *nm inv wood*
boisson *nf drink*
boîte *nf box; tin*
bon, bonne *adj good*
bonne-maman *nf grandma*
bord *nm* **le ~ de la mer** *the seaside*
bouche *nf mouth*
bouche-à-oreille *nm inv* **le ~** *word of mouth*
boucher, -ère *nmf butcher*
boucherie *nf butcher's shop*
bouchon *nm cork*
bouillir *vi to boil*
boulanger, -ère *nmf baker*
boulangerie *nf bakery*
bout *nm end; tip*
briser *vtr to break*
brouillard *nm fog*
bruit *nm noise*

brûler *vtr to burn*
bureau *nm office*
ça *that; this*
caisse *nf cash desk*
carrefour *nm crossroads*
carte *nf card;* ~ **à puce** *smart card*
en tout cas *phr in any case*
case *nf box (on form)*
casserole *nf saucepan, pan*
cave *nf cellar*
céder *vtr* ~ **le passage** *to give way*
celui /celle /ceux /celles *pron the ones*
celui-ci/ celle-ci/ ceux-ci/ celles-ci *this one; these*
celui-là *pron that one*
cent *adj a hundred*
chacun, -e *each*
chambre *nf bedroom; room*
champignon *nm mushroom*
change *nm exchange rate*
chaque *each, every*
charcuterie *nf pork butcher's*
se charger *v refl (+ v être)* **se** ~ **de** *to take responsibility for*
chat *nm cat*
château *nm castle*
chaud *adj hot*
chaussure *nf shoe*
chauvin ~**e** *adj chauvinistic*
cher, chère *adj dear*
chercher *vtr to look for*
cheveu *nm hair*
chèvre *nm goat's cheese*
chez *prep* ~ **qn** *at sb's place*
chien *nm dog*
chiffre *nm figure*
chinois, ~e *adj Chinese*
chômage *nm unemployment*
chose *nf thing*
chou *nm cabbage*
ciel *nm sky*
clos *adj closed*
cocher *tr to tick*
coffre *nm (of car) boot*
coin *nm corner*
collège *nm secondary school*
combien de *how many, how much*
comme *conj as*
comment *adv how*
comprendre *vtr to understand*
compter *vtr to count*
concours *nm inv competition*

conduire *vtr to drive*
conduite *nf (of vehicle) driving*
confiture *nf jam*
connaître *vtr to know*
conseil *nm advice*
contre *prep against*
convenu, -e *adj agreed*
copain, copine *nmf friend; boyfriend/girlfriend*
corps *nm inv body*
à côte *phr nearby*
se coucher *v refl (+ v être) to go to bed*
coup *blow;* **donner un** ~ **de pied** *to kick*
couper *vtr to cut;* **se couper** *to cut oneself*
couramment *adv fluently*
courir *vi to run*
court ~**e** *adj short*
couteau *nm knife*
coûter *vtr to cost*
couvert *adj [sky] overcast;* **mettre le** ~ *to lay the table*
crêpe *nf pancake*
crever *vtr puncture*
croire *vtr to believe*
cuillère *nf spoon*
cuillerée *nf spoonful*
cuire *vtr to cook*
cuisine *nf kitchen; cooking*
dans *prep in*
déboucher *vtr to uncork*
début *nm beginning; start*
découvrir *vtr to discover*
défense *nf '*~ **de fumer'** *'no smoking'*
défi *nm challenge*
dehors *adv outside*
déjà *adv already*
déjeuner *vi to have lunch; nm lunch*
demain *adv tomorrow*
demander *vtr to ask for*
déménagement *nm moving house*
déménager *vtr to move (furniture)*
demeurer *to reside, to live*
demi, ~e *nmf half*
demi-heure *nf half an hour*
demi-tarif *adv half-price*
dent *nf tooth*
dentifrice *nm toothpaste*
dépanner *vtr to fix [car, machine]*
départ *nm departure*
déprimer *vtr to depress; vi to be depressed*
depuis *adv since*
dernier, -ière *adj last*
derrière *prep behind*

dès que *phr as soon as*
descendre *vtr (+ v avoir) to go down, to come down sth; vi to go down (+ v être)*
désolé *pp adj sorry*
dessous *adv underneath;* **en dessous** *phr underneath*
dessus *adv on top*
devant *prep in front of*
devenir *vi (+ v être) to become*
deviner *vtr to guess*
devoir *vaux to have to*
diététique *adj dietary; nf dietetics*
dingue *adj (person) crazy (slang)*
dire *vtr to say*
doigt *nm finger*
donc *conj so, therefore*
donner *vtr to give*
dormir *vi to sleep*
dos *nm inv back;* **mal de** *~ backache*
douche *nf shower*
droit, -e *adj straight*
droite *nf right;* **tourner à** *~ to turn right*
dur, -e *adj hard*
durée *nf length*
eau *nf water*
ébullition *nf boiling*
école *nf school*
écrire *vtr to write*
éditeur, -trice *nmf editor, publisher*
en effet *phr indeed*
église *nf church*
embouteillage *nm traffic jam*
embrasser *vtr to kiss*
embrumé, ~e *adj misty*
emmener *vtr to take*
emploi *nm job; employment*
employé, ~e *nmf employee*
emporter *vtr to take [object];* **pizzas à** *takeaway pizzas*
en *prep in; into*
encore *adv still; again*
endroit *nm place*
enfant *nmf child*
enfin *adv finally*
ennuyeux, -euse *adj boring*
enregistrer *vtr to check in (baggage)*
enseignant, ~e *nmf teacher*
enseigner *vtr to teach*
ensoleillé *adj sunny*
ensuite *adv then*
entendre *vtr to hear*
entier, -ière *adj whole*

entre *prep between*
entrée *nf entrance; starter*
entrer *vi to come in*
envie *nf avoir* ~ **de qch** *to feel like sth*
envoyer *vtr to send*
épais, épaisse *adj thick*
épicerie *nf grocer's (shop)*
éplucher *vtr to peel*
époux *nm inv husband*
équilibre *nm balance*
équipage *nm crew*
équipe *nf team*
escalier *nm staircase; stairs*
Espagne *nf Spain*
espagnol, -e *adj Spanish nm l'* *Spanish*
espérer *vtr to hope*
essayer *vtr to try*
essence *nf petrol*
essuie-glace *nm windscreen wiper*
étage *nm floor*
été *nm summer*
être *vi (+ v avoir) to be*
étudiant, -e *nmf student*
extrait *nm (from book, film) extract*
fabriquer *vtr to make*
en face de *phr en* ~ **de l'église** *opposite the church, across from the church*
facile *adj easy*
façon *nf way;* **de toute** ~ *anyway*
faim *nf hunger* **avoir** ~ *to be hungry*
faire *vtr to make*
faire-part *nm inv announcement*
faisable *adj c'est* ~ *it can be done*
au fait *phr by the way*
falloir *v impers il faut qch/gn we need sth/sb*
familial, -e *adj (meal, life, firm) family*
famille *nf family*
fatigant, ~e *adj tiring*
fatiguer *vtr to make [sb/sth] tired*
fauteuil *nm armchair;* **roulant** *wheelchair*
faux, fausse *adj wrong*
féliciter *vtr to congratulate*
femme *nf woman*
fenêtre *nf window*
fer *nm iron;* ~ **à repasser** *iron*
ferme *nf farm, farmhouse*
fermer *vtr to close*
fête *nf public holiday; name-day*
feu *nm fire*
février *nm February*
fille *nf daughter; girl*
fillette *nf little girl*

fils *nm inv* son
fin, fine *adj fine; [slice, layer]* thin
finir *vtr to finish*
fois *nf inv (with numerals)* **une ~** *once;* **deux ~** *twice*
fort, -e *adj strong*
fou, folle *adj mad*
four *nm oven*
fourchette *nf fork*
frais, fraîche *adj cool; cold; fresh*
fraise *nf strawberry*
framboise *nf raspberry*
frère *nm brother*
frigo *nm fridge*
froid, -e *adj cold*
fromage *nm cheese*
gagner *vtr to win*
galette *nf pancake*
Galles *nf pl* **le pays de ~** *Wales*
gamin, -e *nmf kid*
garçon *nm boy*
gâteau, *pl* **-x** *nm cake*
gauche *nf left*
genou, *pl* **-x** *nm knee*
genre *nm sort, kind, type*
gens *nm pl people*
gestion *nf management*
gîte *nm shelter;* **~ rural** *self-catering cottage*
gonflé, -e *adj inflated*
gonfler *vtr to inflate [tyre]*
goût *nm taste; palate*
goûter *nm snack*
grand, -e *adj [person, tree, tower]* tall
grand-mère *nf grandmother*
grand-père *nm grandfather*
gras, grasse *adj [substance]* fatty
gratter *vtr to scratch*
gratuit, -e *adj free*
grave *adj [problem, injury]* serious
gris, -e *adj grey*
gros, grosse *adj big, large; thick*
habiller *vtr to dress;* **s'habiller** *v refl (+ v être) to get dressed*
habitation *nf house*
halle *nf covered market*
haricot *nm bean;* **~ vert** *French bean*
haut, -e *adj high; tall*
hébergement *nm accomodation*
héberger *vtr to put [sb] up*
heure *nf hour;* **l'~ d'arrivée** *the arrival time;* **~s d'ouverture** *opening times*
hier *adv yesterday*

histoire *nf history*
hiver *nm winter*
homme *nm man*
hors-d'oeuvre *nm inv starter*
humide *adj damp*
immatriculation *nf registration*
immeuble *nm building*
immobilier *nm* **l' ~** *property*
imprimerie *printing*
incendie *nm fire*
infirmier *nm male nurse*
infirmière *nf nurse*
information *nf* **écouter les ~s** *to listen to the news*
inquiet, -iète *adj anxious; worried.*
s'inquièter *v refl (+ v être) to worry*
interdit, -e *pp adj prohibited, forbidden*
intéresser *vtr to interest* **ça ne m'intéresse pas** *I'm not interested*
irlandais, -e *adj Irish nm Irish*
italien, -ienne *adj Italian nm Italian*
jamais *adv never*
jambe *nf leg*
jambon *nm ham*
jardin *nm garden*
jaune *adj yellow*
je *(j' before vowel or mute h) I*
jeu, -x *game*
jeu-concours *nm competition*
jeudi *nm Thursday*
jeune *adj young*
jeunesse *nf youth*
joli -e *adj (gen) nice; [face]* pretty
jouer *vtr to play*
jour *nm day*
journal, *pl* **-aux** *nm newspaper*
journée *nf day*
juillet *nm July*
jus *nm inv juice*
jusque-là *adv until then, up to here*
juste *adv right, just*
justement *adv precisely*
là *adv there; here*
là-bas *adv over there*
laisser *vtr to leave*
lait *nm milk*
lancer *vtr to throw*
large *adj broad; wide*
lavabo *nm washbasin, washbowl*
laver *vtr to wash* **se laver** *v refl (+ v être) to wash;* **se ~ les mains** *to wash one's hands*
le, la (l' before vowel or mute h), *pl* **les** *the*
lecture *nf reading*

léger, -ère *adj light*
lent, -e *adj slow*
lequel/ laquelle/ lesquels/ lesquelles *adj who; which*
se lever *v refl (+ v être) to get up*
liaison *nf link*
librairie *nf bookshop*
libre-service *adj inv self-service*
lieu *nm place;* **au lieu de** *phr instead of*
lire *vtr to read*
livre *nm book*
locataire *nmf tenant*
location *nf renting*
logement *nm accommodation*
loin *adv a long way,* **c'est trop ~** *it's too far*
loisir *nm spare time; leisure*
Londres *n London*
longtemps *adv a long time*
louer *vtr [owner, landlord] to let; to rent out*
lourd, -e *adj heavy*
lumière *nf light*
lundi *nm Monday*
lune *nf moon*
lunettes *nf pl glasses; ~* **de soleil** *sunglasses*
lycée *nm secondary school (school preparing students aged 5-8 for the baccalaureate)*
madame, *pl* **mesdames** *Mrs; a woman whose name you do not know*
mademoiselle, *pl* **mesdemoiselles** *Miss; woman whose name you do not know*
magnétophone *nm tape recorder*
magnétoscope *nm video recorder, VCR*
maigre *adj [person] thin; [cheese] low-fat*
main *nf hand*
mairie *nf town council*
mais *conj but*
maison *nf house; home*
mal *nm mpl* **maux** *adj inv wrong; pain;* **avoir ~ partout** *to ache all over;* **avoir ~ à la tête** *to have a headache*
malade *adj [person] ill, sick*
malgré *prep in spite of, despite*
malheureusement *adv unfortunately*
Manche *nf the Channel;* **le tunnel sous la ~** *the Channel tunnel*
manger *vtr to eat;* **il n'y a rien à ~ dans la maison** *there's no food in the house*
manière *nf way;* **d'une ~ ou d'une autre** *in one way or another*
manoir *nm manor (house)*
manquer *vtr to miss*
manquer de *v + prep to lack;* **on ne manque de rien** *we don't want for anything*

manteau, *pl* **-x** *nm coat*
marcher *vi to walk; to work;* **ma radio marche mal** *my radio doesn't work properly*
mardi *nm Tuesday*
marée *nf tide;* **à ~ haute/basse** *at high/low tide*
marémoteur, -trice *adj tidal;* **usine marémotrice** *tidal power station*
mari *nm husband*
marié, -e *pp adj married*
se marier *v refl (+ v être) to get married* **(avec qn** *to sb)*
mars *nm inv March*
matin *nm morning*
mauvais, -e *adj bad*
mécanicien, -ienne *nmf mechanic*
Méditerranée *nf* **la (mer) ~** *the Mediterranean*
meilleur, -e *adj better; best;* **le ~ des deux** *the better of the two*
mélanger *vtr to mix*
même *adj same; adv even; phr* **agir** *or* **faire de ~** *to do the same*
ménage *nm household; housework;* **faire le ~** *to do the cleaning*
mensuel, -elle *adj monthly; nm monthly magazine*
menteur, -euse *nmf liar*
mentir *vi to lie, to tell lies*
mer *nf sea*
merci *nm thank you*
mercredi *nm Wednesday*
mère *nf mother*
météo *nf weather forecast*
métier *nm job; profession*
métro *nm underground*
mettre *vtr to put*
meuble *nm des ~s furniture*
meublé *nm furnished flat*
meubler *vtr to furnish*
miam-miam *excl yum-yum!*
micro-ondes *nm inv microwave*
midi *nm twelve o'clock, midday, noon; lunchtime;* **le Midi** *the South of France*
miel *nm honey*
le mien, la mienne, les miens, les miennes *mine*
mieux *adj inv better;* **le ~, la ~, les ~** *the best*
milieu *nm middle;* **au ~ da la nuit** *in the middle of the night*
mille *adj inv a thousand, one thousand*
milliard *nm billion*
mince *[person, leg] slim, slender*
Minitel® *nm Minitel (terminal linking phone users to a database)*

minuit *nm midnight*
mi-temps *nm inv part-time job;* **elle travaille à** *~ she works part-time*
mobilier, -ière *adj biens ~s movable property*
mobylette® *nf moped*
moi *I, me;* **c'est** *~ it's me*
moi-même *myself*
moins *minus;* **il est huit heures** *~ **dix** it's ten (minutes) to eight; adv (comparative) less*
à moins de *phr unless*
au moins *phr at least*
mois *nm inv month*
moitié *nf half;* **à** *~ **vide** half empty*
môme *kid; brat (slang)*
mon, ma *pl **mes** my*
monde *nm world; people;* **tout le** *~ everybody*
moniteur, -trice *nmf group leader*
monnaie *nf currency; change*
monsieur, *pl **messieurs** nm Mr*
montagne *nf mountain*
monter *vtr (+ v avoir) to go up sth; vi (+ être);* **tu es monté à pied?** *did you walk up?*
montrer *vtr to show*
mordre *vtr to bite*
morsure *nf bite*
mort *nf death*
mort, -e *adj dead;* **je suis** *~ **de froid** I'm freezing to death*
mot *nm word*
moule *nf mussel*
mourir *vi (+ v être) to die*
moyen, -enne *adj [height, size] medium; medium sized; [price] moderate*
municipal, *~e adj [council] local, town*
mur *nm wall*
musée *nm museum; art gallery*
nager *vtr to swim*
nageur, -euse *nmf swimmer*
naissance *nf birth*
naître *vi (+ v être) to be born;* **elle est née le 5 juin** *she was born on 5 June*
naturellement *adv naturally*
né, -e *pp see naître*
nécessaire *adj necessary*
neige *nf snow*
neiger *v impers to snow;* **il neige** *it's snowing*
n'est-ce pas *adv c'est joli,* ~? *it's pretty, isn't it?*
net, nette *adj [price, weight] net*
nettoyage *nm cleanup*
neuf *nine*
neuf, neuve *adj new*
neveu, *pl **-x** nm nephew*

nez *nm nose*
ni *conj nor, or*
Noël *nm Christmas;* **'Joyeux** *~' Merry Christmas*
noir *adj black*
nom *nm name;* ~ **et prénom** *full name*
nombre *nm number*
nombreux, -euse *adj numerous, many*
non *adv no*
nord *adj inv north; northern*
nord-africain, -e *adj North African*
nord-ouest *adj inv northwest*
notaire *nm notary public*
notre, *pl **nos** our*
nourriture *nf food*
nous *(subject) we; (object) us*
nous-même, *pl **nous-mêmes** ourselves*
nouveau (**nouvel** *before vowel or mute h),* **nouvelle** *adj new*
nouveau-né *adj newborn*
nuage *nm cloud*
nuageux, -euse *adj [sky] cloudy*
nuit *nf night*
nulle part *phr nowhere*
nullement *adv not at all*
numéro *nm number;* ~ **de téléphone** *telephone number;* ~ **d'abonné** *customer's number;* ~ **d'appel gratuit** *freefone number*
obligatoire *compulsory; inevitable*
occupant, -e *occupant*
occupé, *~e [person, life] busy; [seat] taken; [phone] engaged*
s'occuper *v refl (+ v être)* **s'~ de** *to see to, to take care of [dinner, tickets]*
oeil, *pl **yeux** nm eye*
offre *nf offer;* **répondre à une** *~ **d'emploi** to reply to a job advertisement*
oignon *nm onion*
oiseau, *pl **-x** nm bird*
oncle *nm uncle*
onze *eleven*
orage *nm storm*
orageux, -euse *stormy; thundery*
ordinaire *adj ordinary*
ordinateur *nm computer*
oreille *nf ear*
oreiller *nm pillow*
organisateur, -trice *nmf organizer*
orthographe *nf spelling*
os *nm inv bone*
ou *conj or*
où *adv where*
oublier *vtr to forget [name, date, fact]*

ouf *phew!*

oui *yes*

outil *nm tool*

ouvert, -e *adj open*

ouvrable *adj [day] working; [hours] business*

ouvre-boîtes *nm inv tin-opener*

ouvier, -ière *nmf worker; workman*

ouvrir *vtr to open*

paiement *nm payment*

pain *nm bread*

pancarte *nf notice*

panier *nm basket*

panneau *nm sign;* ~ **indicateur** *signpost*

pantalon *nm trousers*

papeterie *nf stationer's (shop), stationery shop*

papier *nm paper*

Pâques *nm, nf pl Easter*

par *prop* **elle est arrivée ~ la droite** *she came from the right;* **régler** *or* **payer ~ carte de crédit** *to pay by credit card*

paradis *nm inv heaven; paradise*

paraître *vi to appear, to seem, to look*

parapluie *nm umbrella*

parc *nm park*

parce que *phr because*

pardon *nm forgiveness; pardon;* **je te demande ~** *I'm sorry ~* **!** *sorry!*

pare-chocs *nm inv bumper*

pareil, -eille *adj similar*

paresse *nf laziness*

paresseux, -euse *adj lazy*

parfait, -e *adj perfect*

parfaitement *adv perfectly*

parfois *adv sometimes*

parier *vtr to bet*

parisien, -ienne *adj Parisian*

parler *vtr to speak*

parmi *prep among, amongst*

part *nf (of food) slice, helping*

partager *vtr to share*

partir *vi (+ v être) to leave*

partout *adv everywhere*

pas *adv* **je ne prends ~ de sucre** *I don't take sugar*

passager, -ère *nmf passenger*

passant, -e *nmf passer-by*

passer *vtr to cross; to go through*

patin *nm skate;* ~ **à roulettes** *roller skate*

pâtissier, -ière *nmf confectioner, pastry cook*

patron, -onne *nmf boss*

pauvre *adj poor*

payer *vtr to pay for*

pays *nm country*

péage *nm toll*

peau *nf skin*

pêche *nm peach;* **avoir la ~** *to be feeling great*

pêcher *vtr to go fishing for*

peine *nf sorrow, grief;* **avoir de la ~** *to feel sad or upset*

pellicule *nf film*

se pencher *v refl (+ v être) to lean*

pendant *prep for;* **je t'ai attendu ~ des heures** *I waited for you for hours*

penser *vtr to think*

Pentecôte *nf Whitsun*

perdre *vtr to lose*

père *nm father*

permettre *vtr ~* **à qn de faire** *to allow sb to do*

permis *nm ~* **de conduire** *driver's licence*

petit, -e *adj small, little; short*

petite-fille *nf granddaughter*

petit-fils *nm grandson*

petits-enfants *nm pl grandchildren*

peu *adv not much*

peut-être *adv perhaps, maybe*

phare *nm headlight*

pharmacie *nm chemist's (shop)*

pharmacien, -ienne *nmf (dispensing) chemist*

pièce *nf room*

pied *nm foot*

pierre *nf stone*

piéton, -onne *adj pedestrianized; nmf pedestrian*

piqûre *nf injection, shot; sting; bite*

placard *nm cupboard*

plage *nf beach*

plaisanter *vi to joke*

plan, *nm map; (in building) plan, map*

planche *nf ~* **à voile** *windsurfing board*

plateau, *pl* **-x** *tray* **(de** *of)*

plein, -e *adj full*

pleurer *vi to cry*

pleuvoir *v impers to rain;* **il pleut** *it's raining*

pluie *nf rain*

la plupart *nf inv most*

plus *adv more;* **le ~ the most; de plus** *phr furthermore;* **une fois de ~** *once more, once again*

plusieurs *adj several*

plutôt *adv rather; fairly*

pluvieux, -ieuse *adj wet, rainy*

pneu *nm tyre*

poids *nm inv weight*

poignée *nf ~* **de main** *handshake*

point *nm ~* **de suture** *(Med) stitch;* ~ **de vue** *point of view*

pointure *nf shoe size*

poire *nf pear*

pois *nm* **petit ~** *(garden) pea*

poisson *nm fish*

poivre *nm pepper*

poivrer *vtr to add pepper to [sauce]*

poli, -e *adj polite*

pomme *nf apple;* **~ de terre** *potato;* **~s frites** *chips*

pompe *nf* **~ à essence** *petrol pump*

pompier, -ière *nm fireman*

pont *nm bridge; deck*

populaire *adj working-class*

portefeuille *nm wallet*

porter *vtr to carry*

portugais *adj Portuguese nm Portuguese*

poulet *nm chicken*

pour *prep to;* **~ faire** *to do; in order to do; for;* **le train ~ Paris** *the train for Paris*

pourquoi *why*

pourtant *adv though*

pousser *vtr to push*

pouvoir *v aux to be able to;* **peux-tu soulever cette boîte?** *can you lift this box?*

pratique *adj practical; convenient*

pratiquer *vtr to play [tennis]; to practise*

préavis *nm inv notice;* **déposer un ~ de grève** *to give notice of strike action*

premier, -ière *adj; first*

prendre *vtr to take;* **je vais ~ du poisson** *I'll have fish;* **aller ~ une bière** *to go for a beer*

prénom *nm first name, forename*

près *adv close;* **à peu ~ vide** *phr practically empty*

presque *adv almost, nearly*

prêt, -e *adj ready*

preuve *nf proof*

prévenir *vtr to tell; to warn*

prévision *nf forecasting;* **~s météorologiques** *weather forecast*

printemps *nm inv spring*

prix *nm inv price*

prochain, ~e *adj next*

proche *adj nearby*

produit *nm product*

professeur *nm (in school) teacher*

profil *nm profile*

se promener *v refl (+ v être) to go for a walk/drive/ride*

promettre *vtr* **~ qch à qn** *to promise sb sth*

prononcer *vtr to pronounce*

propos *nm inv* **à ~, je...** *by the way, I...*

propre *adj clean*

prouver *vtr to prove*

PTT *nf pl (abbr =* **Administration des postes et télécommunications et de la télédiffusion**) *French postal and telecommunications service*

puis *adv then*

quai *nm quay; of river bank*

quand *conj when*

quart *nm quarter*

quartier *nm area; district*

Québécois, -e *nmf Quebecois, Quebecker*

quel, quelle *who; what; which*

quelque *some; a few; any;*

quelquefois *adv sometimes*

quelqu'un *someone, somebody; anyone, anybody*

qui *who; whom*

quitter *vtr to leave [place, person, road]*

quoi *what;* **à ~ penses-tu?** *what are you thinking about?*

quotidien, -ienne *adj daily; nm daily (paper)*

raccrocher *vtr to hang [sth] back up* **~ le combiné** *to put the telephone down.*

raisin *nm grape*

raison *nf reason;* **~ d'agir** *reason for action*

ralentir *vtr, vi to slow down*

rallye *nm (car) rally*

ranger *vtr to put away; to tidy*

rapide *adj quick, rapid*

rapidement *adv quickly; fast*

se raser *v refl (+ v être) to shave*

rasoir *nm* **~ électrique** *electric shaver*

rater *vtr to miss*

rayon *nm department*

recette *nf* **~ (de cuisine)** *recipe*

recevoir *vtr to receive, to get*

reconnaître *vtr to recognize; to identify*

réfléchir à *vtr + prep to think about*

réfrigérateur *nm refrigerator*

regarder *vtr to look at [person, scene, landscape]*

régime *nm diet;* **être au ~** *to be on a diet*

région *nf region; area;* **le vin de la ~** *the local wine*

regretter *vtr o be sorry about, to regret*

rejoindre *vtr to meet up with*

remarquer *vtr to point out*

remercier *to thank (***de qch** *for sth)*

remplir *vtr to fill (up) [container]; to fill in or out [form]*

rencontre *nf meeting; encounter*

rencontrer *vtr to meet [person]*

rendez-vous *nm inv appointment*

renseignement *nm information*
renseigner *vtr* ~ **qn** *to give information to sb*
rentrée *nf (general) return to work (after the slack period of the summer break, in France)*
réparer *vtr to repair, to mend, to fix*
repasser *vtr to iron*
répétitif, -ive *adj repetitive*
répondre *vtr to answer, to reply*
réponse *vtr answer, reply*
repos *vtr rest*
reposer *vtr to rest;* **se reposer** *v refl (+ v être) to have a rest, to rest*
réserver *vtr to reserve, to book [seat, ticket]*
respirer *vtr to breathe in [air]; vi to breathe*
rester *vi (+ v être) to stay, to remain*
résultat *nm result*
retard *nm lateness;* **un ~ de dix minutes** *a ten-minute delay;* **avoir de ~** *to be late*
retour *nm return;* **(billet de)** ~ *return ticket*
retraite *nf retirement*
se retrouver *v refl (+ v être) to meet (again);* **on s'est retrouvé en famille** *the family got together*
réunion *nf meeting*
réussir *vtr to achieve* ~ **à un examen** *to pass an exam*
rêve *nm dreaming; dream*
se réveiller *v refl (+ v être) to wake up*
revoir *vtr to see again*
au revoir *phr goodbye, bye*
rien *nothing;* **se disputer pour un** ~ *to quarrel over nothing*
rire *vi to laugh*
rond, -e *adj [object, table, hole] round*
rond-point *nm roundabout*
roue *nf wheel*
rouge *adj red*
route *nf road, highway*
routier *nm lorry driver*
sage *adj wise, sensible; good, well-behaved*
saison *nf season*
salade *nf lettuce; salad;* ~ **verte** *green salad*
salaire *nm salary; wages*
salle *room; hall;* ~ **d'attente** *waiting room;* ~ **de bains** *bathroom;* ~ **de jeu(x)** *(for children) playroom* ~ **à manger** *dining room;* ~ **de séjour** *living room*
sans *adv without*
santé *nf health;* **à votre ~!** *cheers!*
saucisse *nf sausage*
saucisson *nm* ~ **à l'ail** *garlic sausage*
sauf *prep except, but*

savoir *vtr to know [truth, answer]*
sécurité *nf security;* **en toute** ~ *in complete safety*
selon *prep according to*
semaine *nf week*
sens *nm inv direction, way*
sentinelle *nf sentry*
sentir *vtr to smell*
serveur, -euse *nmf waiter/waitress*
servir *vtr to serve;* **qu'est-ce que je vous sers (à boire)?** *what would you like to drink?*
se servir *v refl (+ v être) (at table) to help oneself*
seul, -e *adj alone, on one's own*
seulement *adv only*
si *nm inv if; adv yes; so* **c'est un homme ~ agréable** *he's such a pleasant man*
siffler *vtr to whistle [tune]*
sinon *an; otherwise, or else*
skier *vi to ski*
sœur *nf sister*
soif *nf thirst;* **avoir** ~ *to be thirsty*
soir *nm evening; night*
soirée *nf evening;* **dans** *or* **pendant la** ~ *in the evening*
en solde *phr* **acheter une veste en** ~ *to buy a jacket in a sale*
soldes *nm pl sales; sale*
sommaire *nm contents*
sommeil *nm sleep;* **avoir** ~ *to be or feel sleepy*
son, sa, *pl* **ses** *his/her/its*
sondage d'opinion *nm opinion poll*
sortir *vi (+ v être) to go out; to come out;* **être sorti** *to be out*
sous *prep under, underneath*
souvent *adv often*
stage *nm professional training; work experience*
studio *nm studio flat*
sud *adj inv south*
suffire *vi to be enough;* **ça suffit (comme ça)!** *that's enough!*
suivant, ~e *adj following; next;* **le** ~ *the following one; the next one*
sur *prep on;* ~ **la table** *on the table*
sympathique *adj nice; pleasant*
syndicat *nm trade union*
tabac *nm tobacco*
taille *nf size*
tant *adv (so) much*
tante *nf aunt*
tard *adv late;* **plus** ~ *later*
tarif *nm rate*
tarte *nf (food) tart;* ~ **aux fraises** *strawberry tart*
tasse *nf cup;* ~ **à thé** *teacup;* ~ **de thé** *cup of tea*

tel, telle *adj such; je n'ai jamais rien vu de* ~
  I've never seen anything like it
télécopieur *nm fax machine, fax*
tellement *adv so*
temps *nm inv weather; time*
tenir *vtr to hold*
terrain *nm ground*
terrasse *nf terrace; s'installer à la* ~ *d'un café*
  to sit at a table outside a café
tête *nf head*
**tien, tienne, le tien, la tienne, les tiens, les
  tiennes** *yours*
timbre *nm stamp*
tirer *vtr to pull*
toi *pron you*
tomber *vi (+ v être) to fall*
tonnerre *nm thunder*
tort *nm avoir* ~ *to be wrong*
tôt *adv [start] early*
toujours *adv always*
tourner *vtr to turn*
tout ~**e** *mpl* **tous** *fpl* **toutes** *everything; all;
  anything*
trafic *nm traffic*
tranquille *adj [person, life, street, day] quiet*
tranquillement *adv quietly*
travail *nm work;* **chercher du/ un** ~ *to look for
  work/a job*
travailler *vtr to work*
traverser *vtr to cross*
très *adv very*
triste *adj sad*
trop *adv too; too much*
trouver *vtr to find*
tutoyer *vtr to address [sb] using the 'tu' form*
université *nf university*
urgence *nf urgency; le service des* ~**s, les** ~**s** *the
  casualty department*
utile *adj useful*
utiliser *vtr to use*
vacances *nf pl holiday*
vache *adj mean, nasty (slang) nf cow*
vachement *adv really; il a* ~ *maigri he's lost a
  hell of a lot of weight*
valise *nf suitcase*
véhicule *nm vehicle*
vélo *nm bike;* ~ **tout terrain, VTT** *mountain
  bike*
vendeur, -euse *nmf shop assistant*

vendre *vtr to sell*
vendredi *nm Friday*
venir *v aux* **venir de faire** *to have just done;* **elle
  vient de partir** *she's just left; vi (+ v être) to come*
vent *nm wind*
vente *nf sale*
ventre *nm stomach;* **avoir mal au** ~ *to have
  stomach ache*
vérifier *vtr to check*
verre *nm glass*
vers *prep toward(s)*
vert, ~**e** *adj green*
vêtement *nm piece of clothing*
veuf, veuve *adj widowed*
viande *nf meat*
vide *adj empty*
vie *nf life*
vieux, vieille *adj old*
ville *nf town; city*
vin *nm wine*
virage *nm bend*
vite *adv quickly;* ~! *quick!*
vitesse *nf speed*
vivre *vi to live*
voici *prep here is, this is; here are*
voilà *prep here is, this is; here are*
voir *vtr to see*
voisin, ~**e** *nmf neighbour*
volant *nm steering wheel*
vomir *vtr to vomit*
votre, *pl* **vos** *your*
vôtre: mes biens sont ~**s** *all I have is yours*
vouloir *vtr to want*
vous *you*
vous-même *yourself*
vouvoyer *vtr to address [sb] using the
  'vous' form*
voyage *nm trip; journey*
voyager *vi to travel*
voyageur, -euse *nmf passenger*
vrai, ~**e** *true; real, genuine*
y *it;* **il** ~ **a** *there is/are;* **il** ~ **a du vin? il n'** ~ **en a
  plus** *wine? there's none left;* **il n'** ~ **a qu'à
  téléphoner** *just phone*
yaourt *nm yoghurt*
yeux *nm pl see* **oeil**
zéro *nm zero, nought*
zone *nf zone, area;* ~ **d'activités** *business park*
zut! *damn!*